# General Stand Watie's
# CONFEDERATE INDIANS

# General Stand Watie's
# CONFEDERATE INDIANS

by FRANK CUNNINGHAM

Foreword by Brad Agnew

UNIVERSITY OF OKLAHOMA PRESS
NORMAN

Dedicated to my sister "Judy"

(Virginia Stovall Cunningham Brookes)

and

Langley, Lawrence and "Happy" Brookes

from their "Uncle Frank"

**Library of Congress Cataloging-in-Publication Data**

Cunningham, Frank, 1911–
General Stand Watie's Confederate Indians / by Frank Cunningham ; foreword by Brad Agnew.
p. cm.
Originally published: San Antonio : Naylor Co., 1959.
Includes bibliographical references and index.
ISBN 0-8061-3035-0 (pbk. : alk. paper)
1. Watie, Stand, 1806–1871. 2. Generals—Confederate States of America—Biography. 3. Cherokee Indians—Biography. 4. Confederate States of America. Army—Biography. 5. United States—History—Civil War, 1861–1865—Participation, Indian. 6. Confederate States of America. Army. Cherokee Regiment. 7. Oklahoma—History, Military—19th century. I. Title.
E467.1.W43C86 1998
973.7'42—dc21 98-17396
CIP

The paper in this book meets the guidelines for permanence and durability of the Committee on Production Guidelines for Book Longevity of the Council on Library Resources, Inc. ∞

Published by the University of Oklahoma Press, Norman, Publishing Division of the University. First published in 1959 by The Naylor Company.  Manufactured in the U.S.A. First printing of the University of Oklahoma Press edition, 1998.

3 4 5 6 7 8 9 10

# Contents

## PICTURE CREDITS

From the *National Archives*:

Sterling Price, E. Kirby-Smith, John Sappington Marmaduke, Stand Watie, Benjamin McCulloch, S. B. Maxey, Albert Pike, Franz Sigel, James Blunt, Frances J. Herron, Confederate Generals in Mexico.

From *Library of Congress:*

William Steele, James M. McIntosh, William Y. Slack, Earl VanDorn, M. Jeff Thompson, Jo O. Shelby, William Clarke Quantrill, William L. Cabell, R. M. Gano and Douglas H. Cooper.

From *Oklahoma Historical Society:*

Stand Watie, Tandy Walker, Samuel Garland, John Jumper, Samuel Checote, Black Dog and Wife, George Washington Grayson, Winchester Colbert, Captain George Washington, W. P. Adair, E. C. Boudinot, Southern Cherokee Commission in 1866, Nannie Watie, Jacqueline Watie, Saladin Watie, Watie children, John Ross, Opthleyoholo and Rose Cottage.

From *T. L. Ballenger:*

Sarah Watie (copied from *The Life of General Stand Watie* by Mabel Washbourne Anderson) and Colonel William A. Phillips (copied from *A History of Oklahoma* by Joseph Bradfield Thoburn and Issaac M. Holcomb).

# Foreword

To many who have studied the conflict, Indian Territory was little more than a backwater of the Civil War. Neither the North nor the South committed significant resources to the region during the war, and historians paid little attention to the area for decades following Appomattox. Nonetheless, in terms of destruction, casualties, and significance, the Civil War affected Indian Territory and its people as profoundly as it touched Georgia or South Carolina and their citizens. Wiley Britton, Annie Heloise Abel, and a few other pioneering historians first documented the role of American Indians in the Civil War. Their accounts illuminate the leadership and exploits of a mixed-blood Cherokee who had already distinguished himself as a steadfast champion of a lost cause before the first shots were fired at Fort Sumter.

In 1839 Stand Watie was catapulted into the leadership of the party opposing Cherokee Chief John Ross and his full-blood faction. The assassination of Watie's brother, uncle, and cousin by Ross's supporters ignited an intratribal civil war that raged for years until Watie agreed to a truce that left Ross in control of the Cherokee Nation. The uneasy peace, which lasted for a decade and a half, collapsed when the Cherokee Nation was swept up in the conflict that divided the union and propelled the United States into the Civil War.

Stand Watie was fifty-three when the conflict began in 1861. Despite the forced removal of his people from their ancestral homeland in the South, Watie, an early advocate of the Southern cause, disregarded John Ross's efforts to maintain neutrality and instead raised troops for the Confederacy. During the war, Colonel Watie won the praise of his white allies who previously had doubted the fighting ability of most Indian units. He also earned the grudging respect of his Union opponents with daring raids and ambushes. In 1864, officials in Richmond acknowledged his ability when they promoted him to brigadier general. Their faith was not misplaced, for

Watie continued to resist Union efforts to subdue Indian Territory and the Western border region despite flagging support from the Confederate government. Reduced to employing guerrilla tactics, Watie—the only Indian general in the Civil War—continued to resist until late June of 1865, two months after Robert E. Lee surrendered to Ulysses S. Grant.

Watie's exploits did not capture the public imagination in the half century following the end of the Civil War. Most Americans fascinated by the exploits of Lee, Grant, Stonewall Jackson, William Tecumseh Sherman, J. E. B. Stuart, Philip Sheridan, and other officers dismissed Watie and his accomplishments, if they had even heard of him. Fifty years after the war, Mabel W. Anderson, Watie's grandniece, wrote a brief biography of her relative, which devoted a single, twenty-two-page chapter to his Civil War exploits. Unfootnoted, with no bibliography, Anderson's work was an uncritical tribute to Watie and an attempt to provide "a more accurate study of the early history of the Cherokees and other Oklahoma Indians, and of the men who made that history."

Almost another half century passed before Watie's military career received a more detailed examination in Frank Cunningham's book, *General Stand Watie's Confederate Indians*. Published in 1959, on the eve of the centennial of the Civil War, Cunningham's volume sought to place Watie's name "in the front ranks of those who revere the dauntless courage of the men of the Confederacy." Unlike Anderson, Cunningham reveals the conflict in Indian Territory in greater scope and detail. He sets the stage for the combatants to relate their campaigns, hardships, and sacrifices in their own voices. Political officials, refugees, and others affected by the war also describe events from their perspective. Drawing from official reports, letters, and memoirs, Cunningham breathes life into a theater of war overshadowed by campaigns waged east of the Mississippi. Wilson's Creek, Pea Ridge, Honey Springs, and Cabin Creek lacked the scale of the battles that raged in Virginia and Pennsylvania, but Indians who fought on both sides displayed no less courage than their counterparts at Chancellorsville or Gettysburg. The Indian general who emerges from the pages of Cunningham's work may not be as thoroughly documented as Lee or Grant, but there is no doubt about his perseverance and devotion to the Southern cause.

As its title suggests, the book's focus is not exclusively on Watie. It seeks to emphasize the contributions of the American Indians who fought in the Civil War, particularly those who served in Confederate units. After surveying Watie's background and tribal divisions in Cherokee history, Cunningham explores events that prompted the Five Civilized Tribes of Indian Territory to ally with the Confederacy. The remainder of the book describes the role of American Indians in the Civil War, emphasizing Stand Watie's leadership.

Cunningham wrote almost a century after the Civil War, but the passage of time had done little to moderate his Southern sympathies. From the first chapter the reader has no doubt which way Frank Cunningham's grandfather shot in the Civil War. While his partisanship may color his evaluation of the motives and actions of the belligerents, it does not seem to have clouded his objectivity in describing the conduct of the war in Indian Territory. He may call Pin Indians "devilish" and rail against "lunatic abolitionists," but he acknowledges Union victories and does not make excuses for Confederate failures.

It is not surprising that Cunningham, a journalist, should write with more verve and less restraint than a professional historian, but his tendency to conjure certain details (the dialogue between J. E. B. Stuart and the "Cherokee political leader" in Chapter 2 and the description of Douglas Cooper pouring himself a "couple of stiff drinks" in Chapter 6) should have been left to novelists. While Cunningham provides a colorful overview of the Civil War in Indian Territory and the border region, readers should be alert to the presence of occasional errors in detail. The author also wrote in an era before Americans became sensitive to the feelings of minorities and consequently used a few terms that are now considered pejorative. The absence of footnotes may frustrate individuals who would like to delve deeper into Watie's career, but the text usually indicates the sources of the passages, and the bibliography does offer a starting point for further study of Stand Watie. All in all, the book's shortcomings do not diminish the author's attempt to focus public attention on an overlooked Cherokee warrior and the men who fought in Indian Territory.

Since publication of *General Stand Watie's Confederate Indians,* many articles, theses, dissertations, and other works have shed light on the Confederate general's military career. Two biographies in particular, Kenny A. Franks's *Stand Watie and the Agony of the Cherokee Nation* and Wilfred Knight's *Red Fox: Stand Watie and the Confederate Indian Nations during the Civil War Years in Indian Territory,* contribute additional detail to Watie's story. Nevertheless, the Civil War in the West remains an overlooked theater of action, and it is hoped that this republication of Cunningham's book will spur increased interest in the conflict in Indian Territory and the Indian general who distinguished himself there.

Brad Agnew

*Northeastern State University*

# Acknowledgments

I am deeply appreciative to Dr. William D. McCain, the distinguished Southern educator and patriot, president of Mississippi Southern College, for his splendid and gracious Foreword.

My debt is to the noted bookman, Robert "Bob" Campbell, Westwood Village, Los Angeles, for his aid in helping me locate out-of-print books, and to the top rank novelist and authority on the Indian Wars, Paul M. Wellman, for lending me his personal copy of *Cherokee Cavaliers.*

My fullest thanks most assuredly go to Mrs. C. E. Cook, Curator of the Oklahoma Historical Society and officer of the United Daughters of the Confederacy, for her vital help in obtaining pictures of the Indian leaders and the Watie family, as well as her all around interest in the book. And no one could have been more co-operative than the well-known historian Carolyn Thomas Foreman, widow of the illustrious Grant Foreman, who not only gave me permission to quote from her excellent book *Park Hill,* but who took the trouble to send me notes on Stand Watie from regional publications she felt I might have by chance overlooked. One is especially conscious of Mrs. Foreman's courtesy when it is revealed that her sympathies were with Chief John Ross, bitter opponent of Stand Watie.

Other thanks to Oklahoma people must include Mary Stith, editor, University of Oklahoma Press, for leads in locating pictures; Savoie Lottinville, director, University of Oklahoma Press; and T. L. Ballenger, writer and Indian authority at Tahlequah.

My gratitude for their courtesy is expressed to the staff of the History Department, Los Angeles Public Library and especially to Irwin L. Stein, who was ever on the outlook for a new reference lead, and who can recite the battle of Pea Ridge from first to last bullet and whose personal interest is in Jefferson Davis; that is, the Union General Jefferson C. Davis.

I also found assistance in the libraries at Santa Monica, Beverly Hills, San Francisco and Pasadena.

From his personal files, Seale Johnson, president of McCowat-Mercer Press, made available the Pea Ridge pictorial material.

For encouragement on the book project, my thanks to Dr. Joseph W. Hough, president of Sequoia University and Fremont College, formerly active in education in Oklahoma.

In Washington, D.C., my appreciation goes to Virginia Daiker, Reference Librarian, Library of Congress; Josephine Cobb, Audio-Visual Records Branch, National Archives; and Remington Kellog, Director, Smithsonian Institution, United States National Museum.

Direct quotations from other books in *Confederate Indians* bring my appreciation to their publishers.

And finally, a word of gratitude to my mother, Mrs. Frank Henry Cunningham, who, since my first book was published in 1943 vows on her huge family Bible which rests on a marble-topped table, she will never live through another non-fiction book project. But, fortunately, she always has and then, after publication, buys copies by the wagon-load to show what "son" has been doing while most everyone else she knows is building space rockets, splitting or playing around with atoms, buying $50,000 homes as used-car lot salesmen, working in some exotic land for the State Department or the CIC, getting rich on housing developments or winning fortunes on Quiz TV shows.

In her more outspoken moments she voices her lament that while "son's" manuscripts are long on Southern sympathies, they are short on Southern sex!

INDIAN CHIEFS and red man warfare have written their stirring saga into American history though to many of today's readers James Fenimore Cooper's forest redskins have been far overshadowed by the Plains Indians, the "heavies" of countless western novels and motion pictures, as well as the heroes of some stories and an occasional photoplay.

One making a survey of Indian leaders in the United States will soon find himself becoming familiar with such names as Powhatan, the Great Sachem of Virginia, who had eleven daughters and twenty sons and whose most famous child was the Indian princess, Pocahontas; Opechancanough, the scourge of Virginia, the younger brother of the famed Powhatan and Chief Sachem of the Chickahomminies; Sassacus and Uncas, rival chieftains of the Pequot Rebellion, and the latter the Mohegan ally of the Connecticut settlers; King Philip of "King Philip's War;" and the Ottawa leader against the British, mighty Pontiac; Massoit, chief of the Wampanoags and friend of the Puritans; Red Jacket, the great warrior of the Senecas; and Logan, the mighty orator and warrior of the Mingoes, betrayed by certain white men in return for his friendship to the invading race.

One would have to recall Captain Joseph Brant, the warrior chief of the Mohawks; Little Turtle, the Miami conqueror of St. Clair; the heralded Tecumseh, Shawnee soldier, diplomat and orator, ally of the British in the war of 1812; Weatherford, the Creek conspirator and fearless fighter; Black Hawk, the leader of the Sacs and Foxes and top warrior of the Black Hawk Rebellion; Osceola, the Creek leader of the Seminoles defeated only by means of a white flag violation in the Florida War; Roman Nose, the Custer of the Cheyennes; Geronimo, the wily Apache who led the cavalry many a chase; and Sequoyah, the amazing genius of the Cherokees, son of a Dutch ancestry Indian trader and a Cherokee mother, who was granted a literary pension of $300 a year out of the Cherokee National Treasury, probably the initial literary pension in American history and most assuredly the first and only one to be granted by an Indian tribe.

Then there are Red Cloud, the tall, eloquent fighting chief of the Ogala; Chief Joseph of the Nez Perce up in the Pacific Northwest and the mighty Sitting Bull, general of the Great Sioux Rebellion with its epic Indian victory over Custer at Little Big Horn, and his able lieutenant Crazy Horse, and Quanah Parker, eagle of the "Lords of the Plains," the Comanches.

Yes, anyone who has "read up" on the Indians will recognize all these names of outstanding fighters and leaders and he'll be acquainted with many in addition whose contributions to history are somewhat comparable.

Yet, will he know the story of the three-quarter Cherokee statesman and fighter who was the Principal Chief of the Southern Cherokee, who was the major Indian leader on the side of the Confederacy in the War for Southern Independence, and who rose to be a Brigadier General in the Secessionist army? And whose name and exploits were at one time as feared in the strife-torn lands of the border as those of Charles Quantrill!

A fearless raider about whom Sherman J. Kline, in an article in the *Americana,* said, "His operations have been likened to those of Francis Marion, who conducted many successful raids in South Carolina during the Revolutionary War, and who became widely known as the 'Swamp Fox.'"

James Street in *The Civil War,* when he mentioned his favorite Confederate generals, wrote, "Gimme Old Jack Jackson or Nathan 'ygod Bedford Forrest helling for leather. Or Stand Watie, the Cherokee. Who can help loving a man with a name like that – General Stand Watie."

A man on whose death in 1871, Judge John F. Wheeler wrote in the Fort Smith, Arkansas, *Herald*: "He was never known to speak an unkind word to his wife or children. He was never morose under any circumstances, and was kind to a fault. His house was the home of every Cherokee . . . there never lived a better man . . ."

Even after April 9 at Appomattox Court House where the immaculate gray-clad Robert E. Lee, after having received a message from General John Gordon . . . "my command has been fought to a frazzle, and I cannot long go forward," commented grimly, "There is nothing left for me to do but to go and see Grant, and I had rather die a thousand deaths;" even a few days later, on April 18, after Joseph E. Johnston surrendered the Army of the South to William T. "scorched earth" Sherman near Durham Station in North Carolina; indeed even after E. Kirby-Smith, known as "the last Confederate General to surrender" – (actually by General Simon Bolivar Buckner who had replaced Kirby-Smith) – had hauled down the Stars and Bars of the Army of the Trans-Mississippi in May and the vast undefeated Rebel Texas lands fell; yes, after all these Southern capitulations, *this Confederate Indian leader still held out!*

Despite the verdict of most histories, E. Kirby-Smith was not the last Confederate General to surrender. Edward A. Pollard, editor of the Richmond *Examiner,* wrote in his book, *The Lost Cause,* that "With the surrender of General Smith the war ended, and from the Potomac to the Rio Grande there was no longer an armed soldier to resist the authority of the United States."

But there was!

This Indian General kept holding out. A short time previously he speculated that even though the South had lost in the West, the East and the Deep South, Kirby-Smith had some 36,000 well-fed troops with the possibility that this force could be raised to 90,000 if the still fighting, but retreating C.S.A. soldiers could reach Kirby-Smith's territory.

This Indian General was so resolved that the Indian allies of Richmond could win out over their enemies — both white and Indian — that even at the time of Lee's abandoning the struggle he was preparing to raise an army of 10,000 men to invade the abhorred abolitionist land of Eastern Kansas.

Yes, one Confederate Army brigade refused to quit! This was the Indian Brigade with headquarters in the Choctaw Nation, commanded by a warrior small in stature, of little talk but an eloquent writer, and with strong lion-like features that heralded the innate courage which never ordered a charge that he did not lead.

This was a man born December 12, 1806 at an old home on the Coo-sa-wa-tee stream, near the present site of Rome, Georgia; a man at birth named either Ta-ker-taw-ker, meaning "to Stand Firm — Immovable," or De-gata-ga, conveying the meaning that two persons are standing so closely united in sympathy as to form but one human body. He was the son of Uweti, also known as David-oo-Wa-tee, and Susannah Reese. His mother was one-half white, a member of the Moravian Church, and a descendant of the well-known Reese family of North Carolina and Georgia.

Skilled as a ball player and an excellent rider, the lad soon became known as Stand, though he spoke only his native tongue until he was twelve, and his companions at the Brainerd Mission School in Tennessee little realized that he was to grow up to be one of the foremost names in the history of the Cherokee Nation, a name that, alas, has been obscured by the passing years, perhaps because of the bright light brought forth by the same Sequoyah for, as the Creek Indian poet and editor of the Muskogee *Morning Times,* Alex Posey, wrote in his *Ode to Sequoyah*:

"The names of Watie and Boudinot —
The valiant warrior and gifted sage —
And other Cherokees, may be forgot . . ."

But the name of Brigadier General Stand Watie, the only Indian General in the service of the Confederacy, should ever stand in the front ranks of those who revere the dauntless courage of the men of the Confederacy, men such as General Jo Shelby, who rode into Mexico rather than surrender, and who would say to their scouts returning to report on the enemy:

"Did you see them?"

"Yes, General."

"Did you count them?"

"No, General."

"Then, suh, we'll fight them, by heaven!"

Morris L. Wardell wrote in his *Political History of the Cherokee Nation* that in rating the entire Indian leadership in the War between the States that General Watie stood out as the most prominent, the most highly respected and the most aggressive, certainly as high a tribute as could be paid the Confederate leader.

And Confederate General Douglas H. Cooper, who finally rose to command all the Indian troops, said after the war's end, "General Watie was not only a soldier, brave and efficient and courageous, but he was a great man, whose honor and integrity were above reproach."

As with all the Confederate leaders, defeat continually could not be staved off and in late June 1865, General Stand Watie struck his colors to Lieutenant Colonel Asa C. Matthews, at Doaksville, which had been the capital of the Choctaw Nation from 1850-63; *the last Confederate General to surrender!*

Behind him were the battles and skirmishes in which his Indian Army of battling mixed-breeds, chiefs of whom had lived as Southern gentlemen, with prosperous plantations, expensively furnished, with faithful white wives who dressed in fancy silks to match their husbands' frock coats and high hats, with slaves, many of whom remained true to their masters, and a passionate devotion to States Rights not exceeded by the most ardent South Carolinian, had marked — sometimes with shotgun and tommyhawk — a bloody campaign encompassing such places as Wilson's Creek, Bird Creek, Pea Ridge, Spavinaw, Newtonia, Fort Wayne, Fort Gibson, Honey Springs, Webber's Falls, Poison Spring, Massard Prairie, and Cabin Creek.

The Five Civilized Tribes which backed the Confederacy — though such action split the Indian Nations into warring factions in some cases — lost more men in proportion to the number enlisted than any Southern state.

Who can question whether these deaths were in vain for Mabel Washbourne Anderson wrote in *Life of General Stand*

*Watie,* a slim volume first published in Oklahoma in 1915 and now practically unobtainable in the book market:

"Sherman's terrible raid, on a smaller scale, might have been repeated in the Indian Territory and Texas had it not been . . . for General Watie and his command. His brigade was like a stone wall between Texas and the foe."

Had Watie's stout but sinewy defense in the Indian Territory been broken and his headquarters in the Choctaw Nation smashed, the horror of the Southern hated Sherman, who had been a college president in the South before the war, could well have been over again, for along with the white Northern troops, the foes of the half-breed Indians who fought under the Confederate flag were the full-blooded Indians – the depised Pins who were loyal to the Union. Whether to line up for Lincoln or Davis was not the first question on which the rival Cherokees had taken sides – and arms – and blood!

And to tell the whole story of this little known part of the War between the States one must delve briefly into Cherokee history.

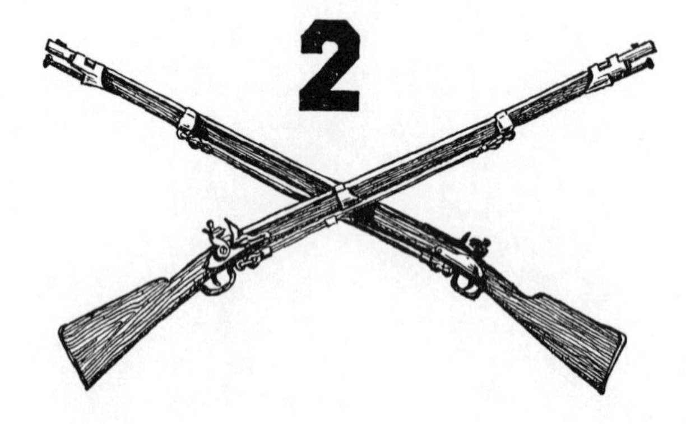

ORIGINALLY, THE CHEROKEES, had been the allies of the British. They had sided with the English in early Colonial struggles, fought a Border war in the South around 1760, but sued for peace after fourteen of their villages burned.

G. E. E. Lindquist in *The Red Man in the United States,* wrote:

"The Cherokee Indians of North Carolina have behind them probably a longer history of white civilization than any other tribe. Eight of their chiefs returned to England with Oglethorpe after his expedition of 1733. Two years later Wesleyan missionaries were made welcome by the tribe. Their first treaties with the white man were made with George III and their earliest diplomatic relations with the United States came in 1785 when boundaries were established and 15,000 families were settled on

Cherokee lands by the treaty of Hopewell. As early as 1800 the Cherokees were manufacturing cotton cloth. Each family had a farm under cultivation. There were districts with a council house, judge and marshal, schools in all villages and churches of several denominations. Many of the Indians were Christians and were said to lead exemplary lives."

Edward Everett Dale discussed in *Oklahoma – a Guide to the Sooner State* the fact that the Indians of the Five Civilized Tribes were alertly cognizant of the favorable geographic position of their lands – east of the Mississippi – and they were adept at playing nation against nation in an effort to hold a balance of power. This involved France, England and Spain as well as Florida, Louisiana, the Carolinas and Georgia.

Scotch families had emigrated following the uprising of 1745 and in the Revolution many of these people had remained "true to the old flag." When the Continental Army triumphed, a large number of the Loyalists fled into the Cherokee country and the unmarried men soon were husbands of the Cherokee women, frequently Christians as the Moravian Church had been in the Cherokee country since 1740. It was the white blood – so often of the best Scotch families – which was to produce the aristocratic mixed-bloods who were to play the most prominent roles in coming Cherokee history.

After General Pickens had subdued their Tory tendencies, the Cherokees acknowledged the sovereignty of the United States by the Treaty of Hopewell, signed November 28, 1785.

On March 30, 1802 the United States guaranteed the Cherokees the possession of all lands not ceded by them, recognized their right of self-government and gave the Cherokees the power to throw out all intruders on their lands. Certainly the Cherokees, now with their independence assured, could want no more from the United States.

There was soon to be a tragic complication. Only some three weeks later, on April 24, the United States, completely ignoring the agreement with the Cherokees, entered into one with Georgia saying, "the Indians' lands within the state of Georgia shall be given up as soon as could be done peaceably and on reasonable terms."

Such was the double-cross. In a sense, both the Indians and Georgia were double-crossed in that Georgia had ceded valuable lands in return for the assurance from the United States that the Indians would move.

Fifteen years later, in 1817, the Indians had made little effort toward departing and Georgia was getting impatient. The Lower Cherokees, the farmers, paid no heed to the suggestions from Georgia that they move, but the Upper Cherokees, the hunters, traded their lands for western hunting grounds.

Still, that deflection left in possession of the Cherokees and the Creeks an area amounting to one-fourth the present state of Georgia.

Both the tribes had laws forbidding any individual to sell land as such sales must be by the tribe. Little difficulty was encountered in enforcing this law as there were few lawbreakers. Violators were promptly executed. The Creeks and the Cherokees also had the death penalty for anyone who married a Negro.

Every possible pressure was exerted on the two tribes and, in 1826, on January 24, Creek Chief William McIntosh sold all the Georgia and part of the Alabama lands for $400,000. That he was the Chief made no exception to the law. He was put to death. But a short time later the Creeks had to give in to Georgia, which invoked the theory of nullification to block Federal control of state matters.

New Echota, the Cherokee capital, was established in 1819 and soon prospered in the fertile Georgia lands. Sequoyah, in 1821, after six years' work completed his form of written language for the Cherokees – it had eighty-four characters corresponding to Cherokee sounds. The year before, the Cherokees formulated a civilized government with a paid legislature and a code of laws. At that time they were still skeptical of Sequoyah's project, but, once he had shown them how he could communicate with his six-year-old daughter by means of it, the National Council became enthusiastic. In 1827 the Indians drew up a Constitution and took the name Cherokee Nation.

Any self-respecting Nation needed a means of propaganda and in 1828 the National Council established a newspaper, the Cherokee *Phoenix*. For editor, the Council named Stand Watie's brother, Elias Boudinot, who had been teaching school. Setting a pace for newspaper salaries, the Cherokees paid their editor $300 a year; the first issue of the *Phoenix* was February 21 and a brilliant career in Cherokee annals commenced.

Elias, born in 1802, was given an Indian name meaning stag or male deer, and he became known as Buck Watie. When he was educated at the Foreign Mission School in Cornwall, Connecticut, by a Philadelphia philanthropist, Elias Boudinot, Buck Watie took his benefactor's name. In Connecticut he fell in love with Harriet Gold, a daughter of one of the town's leading families, and married her.

Under Editor Boudinot, the *Phoenix* was printed with parallel columns in Cherokee and English and became known throughout not only the South but the Eastern literary world.

Stand Watie's brothers, besides Elias, were John, Thomas and Charles; and his sisters, Nancy, Mary and Elizabeth. His uncle Major Ridge, was a brother of Stand Watie's father. He married the Cherokee maiden, Princess Sehoya, was appointed a Major in the United States Army by General Andrew Jackson, and for many years was speaker of the Cherokee Council.

In early manhood, Stand Watie had a close friendship with Sheriff Charles Hicks. When a notorious desperado murdered Hicks, Deputy Sheriff Watie hunted down the slayer and killed him.

From December 20, 1828 to December 22, 1830, the Georgia authorities passed a series of laws designed to force the Cherokees out of the state. Some measures were these: Cherokee laws, usages, legislative assemblies and court were abolished; Cherokees were declared unacceptable for making contracts with white men and if the Cherokees put in action their death law for private land sales, the Georgia authorities would treat this as murder; Georgia laws and jurisdiction were extended over all inhabitants of the Cherokee Nation; Cherokee improvements and gold mines were confiscated; and white men were forbidden to enter Cherokee country without a license from the Georgia governor and the taking of an oath of allegiance to Georgia.

If all this were not capable of disrupting the Cherokee Nation, Georgia ordered the Cherokee lands surveyed for a distribution by lottery among Georgia citizens!

Chief John Ross and the other Cherokee leaders felt under no compulsion to obey these drastic demands made on their independent Nation. They appealed to President John Quincy Adams, but, as he was going out of office, he relayed the supplication to incoming President Andrew Jackson. Chief Ross, told that Jackson said the Cherokees must submit or move, said he would sell for $20,000,000, which was more money than Napoleon wanted for the Louisiana Territory!

Finally the Cherokees got several of their cases before the United States Supreme Court, lost the first one and then in March 1832, the Court apparently reversed itself, holding that "all acts of the Georgia legislature with respect to the Cherokees were unconstitutional and in violation of the treaties and laws of the United States . . ."

It was then that Andrew Jackson is alleged to have said, "John Marshall has made his decision — now let him enforce it!"

In 1832, when Elias Boudinot went to the East on a lecture tour, Stand Watie, who had become well-known in the Nation as clerk of the National Supreme Court in 1829, was put in charge of the *Phoenix*. The Cherokees were becoming hotly involved in an intra-Nation controversy over the question of whether they should accede to the Georgia demands. From the East, Elias wrote Stand not to write anything controversial regarding the national political election — involving Henry Clay and Andrew Jackson — as Boudinot did not wish the Cherokees entangled in more politics.

Nevertheless, Chief John Ross displaced Elias Boudinot as editor and Elijah Hicks headed the *Phoenix*. Watie and Boudinot, who favored selling the land and leaving Georgia, could not allow their means of possible political control to slip out of their hands, and, with the aid of Georgia authorities seized the *Phoenix* and put its editorial policy back behind emigration.

The feeling over emigration was extremely bitter and many of the Cherokees did not agree with the so-called Treaty Party headed by Stand Watie, Elias Boudinot and Major Ridge. These men, themselves, would have preferred to stay in Georgia, but they realized that removal was inevitable as those in Georgia who demanded the Cherokee lands had the power in Washington to thwart the Cherokee Nation. The Treaty Party men were the mixed-breeds, often actually more Southern than Indian, and equally as prosperous as many of the white planters who lived adjoining the Cherokee Nation. Cherokees owned valuable land, trading posts and ferries. Major Ridge was wealthy and his son, John Ridge, had erected a schoolhouse at his own expense on the land where stood "Running Waters," his home.

Chief John Ross and his full-bloods also had prospered, but they had no feeling for Southern white life in the sense of kinship. They were for the Cherokee Nation as a political entity come hell and high water. Equally as much for the continuation of the Cherokee Nation, the Treaty Party contended that to defy the United States Government would, in the end, mean the total oblivion of the Nation. It was far better, they maintained, to move the Nation, than to lose the Nation!

It is rather odd that in 1861 it was the mixed-blood element who fought the United States – Northern half – for the love of the South they had been forced to leave.

Benjamin F. Currey, Government Superintendent for the Cherokee removal, reported on a meeting held May 14, 1833, by the Cherokee Council to hear a review of the work of the Washington Cherokee delegation. Currey stated in his dispatch to the Commissioner of Indian Affairs:

"Old Major Ridge is the great orator of the nation. He dismissed the meeting, after giving a concise and well-arranged history of their present condition compared with what it had been; the probability of their being called on in a few months for the last time, to say whether they will submit always to the evils and difficulties every day increasing around them, or look for a new home, promising them freedom and national prosperity, advising them to bury party animosity, and, in case they should conclude to seek a new home, to go in the character of true friends and brothers . . ."

Currey added as his own observation, "Past experience has shown Ross and his party hold no pledge sacred."

This observation by the Government Superintendent most certainly lends support to the Watie-Ridge-Boudinot faction in its conflict with John Ross and his adherents.

On December 29, 1835, without the consent of Chief John Ross, the Treaty of New Echota was signed by the Treaty Party leaders and the Georgia Cherokee Nation lands were sold for $5,700,000. The Nation pledged that it would leave Georgia in not more than three years and re-establish itself in the Indian Territory that is now Oklahoma. When John Ridge – his father, and Chief Ross, then friends, had fought side by side leading a canoe attack against the Creeks at Tohopeka – signed the treaty, he said after he put down his pen, "John Ridge signed his death warrant when he signed that treaty and no one knew it better when he signed his name on that paper. John Ridge may not die tomorrow . . . but sooner or later he will have to yield his life as the penalty for signing."

It is significant to observe that it was Major Ridge, one of the staunch defenders of the rights of the Cherokees, who, in 1829, introduced into the council at New Echota, a measure decreeing death to any member who would sign a treaty agreeing to give up their country in the East. This measure was adopted.

Commented Grant Foreman in an article in *Chronicles of Oklahoma*:

"The fact that he [Major Ridge] was one of the few unauthorized private individuals of the tribe who did at last in 1835 sign what purported to be a treaty of removal is an indication of the desperate straits to which the Indians were reduced and of the heroic measures their leaders were willing to enter into. . ."

Unfortunately for the leaders of the Treaty Party, brilliant and honorable as they were, the methods by which the government moved the last of the Cherokees only widened the rupture between the two factions. In the spring of 1838 General Winfield Scott, with 4,000 Federal and State troops and 4,000 volunteers came to New Echota to begin the removal. Fifteen thousand Cherokees signed, to no avail, a petition which said in part:

"Are we to be hunted through the mountains like wild beasts, and our women, our children, our aged, our sick to be dragged from their homes like culprits, and to be packed into loathsome boats for transportation to a sickly clime?" (Reports coming to Georgia were that the 3,000 Cherokees already there were not being welcomed by the half-wild Indians who were their western neighbors.)

The unjust treatment given the Cherokees met with considerable opposition in Southern circles and General John Ellis Wool, of the United States troops, commented:

"The whole scene since I have been in this country has been nothing but a heart-rending one, and such a one as I would be glad to be rid of as soon as circumstances will permit. Because I am firm and decided, do not believe I would be unjust. If I could, and I could not do them a greater kindness, I would remove every Indian tomorrow beyond the reach of the white man, who, like vultures, are watching, ready to pounce upon their prey and strip them of everything they have, or expect from the government of the United States. Yes, sir, nineteen-twentieths, if not ninety-nine out of every hundred, will go penniless to the West."

Even Major Ridge, the principal signer of the treaty, felt he should protest and he wrote the President:

". . . Even the Georgia laws, which deny us our oaths, are thrown aside, and notwithstanding the cries of our people . . . the lowest classes . . . are flogging the Cherokees with cowhides, hickories, and clubs. We are not safe in our houses — our people are assailed day and night by the rabble . . . the women are stripped also and whipped without law or mercy . . . send regular troops to protect . . . our people as they depart for the West . . . or . . . we shall carry off nothing but the scars of the lash on our backs, and our oppressors will get all the money. We talk plainly, as chiefs having property and life in danger, and we appeal to you for protection."

General Dunlap, Tennessee troop commander, called out in case there was a Cherokee uprising, said his soldiers would never enforce the treaty at the point of the bayonet.

The last of the Cherokees, like cattle, were driven from their lands by the soldiers. One quarter of these civilized Indians — who had established their high culture in Georgia — died during or immediately after emigration. Some died of broken hearts as they loved their homes and their lands. The "trail of tears" made by the Cherokee stains a dismal page in Indian relations. Not realizing that the Treaty Party had acted unselfishly and solely in behalf of the Nation — for these men lost their homes as did the others — the bitter full-blooded aligned with Chief Ross, angry and unhappy in the alien new land awaited their time for revenge.

Stand Watie had married twice before the Cherokees left for the West. His wife Betsy died in childbirth, as did the child, late in March, 1836, and he afterwards married the former wife of Eli Hicks, Isabella, but they separated when Watie, with the Ridges emigrated by water to the Western lands in 1837.

In June, 1839, at Double Springs, the Ross faction held a secret council, put a commander over each hundred men of their Knights of Death, or secret police, and vowed to wipe out the leaders of the Treaty Party!

On the morning of June 22 a company of riders rode up to the Honey Creek home of John Ridge in the northwest section of the Nation, and over the cries of Sarah Northrup, his wife from Cornwall, Connecticut, dragged him from his bed. With twenty wounds in his body, Ridge died on the ground. Twelve-year-old John Rollin Ridge came to his mother and vowed he would have vengeance for his father's murder.

Elias Boudinot and Reverend S. A. Worcester, with whom he had translated a number of gospels, had been working on a translation of St. John at the minister's house at Park Hill. Three men rode up and asked Boudinot if he would ride with them to help secure medicine. A short time later, a hired man heard Boudinot scream and Worcester and Delight Boudinot, his wife, found Elias among the tall grasses, stabbed in the back and his head bashed in with a hatchet. Alive, he died before he could speak to them. So in violence was killed the scholarly former editor of the *Phoenix*, the author of the novel in Cherokee, *Poor Sarah, or the Indian Woman.*

On that bloody morning it was poor Delight Boudinot, her new home half built, left with five children not of her bearing!

The assassins still had to reach Stand Watie and Major Ridge.

Carolyn Thomas Foreman relates in *Park Hill* how this warning was rushed to Watie:

". . . the life of Stand Watie was saved by an older son of the Worcesters. The lad, after seeing the death of the family friend, mounted his father's horse, 'Comet,' and rode as rapidly as possible to a store kept by Watie a mile from Park Hill.

"Calling the man aside, near the sugar barrel, as if it were the object of his visit, the boy quickly told the news, in low tones, meantime in louder ones bargaining for sugar, as some of the anti-treaty party were in the store. Stand Watie escaped through the back door, found 'Comet' where the lad had left him tied in a thicket, mounted and fled."

Mrs. Foreman continued:

"Mary Worcester Williams, when a young girl, saw another escape of this man. While standing in the door of her father's smoke house trembling with fear, she watched a party of Indians as they searched for Stand. He had been to visit his sister, Mrs. John Wheeler, not far from the Worcester home for which he was bound. Between the houses there was an orchard and close to the orchard fence there was a deep pit called the 'Devil's Sink-hole,' which the children believed to be bottomless. This was hidden from view of persons passing along the path by a growth of underbrush.

"While walking along the path Watie heard the enemy approaching, so he rushed to the pit, over which saplings had been spread to keep people or animals from falling within; he was a man of amazing strength and was able to work himself along by hanging to the poles until, over the hole, he lowered himself from sight until fifty mounted Indians had passed in single file. After the sound of horses had died away Stand pulled himself up and returned to his sister's house which the red men had recently searched."

Watie sped to Fort Gibson, rounded up fifteen men and proceeded — in vain — to seek the assassins. As news of the murders spread, several hundred armed men gathered around Chief Ross' home to protect him should Watie attack.

According to some sources, Watie, knowing his brother was murdered, alone rode to the Boudinot home and entered the yard filled with hostile armed men. At the porch, he lifted the cloth off the dead man's face, then turned away, saying to the crowd, "I would give ten thousand dollars for the names of the men who did this!"

With contempt for his opponents, he rode through them to the road and not a hand was raised against him. Then, looking back at the body for a final time, he put spurs to his horse.

And what of seventy-year old Major Ridge? The Arkansas *Gazette* for August 21 tells the story in an account by John A. Bell and Stand Watie:

"Major Ridge started the previous day to Vineyard in Washington county, Arkansas . . . he was waylaid about 10 o'clock [the same Saturday morning as the other murders] by a party of Indians about five miles out of Cane Hill and shot from a high precipice which commanded the road. It was reported that ten or twelve guns were fired at him; only five balls, however, penetrated his body and head."

Believing there was a well-laid plot to kill all the Treaty Party and its associates, Stand Watie, to whom the Treaty people now looked for leadership, gathered a force at Old Fort Wayne near the Arkansas border, as civil war seemed imminent. Angered men milled back of the stockade where Captain Nathan Boone, son of Daniel Boone, had plotted early Indian boundary surveys. George Lowrey, acting Principal Chief of the Cherokee Nation, in the absence of Chief Ross, wrote Watie protesting the gathering of armed men and asked Watie to "break up without delay your present organization, return to your respective homes and contribute whatever may be in your power to the promotion of order and harmony among our people." Disregarding the Lowrey demand, the Watie faction remained mobilized — while Stand Watie sought help in Washington — until they felt the Ross men were impressed with their potential power.

Shortly after the assassination of the three Treaty Party leaders, the East and the West Cherokees met at Takotokah on July 12 and chose Tahlequah, three miles to the southwest, as their capital, having signed the Act of Union. Tahlequah consisted of a council ground and a camping site and it was not until some four years later, in 1843, that the capital was graced with buildings; three large cabins in which the National Council, Senate and Treasury could meet.

Hatred between the mixed-bloods and the full-bloods limned nearly every face in the Cherokee Nation. Each side strove for favor with the Washington political circles. Around January 1840, Stand Watie and John Adair Bell, who was one of the signers of the Treaty of New Echota, on arriving in the nation's Capitol, lost no time in putting their best foot forward.

Stand Watie quickly purchased an elegant green frock coat and John Bell picked out a mulberry one. Difference in color made no difference in price. The frock coats were about thirty dollars each. Over his green frock coat, Stand Watie wore a new cloth overcoat which had cost almost forty dollars, whereas Bell bought a slightly more expensive beaver overcoat. In addition, the two men donned fancy velvet vests and high grade pantaloons for, most certainly, the wealthy aristocrats of the Indian Territory would want their representatives to be in high style. And there were no more fashionably attired men at the Globe Hotel than Stand Watie and John Bell. Although his companion had to return to the Indian Territory on March 16, Watie continued his stay in the capital until early in May when, after settling a hotel bill of over $300, he started back to his home.

Watie had other accounts to settle back in Indian Territory.

Two years later Stand Watie walked into a grocery store on the Arkansas side of the Indian borderline. In the store was James Foreman, one of the alleged assassins of Major Ridge. Stand Watie killed Foreman, stood trial and was acquitted on a plea of self-defense.

George W. Pascal, who married the daughter of John Ridge, wrote a report on the trial of Stand Watie in which he said:

"Watie is a man of powerful intellect, and great common sense. He is brave to a fault, but not less generous than brave. Few men have more gentle or pacific manners; or bear a more amiable deportment. Under the severest injuries he never makes a threat . . .

"James Foreman was generally reputed a violent man. He was usually believed to have been the murderer of Jack Walker, and the selected leader of the party who slew Major Ridge, both of whom were killed in a most cowardly manner. Indeed while he was thought to be dangerous he was generally conceded to be cowardly."

In a defense plea Alfred W. Arrington, a North Carolinian by birth, a distinguished Arkansas legislator, and who "occupies the very first place as orator in the state," said:

"Not satisfied with declaring [by the Ross element] Stand Watie an outlaw, we expect to prove that he was hunted down and followed up – waylaid, and every attempt made to take his life, until the very moment when James Foreman, one of the leading conspirators, was slain – and that even at the very moment when the conflict commenced the enemies of Stand Watie had freely prepared to take the life of himself and an unoffending brother. That his life was only saved by a gallantry and prowess, alike honorable to the blood which runs in his veins, and the chivalrous age in which he lives. In a word, we expect to prove that if ever there was a case where a man acted in self-defense – from necessity forced upon him by imperilous circumstances, Stand Watie's was the case. . ."

The testimony of James P. Miller described the fight which took place at England's grocery about three miles from Maysville:

"I proposed to Watie that we should go. Stand Watie said we should drink first; called for a glass of liquor. James Foreman picked up the glass and drank, saying, 'Stand Watie, here is wishing you may live forever.' Foreman then handed Watie the glass. Watie took the glass, smiled and said, 'Jim, I suppose I can drink with you, but I understood a few days since that you were going to kill me.' Foreman said: 'say yourself!' and immediately the fight commenced. Watie threw the glass; if any difference first. When Foreman said 'say yourself' he straightened himself from the counter against which he had been leaning, with a large whip in his hand. [Another witness, Hiram Landrum, stated that the whip was large enough to have killed a man.] Foreman fought with the whip while in the house. Drumgoole [Alexander Drumgoole, Foreman's uncle] was working about Watie's back. Some how or another Drumgoole fell out of the door. Foreman jumped out and picked up a board and raised it up. As he raised it, Watie sprang forward from the door, and struck with a knife; I suppose. [Landrum testified that Foreman hit Watie with the board.] I did not see the knife until Watie was on his horse. After Watie struck, Foreman jumped off some fifteen or twenty paces and said, 'you haven't done it yet.' Watie then presented a pistol and fired. Foreman ran about 150 yards, fell in the gap of the fence and died."

Defense witnesses testified that they had heard Foreman say if he "ever met Watie he would put him out of the way" and that Foreman's general character was that of a "bad and dangerous man."

In the defense it was brought out that "his [Foreman's] taking the whip from Drumgoole and wrapping the lash around his hand were signs not to be misunderstood." Also Foreman had sent his half-brother for his guns and "a few minutes later and he would have caused Stand Watie to have been among the martyrs of the treaty party."

Stand Watie's lawyers continually brought out the ill-feeling between the two factions in the Cherokee Nation and traced its continuation from the days of the treaty-signing at New Echota.

David Walker, a defense lawyer, had been a member of the Legislature under the Territorial government and a Senator under the State government. In his argument he contended:

"Watie was upon our own soil. He was assailed by one who had more than once violated that soil which throws its broad mantle of protection over every man of every name and every color who sets his foot upon it. Foreman again sought to stain that soil, and stain it with more innocent blood. He commenced the contest with superior advantages. He was a giant in size and strength accustomed to dangerous and deadly stratagems. Watie was a small man, of peaceful bearing. Foreman was surrounded by his friends — and kindred — Watie alone and unprotected.

"Justice was however on his side and providence decided the battle."

General Ethan Allen Hitchcock, who was sent by the Secretary of War to Indian Territory, during the period of November 1841, to March 1842, to investigate the condition of the Indians recently emigrated there from the Southern states, encountered the Watie-Ross animosity. In *A Traveler in Indian Territory* he wrote:

"Governor Butler had told me of Stanwatie and that he had threatened the life of John Ross; that he is of a cool and determined character and that Ross will not be allowed to pass out of the Nation to Washington if he meets with Stanwatie . . ."

Pierce Mason Butler was the Cherokee agent. A South Carolina governor and a Colonel in the famed Palmetto Regiment, he was killed at the battle of Churubusco in the Mexican War.

Diligently the Cherokees worked at improving their lot politically and the Inter-tribal Council, called by them in 1843, met at Tahlequah for four weeks and was attended by representatives of eighteen tribes.

In 1845 all houses on the public square were ordered moved and the main street laid out. A brick building was constructed to house the Cherokee Supreme Court, but it also provided a home for the Cherokee *Advocate;* however, a brick meeting place for the Supreme Court was no sign that the schism in the Nation had been removed.

That year the Ross faction killed Thomas Watie and James Starr. John Walker Candy, married to Stand Watie's sister, Mary Anne, wrote to Watie in Washington from Park Hill in April 1846 that murders were so numerous in the Cherokee land, news of the killings created as much interest as the death of a roving dog.

When Stand Watie returned from Washington he and Chief John Ross made their peace for the killings which had brought only misery to both factions.

Another angle on the Cherokee picture was given by Cherokee Agent Pierce Butler in his annual report to the Commissioner of Indian Affairs, in which he stated:

"The Cherokees display great mechanical ability; many, even most of the farmers are capable of stocking their own ploughs, helving their own hoes and making gates and doors to their dwellings . . . [of the women] they are no less contributors to the progressive social condition of their own people than are the men; they are fond of spinning and weaving, and manifest great ingenuity in the manufacture of domestic cloth . . . it is a pleasant spectacle and a subject of great congratulation to the friends of these people, to witness on the Sabbath the father, mother, and children clad in the products of their own labor; the material is well manufactured, and in the selection, variety, and arrangements of the colors they exhibit great taste and skill . . ."

Vengeance may be masked by a treaty, not destroyed. John Rollin Ridge, following the murder of his father, had been educated for ten years in New England and Arkansas. This education in no way erased the memory of that horrific morning back in 1839. As his formal education was complete, John Rollin Ridge returned home and was warned that Ross' man, David Kell, was gunning for him. Ridge shot first, killing Kell, and fled to Missouri where, in 1849, he wrote Stand Watie asking permission to make a raid into the Cherokee Nation. Ridge had enlisted a party of white men for the purpose of killing Chief John Ross!

As much as Stand Watie, who represented his people time and time again in the National Council, may have respected John Rollin Ridge's enterprise, he could not put his approval on this raid for murder.

With his plan to eliminate Chief Ross not favored by Watie, John Rollin Ridge traveled to California and two years later was writing for the San Francisco *Golden Era* and soon published a widely sold book, *The Life and Adventure of Joaquin Murrieta.* In practically no time young Ridge — he was born in 1827 — became one of the leading literary figures in California.

In the meantime, in 1843, Stand Watie had married again. His new wife was Sarah Caroline Bell, sister of his good friend, John Adair Bell. Sarah had been born in 1820 in the Old Cherokee Nation east of the Mississippi.

As much as the Cherokees fought against going to the Indian

Territory, they soon found it a good land to pioneer and the prosperity of Georgia was renewed. Over all this was a land of beauty, variety and contrast. There were the timbered mountains and spark-sprinkled lakes; there were cypress and pine; and there were also treeless level prairies with mesquite and sage brush.

With the Cherokees becoming well-established, the Cherokee newspaper was revived by the Council October 25, 1843, renamed the Cherokee *Advocate* and published its first edition – four pages of six columns – on September 26, 1844.

The prospectus for the *Advocate* read in part:

"The history of the Indian tribes, but most especially that of the Cherokees, is replete with instances at once striking and commanding. The mystery that surrounds their origin, their former warlike character, their manly freedom, their firm adherence to their natural and political rights, their fond attachment to their homes – the homes of their forefathers – their rude expulsion from those homes, their sudden transition from savage to civilized life, their rapid improvement in education, agriculture and domestic arts, their present condition and the influence which, from their location, friendship and intercourse, they must and will exert over the great Indian population, extending north and south along the great western border of the United States and back to the Rocky Mountains, cannot fail to kindle a lively interest in the breast of the philanthropists, awaken a general thirst for more familiarity with them, and arouse their protectors to the important but often forgotten fact, that they have no trifling duty to perform towards this people. To those, then who take any concern in whatever relates to the Cherokees and neighboring Indians, and who are desirous to being regularly and accurately made acquainted with passing events among them, the Cherokee *Advocate* is recommended.

"Our location . . . to the Creeks, Chickasaws, Choctaws, Osages, Senecas, Delawares and other Indians . . . will enable us . . . to furnish the readers . . . with the latest and most correct border news . . ."

But the *Advocate* missed by a month being the first paper in the new Cherokee Nation. Reverend Evans Jones – a strong pro-Ross man – published the Cherokee *Messenger* at the Cherokee Baptist Mission known sometimes merely as Baptist and more often as "Breadtown," for it was from the Mission that bread was distributed. Jones was to decry Stand Watie's influence until the Confederate Indian troops put him to a long awaited — by the Secesh faction — flight.

The *Advocate* was edited by William Potter Ross, an excellent writer, a Princeton graduate, and a nephew of Chief John Ross. The paper naturally tended to favor the anti-Watie faction in the Nation — so it was that Watie had both the *Advocate* and *Messenger* critical of him! The *Advocate* came out regularly until September 18, 1853, when it was suspended for lack of funds. Five years after the end of the War between the States the *Advocate* was resumed and it was published until 1906.

Even his success in the Golden Bear State could not erase John Rollin Ridge's love for his Cherokee Nation. In 1854 from Marysville, Ridge — who often was known in the literary world as Yellow Bird — wrote Stand Watie asking him to aid in the financing of an Indian newspaper to be published in Arkansas.

Ridge brought out that he wanted to write the history of the Cherokee Nation from the Indian point of view and not the white man's for the white man, Ridge contended, would make such a history too much a justification of the white man's actions. Too, Ridge felt that with a newspaper he could record the memory of the relatives so that their deeds would remain for the world to know. Certainly, Ridge emphasized, it was unthinkable that men such as Watie and himself would allow the deeds of their people to be forgotten when they could — with their own paper — awaken readers at home and abroad to what they had to relate.

John Rollin Ridge was to continue his notable career in California journalism and not to become the publisher of a Cherokee newspaper. For although Stand Watie encouraged him in the project, he was expanding his own planting operations and could not assist financially. He was to acquire three places on the Spavinaw and around 1860 commenced construction of a substantial new home.

But Watie could discern sinister shadows creeping out from the East and North toward Indian Territory. Men had fought before in the Territory in the feuds between Watie's group and the Ross clan, but there was something far more ominous in these shadows as if the Arkansas River were to run with blood and spill out over the Indian plantation lands. Cherokees had watched the famed Second Cavalry canter down Tahlequah's Muskogee street in November 1855. Seven hundred and fifty riders from Jefferson Barracks in St. Louis were on their way to Texas to fight in the Indian wars.

When some of the cavalrymen reined up in front of the National Hotel, built in 1848 by a Mormon Bishop and two followers run out of the East, the Cherokees welcomed them.

"Mind telling me who's in command?" queried a Cherokee political leader who had come out to watch the column.

"Colonel Albert Sidney Johnston, suh," came the reply from a young Lieutenant. "Our second-in-command will join us in Texas. He's detained at Fort Leavenworth on a court-martial case – he's Lieutenant Colonel Robert E. Lee."

The Cherokee looked questioningly toward a Captain talking to a Lieutenant.

"That's Captain E. Kirby-Smith," the young officer volunteered, "and he's talking to Lieutenant John B. Hood. Beg yore pardon, suh, but you look mighty like a Georgia man. I'm from Virginia myself."

The Cherokee smiled, looked around for any close-by Ross men, and then said, "Good, Lieutenant, I'm one of Stand Watie's men and we're on the South's side. Be kind enough, if it please you, to get whatever fellow officers you like and we'll step into the National. I've got a room there and I'll be much obliged if you'll allow me to treat you all to something to quench a long dry thirst, Lieutenant –," the speaker halted and fumbled for his words.

"Indeed, suh, I'm begging yore pardon for having neglected to introduce myself. True hospitality like this could not be exceeded along the faraway banks of the mighty rolling James. I'm Lieutenant Stuart, suh. And since you're one of Stand Watie's friends, just call me what my other friends do, 'Jeb.' "

Stand Watie was not the only Cherokee leader worried by shaping developments. Old Chief John Ross questioned the effects of the conflicting political philosophies of the North and the South on the Indian Territory.

Fortune had been most kind to the old Chief who, though he headed the full-bloods, had a Scotch father and a quarter-blood mother! Actually John Ross, born in 1790, near Lookout Mountain in Tennessee, had far less Indian blood in him than Stand Watie! True, he had taken a Cherokee as his first wife, but, in

1845, he had married Mary B. Stapler, a Delaware Quaker.

The New York *Tribune*, September 5, 1844, wrote up the Ross wedding which had been at Hartwell's Washington House in Philadelphia:

"Another grand wedding party has 'come off' at this delightful house, so celebrated for affairs of this nature.

"John Ross, the celebrated Cherokee chief, was married in the President's parlor of this Hotel last night to Miss Mary B. Stapler of Wilmington, Delaware. He is about 55 and she is only 18 years of age; she is a very beautiful girl and highly accomplished; and belongs to the Society of Friends, or did. Her father was formerly a highly respected Quaker merchant of this city.

"She was given away by her brother and attended by her sister and a niece of John Ross as bridesmaids. He had collected several of his daughters and nephews from boarding schools, &c. in New Jersey to be present at the wedding; and after the ceremony a family party of 20 of the Ross's (all half breed Indians) sat down to a most sumptuous banquet for the preparation of which he had given Hartwell a *carte blanche* and a most elegant affair it was. Ross is considered to be worth half a million dollars. He proposes to sojourn with his beautiful bride at this excellent hotel for a short time; after which he goes straight to his wild home in the South Western prairies."

His "wild home," as the New York newspaperman put it, is fully described in *Park Hill*:

"Situated on high ground overlooking a wide sweep of the country, the white house [Rose Cottage] surrounded by a fence covered with rose vines, must have surprised and delighted the young wife. The cottage could hold forty guests in comfort. It was approached by a driveway half a mile in length which was bordered with many varieties of roses that Ross bought during his travels. In the spring and summer the lane was a riot of bloom and the air was filled with fragrance. His orchard contained a thousand fine apple trees and his stables were as large as public stables in a city. The hitching racks in a space reserved for that purpose had room for fifty horses without crowding. The house was furnished with mahogany and rosewood, imported china and beautiful silver. The grounds were planted with shrubs and choice flowers, while the kitchen, garden and orchard were on a scale large enough to supply demands of the family, guests and a retinue of house and field servants. In connection there was a kiln, a smokehouse, a dairy, blacksmith shop, laundry and cabins for the Negroes.

"The Ross family lived in great style, gave dinners to which many guests were invited and kept open house. The plantation included a thousand acres, was worked by slaves and was immensely profitable."

Rose Cottage, at Park Hill, some four miles south of Tahlequah, was two-stories with four massive, tall white columns supporting the center porch. His hundred slaves looked on as Chief Ross and his youthful bride went riding in a fine coach topped by a black lad in livery. The house servants marvelled at the $10,000 worth of furniture in Rose Cottage which had been shipped from the East.

Chief John Ross was handsomely and safely ensconced in beautiful Rose Cottage supported by the Keetoowah, the secret society of the Pins with 2,000 members. Ross knew that the Keetoowah was sponsored by Northern abolitionists who urged the Indians to remain true to their customs and their gods – as long as they also were true to the North and abolition! The Pins were identified by crossed pins which they wore on their coat lapels or calico shirts. Chief John Ross' cognition was that Stand Watie's Knights of the Golden Circle looked at these men with their Pin insignia and intuitively measured them – for their graves!

Chief Ross in his mansion at Park Hill, entrapped in the conflicting currents of Pin and mixed-blood, of States Rights and Federal Power, of the disturbing influence of the "horse Indians" on the great plains to the West, knew not where to turn. As the Principal Chief of the Cherokee Nations, his answer could well hold the destiny of his people.

At his large new house on the Spavinaw, Stand Watie, too, was reaping the fortunes of his ability. His home was not the mansion owned by Chief Ross, but it was the showplace of the mixed-bloods who often thronged his home as welcome guests. Stand Watie and Sarah had five children; three boys, Saladin, going on fifteen or so; Cumiskey, around eleven; and the youngest son, Watica; and two young daughters, Minnehaha Josephine, and Jacqueline. Minnehaha, the elder, could read the Bible fluently and quote Latin.

Gyrated in the political maelstrom, Chief Ross groped for a

way to secure himself and his Cherokee Nation from being sucked under. Contrastingly, Stand Watie groped for nothing. In what was a malevolent whirlpool to Ross, Stand Watie perceived as a new road to freedom — freedom from the domination of the Cherokee Nation by the Pins and freedom for the South from the oppressive threats of the Black Republicans and Kansan abolitionist cut-throats!

Stand Watie's confounded Pin enemies had watched him live through the crimson, feuding years unscratched, and they had come to avow that no bullet ever fired by them could kill Stand Watie!

As far as Watie was concerned, the Yankees could sustain the same thesis!

3

WITH THE FRENZIED abolitionists whipping up an emotional malice against the Southerners supporting States Rights and refusing to bow before the outcries of fanatics, the boiling political kettle spilled over into far remote Indian Territory, the land of the Five Civilized Nations; the Cherokee, Seminole, Creek, Choctaw and Chickasaw.

The Superintendent of Indian Affairs at Fort Smith, Arkansas, Elias Rector, was a Southerner and Douglas H. Cooper, a hard-drinking Mississippian, a Franklin Pierce appointee, was the Choctaw and Chickasaw agent. Others working openly for Secession were John Crawford, Cherokee agent; William Quesenbury, Creek agent; Samuel M. Rutherford, Seminole agent; and Matthew Leeper, Wichita agent.

These agents of the Washington government felt secure in that the rather inaccessible nature of the Indian Territory would cloak their activities in behalf of the South. Troops had been withdrawn from the Indian frontier and in May 1860, several of the forts were abandoned and others weakened.

The strategists of the South realized that if war were to come, the Secessionists could make good use of the Indian Territory as a storehouse for provisions, a highway to and from Texas, a base for raids into Federal territory and also a possible jumping off place for capturing Colorado. There was some Rebel sympathy in that state as well as an anti-Washington feeling which could be utilized as many citizens were angry because they felt Washington had exposed their state to attack by the wild Plains Indians.

On January 5, 1861 a caucus of Southern senators adopted resolutions advising immediate secession. On the very same day the Chickasaw Legislature suggested that an intertribal conference be held so that the Civilized Nations could arrive at some mutual action in respect to the impending split between the North and the South. Governor Cyrus Harris, of the Chickasaw Nation, sent out a plan to other tribes and the Creek chiefs named a conference for February 17.

Before this date came about, on February 7 the Choctaw Nation had come out for the slave states, saying their (the Choctaws) "natural affection, education, institutions and interests" bound them "in every way to the destiny" of their "neighbors and brethren of the Southern states." The Choctaws had 5,000 Negro slaves.

Bluntly Stand Watie's long time foe, Chief Ross of the Cherokees, replied that the quarrel between the states was of no concern to the Indians.

The Creeks still felt that the split in the Union could be of some import to their nation. The Creek Legislature was composed of two houses, the House of Kings and the House of Warriors and the rulings of the Nation – legislative, judicial and executive – were enforced by a company of light horse.

On February 9, Jefferson Davis, of Mississippi, became president of the Confederacy and Alexander H. Stephens, of Georgia, became vice president, with the president to serve six years and not to be eligible for re-election. And just eight days later, leaders of the Indian Territory met in their conference as the Creeks had proposed, and decided to follow the course set by John Ross, to remain neutral at least for the time being. But, apparently sensing the action to be taken, the pro-Confederate leaders of the Choctaw and the Chickasaw Nations "went fishing."

In less than a month the Provisional Congress of the Confederate States had authorized President Davis to send a special agent to the Indian tribes west of Arkansas.

Davis appointed Albert Pike, a New Englander by birth, who had lived in Arkansas for many years and had been a Captain in the war with Mexico. In this war Pike had recruited his own company of Arkansas cavalry, equipped at his own expense. At the battle of Buena Vista, Pike had given his horse to a military engineer whose mount had been shot out from under him. After the end of the War between the States, Pike's son, Yvon, on going to Washington College (now Washington and Lee University), as a student, met the same man his father had aided at Buena Vista – Robert E. Lee, the college's president!

Albert Pike had won renown in Arkansas both as a writer – he is known as Arkansas' first great author – and as a lawyer. He was well versed in Greek, Latin, French, Spanish and Sanskrit, as well as the Indian languages. His admission to the bar of the Supreme Court of the United States was in 1849, at the same time as the admission of Lincoln and Hannibal E. Hamlin. He was active in the Democratic American Party, the so-called "Know-Nothings" – which upheld States Rights and had as an objective placing the government of the country in the hands of Americans only, part of its platform being, "All offices, civil and military, should be given to native-born Americans, in preference to foreign born."

Despite his Northern birth, Albert Pike was an ardent Secessionist, edited the Arkansas *Advocate,* and wrote:

> "Southrons, hear your country call you!
> Up! lest worse than death befall you!
> To arms! to arms! to arms! in Dixie!
> Lo! all the beacon fires are lighted,
> Let all your hearts be now united!
> To arms! to arms! to arms! in Dixie!
> Advance the flag of Dixie
> Hurrah! Hurrah!

For Dixie's land we'll take our stand,
To live or die for Dixie!
To arms! to arms!
And conquer peace for Dixie!
To arms! to arms!
And conquer peace for Dixie!"

Whether the Indian leaders of the Civilized Nations were ardent readers of Pike's poetry is not recorded, but the mixed-breed plantation type Indians were his good friends and he often hunted with them. This association resulted in Pike being named their lawyer, representing them in Washington. In 1859 he secured for the Choctaws an award by the United States Senate of $2,981,247.

What was the over-all picture of the Indian situation? The Southern Superintendency took in south Kansas and the whole of the Indian Territory, now Oklahoma. Within it were the five great slave holding tribes that had come from South of the Mason-Dixon line; the Cherokees, Creeks, Chickasaws, Choctaws and Seminoles. Also in the Southern area were a few New York Indian families, as well as some groups of Wichitas, Quapaws, Caddoes, Shawnees and Senecas, as well as a few exiled Texas Indians.

Also in the geographic group were the Osages of Southern Kansas, the Black Dog tribe of which supported secession, and some of the wild Plains Indians, the Tonkasas tribe of the "half wild" Wichitas being Secessionists.

In the Central Agency were the Sacs and Foxes, Munsees, Delawares, Shawnees and a variety of small tribes, Weas, Peories, Kaskaskias, Piankeshaws, Potawatomies, Ottawas, the Miamies, Chippewas and the Kaws of north central Kansas.

Generally speaking, most of the tribes north of the thirty-seventh parallel were loyal. The Kansas Indians – except for the before mentioned Osages of the South – were in the Central Agency. This Agency's tribes were those which had come from free states and they stood by the Union. More than one-half of the adult male Delawares enlisted as volunteers and some were to die under Stand Watie's guns. The Quapaws of the detached bands were loyal as well as the Caddoes from the interior country.

Albert Pike went out in May 1861, on his diplomatic mission to negotiate treaties with the Indians and soon he had the unorganized tribes in the Indian Territory, under Agent Andrew J. Dorn, for the Confederacy.

But before he left, Pike had written a letter on May 11, saying: "I foresaw some time ago that the regular troops would be withdrawn, as too much needed elsewhere to be left inactive, and that they would be replaced by volunteers, under men actuated by personal hatred of the South. I do not think that more than five or six thousand men will be sent there [Indian Territory] for a time, but those, I am satisfied, will be there soon. To occupy the country with safety, we ought to have at least an equal force, if we first occupy it, and shall need a much larger one if they establish themselves in it during an inaction. It will hardly be safe to count upon putting in the field more than 3,500 Indians; maybe we may get 5,000. To procure any, or at least any respectable number, we must guarantee them their lands, annuities and other rights under treaties, furnish them arms (rifles and revolvers, if the latter can be had), advance them some $25.00 a head in cash, and send them a respectable force there, as evidence that they will be efficiently seconded by us."

News reached Fort Smith that Senator Lane of Kansas was raising soldiers to take the field on the western borders of Arkansas and Missouri and in May, Lieutenant Colonel J. R. Kannady, commander at Fort Smith, had a problem himself. Would the Cherokees across the border become alarmed at pro-Abolitionist Lane's activities and support the Secesh?

Chief John Ross was quick to assure Colonel Kannady that the Cherokees' treaties and relations with the United States were still being maintained, and he explained his position:

"Weak, defenseless and scattered over a large section of country, in the peaceful pursuits of agricultural life, without hostility to any State, and with friendly feelings towards all, they hoped to be allowed to remain so, under the solemn conviction that they should not be called upon to participate in the threatened fratricidal war between the 'United' and the 'Confederate' States, and that persons gallantly tenacious of their own rights would respect others."

On May 25 the Chickasaw Legislature announced its support of the Confederacy and urged neighbors to form an alliance against "the Lincoln hordes and Kansas robbers against whom [their Southern friends] a war which . . . will surpass the French

Revolution in scenes of blood and that of San Domingo in atrocious horrors."

The Little Rock *Times and Herald* welcomed the support of the Choctaw and Chickasaw Nations in an editorial which said," . . . these noble sons of the west, who armed with long rifles, Tomahawks and scalping knives, swear that nothing but the scalp of the Yankee will satisfy their vengeance."

Meanwhile Senator Lane of Kansas, who had led the "free state army" in the Kansas border war, was organizing moves to rally the loyal Indians in Federal lands as well as those in the Indian Territory who did not follow their leaders in pledging allegiance to Jefferson Davis. Senator Lane had discussed the loyal Indian problem with Abraham Lincoln, who opposed fighting the Southerners with wild Indians; however, later, when the Union refugees from the Five Nations approached him, Lincoln approved Indian-Federal Kansas councils in Leroy, Fort Scott and Humboldt.

By fall, Pike had made treaties of alliance with all of the Five Civilized Tribes except the Cherokee, held in line by Ross but ever liable to explode under the pressure for the Confederacy being applied by Stand Watie. Albert Pike wrote:

". . . at Park Hill, he [Ross] refused to enter into any agreement with the Confederate States. He said it was his intention to maintain neutrality of his people . . . [who] would be destroyed if they engaged in war; that it would be a cruel thing if we were to engage them in our quarrel . . ."

At Fort Wayne, Delaware District, Cherokee Nation, on July 29, Watie had organized his independent command, the First Cherokee Rifles and named Elias C. Boudinot, his nephew, a Major.

Indian Commissioner Pike had failed to sway Ross even though Pike had $100,000 to be used in obtaining Southern control of the Indian Territory. Prior to Pike's call, Ross had rejected all efforts by Brigadier General Ben McCulloch, Confederate Indian Territory commander, to win the Cherokee Nation.

Confederate difficulty in getting a treaty with the Creeks had been overcome. Old Chief Opothleyoholo (called by some Chief Hopoeithleyohola) had no confidence in the promises of the Confederacy. On the other side, the Rebel cause was espoused by Chilly and Daniel McIntosh, the sons of wealthy William Mc-

Intosh, Creek Chief in the days of the Georgia removal and Brigadier General under Andrew Jackson. The sons' animosity for the full-bloods was nurtured by the memory of how these Indians had "murdered" their father because of his part in supporting the Georgia removal.

Daniel, 22 years younger than Chilly, was an ordained Baptist minister and a handsome man with long hair curled at the ends, a moustache and a goatee, whose pride was in his Southern planter heritage. With a commission from the Confederacy, Daniel had flown the Dixie flag over the Creek Agency to the ebullient cheers of the regiment he had raised. Meanwhile Chilly had ridden westward under the same flag as an aide to Albert Pike in his quest of the wild Plains Indians.

Unlike the Southern planter-type McIntosh, Chief Opothleyoholo was a blanket Indian who painted his face and could neither read nor write, but, although he opposed the alliance with the Confederacy, paradoxically owned many slaves and cultivated some two thousand acres of land. The eighty-year-old Creek Chief had a keen brain and kept all his business transactions as well as the business of the Creek Nation in his head. The Old Chief unalterably opposed the Confederate treaty and he fondly visioned, if fighting came, a force of full-blood Creeks and Negroes, fused with the support of white troops and free state Indians, promised him by the United States Indian Department.

The Confederate Government at Montgomery did not place all the matters of Indian affairs into the hands of the big-framed, scholarly, flowing-locked Pike. On May 13, 1861, the brave Texas Ranger, Benjamin McCulloch, who had accepted the surrender of Daniel E. Twiggs and the San Antonio armaments, was made a Brigadier General in the Confederate Provisional Army and assigned to command of the Indian Territory. McCulloch wanted to make his base in the Cherokee Nation, but unmoved, Ross felt this would be a violation of his neutrality, which he again proclaimed on May 17, and McCulloch established his headquarters at Fort Smith, given up by the Federals, in Western Arkansas.

Leroy Pope Walker, a native of Alabama, had been appointed Secretary of War for the Confederacy in February 1861, and he wrote a letter from Montgomery, on May 13, 1861, to Major Douglas H. Cooper, now in the Confederate service after his successful "propagandizing" of the Choctaw and the Chickasaw:

"We have commissioned General Ben McCulloch with three Regiments under his command, from the states of Arkansas, Texas and Louisiana, to take charge of the Military District embracing the Indian country. And I now empower you to raise among the Choctaw and Chickasaw a mounted regiment to be commanded by yourself in cooperation with General McCulloch. [This, Cooper did, raising the First Choctaw and First Chickasaw Rifles of which he became Colonel] . . . also . . . raise two similar regiments among the Creeks, Cherokee, Seminoles and other friendly tribes for the same purposes.

"This combined force . . . will be ample to secure the frontiers upon Kansas & the interest of the Indians while to the South of the Red River three Regiments from Texas under a different command have already been assigned to the Rio Grande & Western border . . .

"We have our agents actively engaged in the manufacture of ammunition and in the purchase of arms . . . the arms we are purchasing for the Indians are Rifles and they will be forwarded to Fort Smith."

All the officers in Indian Territory were to cooperate with David Hubbard, the Confederate Superintendent of Indian Affairs, as the Provisional Congress of the Confederate States had created a Bureau of Indian Affairs to be attached to the War Department.

In the meantime Chief Ross had ordered raised 1,200 Home Guards to keep out invaders — be they North or South — from the Cherokee Nation. Colonel John Drew was in command. McCulloch authorized Watie to raise a regiment to protect the northern border, but McCulloch, respecting Ross' stand instructed Watie "not to interfere with the neutrality of the [Cherokee] Nation."

In early August, Colonel Watie and a part of his independent command, aligned with Arkansas troops, were in the battle of Wilson's Creek or Oak Hill and John Benge, the first Cherokee to fall, was killed in action.

To lead up to Wilson's Creek, one must recall that General Nathaniel Lyon, a brave soldier but an undisguised and zealous Abolitionist, had advanced the Federal banner during the summer in Missouri. He had pushed aside all his opposition from St. Louis to Jefferson City, Boonville and Springfield in the contest for Missouri.

Jefferson City, the capital, fell without a fight and Governor Jackson and the pro-Confederate legislature had vanished with the state archives, but Lyon soon found out the Missourians had rallied at Boonville. There, the untrained soldiers under twenty-eight-year-old Colonel John Sappington Marmaduke, who had served with Albert Sidney Johnston in the Utah Expedition, were no match for the regulars far superior in numbers.

Governor Jackson and his government continued to fall back; a column of some 4,000 made up of state officials and Secessionist followers. But the retreating column gained allies. Wealthy Jo Shelby rode in with his troop of horses to lend a military air to the column. Then Senator James Rains marched in with 3,000 volunteers and three guns commanded by Hiram Bledsoe with his sweeping moustache and little goatee.

Jackson's army, without uniforms, flying the Confederate flag on its flanks and the Missouri flag at its center, stopped its march at Carthage to fight General Franz Sigel (ranked by some historians as a Colonel at the time of the battle), who had taught at the German-American Institute in St. Louis, and his Germans, former members of a gymnastic society. In what was actually the first important encounter of arms in Missouri, gold-spectacled, straggly-bearded Sigel was defeated but his gray-clad (the color of the gymnastic uniforms) men made an orderly retreat to Springfield, recently occupied by Lyon, who had hoped to overtake Jackson before he joined forces with Sterling Price and Benjamin McCulloch. Shortly after the Missouri "Patriots Army" victory at Carthage, this Rebel junction took place.

The Confederates conjured up plans to defeat Lyon. They whipped their forces into shape at Cowskin Prairie, near the Indian Territory boundary. Raw recruits were instructed to fire at the breeches button of their foes. The opportunity to strike back at Lyon came on August 10 at Wilson's Creek, or Oak Hill.

On the Southern side, besides such Generals as Ben McCulloch and Sterling Price; the former fifty years old with his white hair reaching his shoulders, hero of the Mexican War, one time California sheriff at Sacramento, and who, the eastern press reported was ready to kidnap Lincoln; the latter, who had assumed command of all the Missouri troops after the victory of Jackson's state militia at Carthage; were along with Stand Watie and his men (there were an estimated nearly one thousand Cherokees and Choctaws in the battle), Jo Shelby and his cavalry, and Coleman Younger. Coleman later was to gain a name along with his brother, James, when they fought under the guerrilla banner of Charles Quantrill, who, at Wilson's Creek, was commanding a group of Indian Territory mixed-bloods.

And on the Northern side was a fellow named Wild Bill Hickock walking around in his high-heeled boots and fresh from the wars in Kansas.

The battle of Wilson's Creek was fought – Missourians against Missourians in the center, Arkansans (commanded by General N. Bartlett Pearce), Texans, Louisianans (Louis Herbert's Pelican Rifles) combatting the Kansans, Iowans and Germans on the flanks.

The Southern army, described by one officer as with "not a tent, not a blanket, nor any clothes, except the few we had on our backs, and four-fifths barefooted," after heavy fighting broke up Sigel's command, captured all his artillery except one piece, and the Rebels combined their forces against General Lyon. The Secesh pressed so hard that Lyon said, "I fear the day is lost," and a short time later fell instantly killed.

With crowded ambulances – casualties at Wilson's Creek totalled 23 per cent of all engaged – the defeated Federals fell back some nine miles to Springfield and that evening General McCulloch sent Major Samuel Sturgis, who had assumed the Union command on Lyon's death, the body of General Lyon, forgotten in the retreat.

Under the command of Sigel the Federals left Springfield and moved – to the sorrow of Union families who had come in for protection – to Rolla, 175 miles to the southeast.

And the partially decomposed body of General Lyon, the surgeons failing to preserve it by injecting arsenic, was left behind at Springfield, no farewell shots being fired for the fallen leader who had been the summer-hero of the Union campaign. A lugubrious Union woman, Mrs. John Phelps, a Congressman's wife, learning Lyon's body was unburied, had it put in a coffin which was placed in her outdoor cellar and covered with straw. Later, fearing Confederate soldiers would molest the remains, she had the coffin buried under cover of night. To complete the story, though, it must be stated that several weeks later doleful relatives of General Lyon were allowed back of the Confederate lines and the body was taken East where, with high honors and ceremonies, it was reinterred in Connecticut.

Wilson's Creek had freed Southwest Missouri from Federal control. Southern sympathizers felt that all of the state could be swept clean of the lunatic abolitionists; however, McCulloch and Pearce took their Confederate forces — Watie and his Indians included — back to Arkansas, a move later admitted by McCulloch as "a great mistake." Sterling Price and his State army were left to continue the fight in Missouri.

Daniel O'Flaherty commented on Wilson's Creek in *General Jo Shelby — Undefeated Rebel*:

"Wilson's Creek was the Bull Run of the West, and its analogy to the first great battle in Virginia is remarkable.

"In both cases the battle was the first conflict on a vast scale in its particular theatre of war; in both cases the Southern troops were panicked into flight in the opening phases of the battle; in both cases they rallied to smash the enemy and hurl him back into the tight ring of defenses of his capital; and in both cases they were so exhausted by the victory they could not follow it up. In Virginia the Confederates lost the opportunity to march on Washington after Bull Run and perhaps end the war by dictating peace terms from the capital; in Missouri they failed to pursue the defeated enemy after Wilson's Creek and retake the Missouri River Valley, which would have brought Missouri into the orbit of the Confederacy, gained control of the vital upper Mississippi, and perhaps saved the heartland of the South from invasion.

"Both Bull Run and Wilson's Creek demonstrated the fatal military weakness of the new Southern nation, its inability to make its victories count."

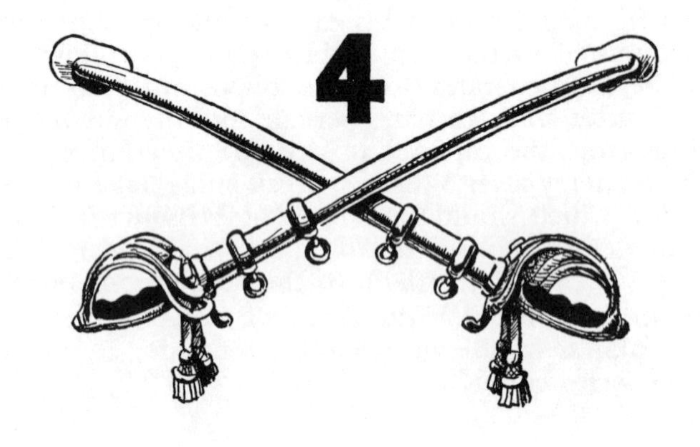
4

WHILE WATIE WAS participating in the Wilson's Creek activities, the squeezing pressure on Ross was beginning to take its toll. Albert Pike had been successful elsewhere in kneading Indians for the Confederacy — even if the fecundity in the case of the wild and "half wild" Plains Indians was impregnated sometimes with canned oysters, sardines, asparagus, green peas, and lobsters, bolts of calico and gingham, a liberal distribution of decks of playing cards and ready-made pants for the chiefs. In August 1861, Pike sent in a strong request for formal Cherokee alliance with the South.

Both Ross and Pike knew that Stand Watie and his friends were advocating such a treaty. And all the principals were well aware of the disaster which had overtaken Lyon and Sigel at Wilson's Creek, and how Stand Watie's position had been subsequently strengthened because he had participated in the Federal defeat.

Ross recognized that the Plains Indians in some cases had rejected his plea to negotiate no treaties with the Confederacy. Plains leaders — Pock Mark, George Washington and Buffalo Hump — bore no actual affection for the Confederacy, but in their eyes at least a glint of Rebel love was ignited by the munificent gifts of diplomat Pike.

When the Federal troops had pulled out of Forts Washita, Arbuckle and Cobb, back in July, Pike, with an impressive escort, had ridden in to over-awe the half-wild Comanches, Osages and Wichitas baffled that the Federal Army officers, Samuel Sturgis and James Totten, would abandon their posts.

Irregular independent Secesh commands, troops made up of half-breed Choctaws and Chickasaws, with English speaking commanders, shared the old Army forts with bands of Texans who had moved into Indian lands. Terrified by the rapid change in their lands, some of the Indians had headed for Kansas and government protection, others had moved westward to the lands of their "wild Indian brothers" and still others preferred to make the future on their home lands. These were the Indians who had come to Pike's grand councils and seen the civilized Indians proudly riding under the Confederate flag.

Both Watie and Ross must have debated whether in behalf of the Southern cause the mutual hatred of the aristocratic Southern planter half-breed Cherokee for his fellow tribesman, the full-blooded Pin, could be effaced?

Seeking some febrifuge against the political fever of the Nation, Chief Ross sent out a call to his people. On August 21, 1861, 4,000 Cherokees gathered at Tahlequah, filed up to the Council house and the open rostrum on the hill, pitched their tents in wind-sheltered valleys. John Ross and his brother Lewis, the Cherokee treasurer, spoke to the crowd and pled for a Confederate alliance. The frock-coated "white" mixed-bloods entertained no notion of opposing the Principal Chief this time since he had switched to Watie's position.

But what of the full-bloods in turbans and calico shirts? Men who looked no part of the Southern civilization as did their half-breed tribesmen with their fair Anglo-Saxon wives.

Ross realized that to side with the Confederacy would cancel the Cherokee treaty with the United States, still owing about $5,000,000 to the Nation for lands vacated in North Carolina, Georgia, and Tennessee. But the Confederate Government had promised to take over the Federal payments, to apply the fugitive slaves laws to their slaves and, if desired, to give the Indian Nations statehood.

Longanimity shattered, the assembled Cherokees gave the answer — union with the Confederacy and the raising of a regiment by Colonel John Drew, a Ross man, for service with General McCulloch. Stand Watie's independent command had already set him high in official Confederate circles.

Had Ross really been won over to the Confederacy? If so why was it that after the treaty was assured Mrs. Ross, a Quaker, violently opposed efforts by the pro-Southern Cherokees to raise a Confederate flag over the Indian council house? Chief Ross upheld his wife.

Even Pike, in his time of triumph, must have had some mistrust of Ross' dulcet tones, and, after the war, Pike said "If Stand Watie and his party took one side, John Ross and his party were in the end sure to take the other, *especially when the other proved itself the stronger.*"

General James G. Blunt, leading the Federal attack on Indian Territory, after he had captured Ross, wrote Lincoln that the Cherokees "had resisted the Confederate agents as long as possible and only the lack of communciations with the Federal government had kept Ross from being loyal."

With the Cherokee Nation now allied with the Confederacy, Stand Watie, still with an independent command, saw General McCulloch at Camp Walker, Benton County, Arkansas, and was given a Colonel's commission and his unit became known as the Cherokee Mounted Rifles.

How excellent an impression Watie and his men made on McCulloch is contained in a report the Brigadier General wrote to Secretary of War Walker in September 1861, in which he stated, "Watie's Regiment is composed of half-breeds, men generally educated and good soldiers in or out of the Nation. I hope the government will continue this gallant man and true friend of our country in the service."

On October 7 the official signing of the Cherokee Treaty of Alliance was held and Albert Pike wrote on this meeting:

"I encamped with my little party near the residence of the Chief unprotected even by a guard and with the Confederate flag flying . . .After the treaties were signed, I presented Colonel Drew's regiment with a flag and then Chief Ross in a speech exhorted them to be true to it; afterwards, at his request, I wrote the Cherokee Declaration of Independence . . . when the flag was presented Colonel Watie was present and after the ceremony the chief shook hands with him and expressed his warm desire for Union and harmony in the nation . . .The same day the Cherokee Treaty was signed, the Osages, Quapaws, Shawnees and Senecas signed treaties, and the next day they had a talk with Mr. Ross at his residence, smoked the great pipe and renewed their alliance, being urged by him to be true to the Confederate States."

Said, in part, the Cherokee alliance:

"The Confederate States of America having accepted the said protectorate, hereby solemnly promises the said Cherokee Nation never to desert or abandon it, and that under no circumstances will they permit the Northern States, or any other enemy, to overcome them and sever the Cherokees from the Confederacy; but that they will, at any cost and all hazards, protect and defend them, and maintain unbroken the ties created by identity of interests and institutions, and strengthened and made perpetual by this treaty."

McCulloch, replying to John Ross' letter of alliance with the Confederacy, said:

"Permit me to congratulate you upon the course you have thought proper to pursue. The people of the Confederate States and those of the Cherokee Nation must share a common destiny. Their interest and institutions are the same. Then, let us as brothers cooperate against a common enemy to us and those institutions, and drive them from our borders whenever they dare approach them."

In an address to Colonel Drew's regiment of mainly full-bloods and Pins at Fort Gibson, John Ross stated:

"On the arrival of the commissioner Pike at this place, the regiment welcomed him and formed his escort to his headquarters at Park Hill, where the treaty was made . . . it secures us advantages we have long sought, and gives us the rights of freemen, to dispose of our lands as we please . . . By negotiating this alliance with the Confederate States, we are under obligations to aid the South against all its enemies, so that the enemies of the South are our enemies . . ."

The Fort Smith *Times and Herald* reported August 29 that George Michael Murrell at Park Hill wrote Major G. W. Clarke, Acting Quartermaster of the Confederate States, "The Cherokees are all right at last, and will have a regiment raised shortly for McCulloch, to go wherever he may order. The Cherokees are more united than they have been for several years."

Murrell, a native of Virginia, owned Hunter's Home, one of the showplaces of the Indian Territory, furnished with importations from France and Italy. A visitor commented, "We thought it beautiful because it had red plush furniture and prisms on the chandeliers. There were large mirrors over the curved mantles and the andirons and fixtures for the fireplace were burnished brass." Other visitors admired the expensive drapes and the imported curtains around the bed and one guest wrote, "Between the parlor and the sitting room there were a hundred canaries in there among the flowers. It was a beautiful sight."

Wealthy Murrell divided his time between Hunter's Home and his plantation on Bayou Goula in Louisiana. The merchant-planter had first married Minerva, eldest daughter of Lewis Ross, brother of Chief John Ross, but when she died at the age of thirty-six, he next married Armanda Melvina Ross, his young sister-in-law. Despite Murrell's relationship with the Ross family, Stand Watie's Rebel raiders never burned the Murrell mansion occupied by Miss Eliza Jane Ross, niece of John Ross, and her mother, during the war.

But, though on the surface, the warring factions of the Cherokees were united, it should be kept in mind that McCulloch warned Pike, in late September to separate the Indian commands under Stand Watie and Colonel Drew "for fear of a collision if they should come into contact with each other." Watie had said at the Tahlequah conference that no peace could come to the Cherokees as long as the Pins remained a powerful political organization.

The tangled situation in the Creek Nation remained troublesome for the Confederacy even though John Ross had written the strong-willed Chief Opothleyoholo, known also as Yo-ho-la, to come "where we may all smoke the pipe of peace and friendship around our great council fire."

Chief John Ross wrote from Park Hill, September 19:

"Opothleyoholo and others. Friends and Brothers . . . with one voice we have proclaimed in favor of forming an alliance with the Confederate States, and shall thereby preserve and maintain the brotherhood of the Indian nations in a common destiny . . . my advice and desire . . . is for all the red brethren to be united . . . by forming an alliance of peace and friendship with the Confederate States of America."

The Creek leader remained adamant in his refusal to join in with the Creek Council in its support of the Confederacy. The pro-Confederate Creeks grew so strong that the Chief fled from the Creek capital to his plantation.

Commissioner Pike, from Park Hill, on October 7 had vainly sought to win over Yo-ho-la with a letter later discovered in the archives of the "Snake" Creek Government of Crazy Snake stating:

"The Confederate States of America hereby offers a free pardon to Hopoithle Yahola and to all Creek and other warriors now under him in arms against the Confederate States and the lawful authorities of the Creek Nation (excepting only Jim Ned, a person half Delaware and half negro, who signed a treaty with them at the Wichita Agency on August 1st), on the condition that they submit and lay down their arms; and if they desire it, a Battalion of the same warriors, under a Lieutentant Colonel to be selected by themselves shall be received in the services of the Confederate States and not marched beyond the limits of the Indian Country without their consent."

Pro-Union refugees from the Seminole Nation – which also had become a Confederate ally – joined the stream of wagons, horses and walking parties which converged on Opothleyoholo. His grass eaten away by the livestock of his uninvited – but not unwelcome – guests, said to number as high as 4,000, including a thousand warriors, the Creek leader was beset with conflicting rumors. One was that the Confederate Indians were preparing to ride upon him and massacre the assembled (thought to be impuissant) Union leaders. Another was that Jim Lane's Kansas troops were on their way to enforce the Union redskins so that they could drive the Rebel tribes from Indian Territory.

The Creek Chief, taking more stock in the first report, poured the National Treasury in a barrel, buried it in the hills, and then ordered a great exodus of his people, authorities on Indian warfare even today debating what the Chief intended to do. Yo-ho-la himself claimed that he was heading for western lands to set up a cow-pen. Watie felt that the Creeks and their refugees were headed eventually for Kansas and Free Territory where they could be reformed and pose a threat to Indian Territory. Had Yo-ho-la not raided the lands of Confederate Indians and driven off their cattle? Had not the homes of pro-South Creeks been burned? And who put the torch to the Indian trading house of John W. Taylor — soon to die in the battle of Round Mounds — openly siding with the South?

Major John Jumper assembled Rebel Seminole fighters eager to battle the Seminoles under Billy Bowlegs and Alligator, both siding with Creek Yo-ho-la. Chilly and Daniel McIntosh rallied the Creeks for vengeance against the depredations of the Old Chief. His seizure of the Creek Treasury brought the retaliatory threat — later countermanded by Cooper — that all of Opothleyoholo's following would forfeit their possessions to a new Creek war chest.

Help arrived from the Confederate Indian ranks around Douglas Cooper's headquarters and soon the expedition started out November 15 from Fort Gibson after the fleeing Creeks and their camp followers. The white Fourth Texas Cavalry led the column — Chilly McIntosh rode in his buggy — which numbered well over a thousand.

The column's advance guard — the Texans — caught up with Opothleyoholo at Round Mounds on November 19 in the late afternoon when approaching darkness was lighted by the Indian campfires. The Southerners charged the Indian camp in the woods and were met with a deadly fire of guns and a volley of arrows. Advancing Confederate Creeks came to the support of the Texans, bewildered by the night fighting. The charge was stopped and the attackers fell back through the brush and tall grass as the loyal Indians picked off the stragglers.

Yo-ho-la, his enemies momentarily halted, ordered a night withdrawal north toward Kansas. His squaws took a firm grip on their hominy pestles and approached the prisoners taken in the night fighting. These captives bound hand and foot knew what fate awaited them.

In the morning Cooper's scouts found them, their heads beaten into unrecognizable pulp, and vowed death to the Yankee Indians when encountered in battle. Booty was plentiful, for retiring Opothleyoholo left behind his buggy, broken down wagons, oxen, ponies, sheep and sacks of supplies.

The first engagement in the Indian Territory was over. Technically it might be called a victory for the defenders as Yo-ho-la had stopped Cooper's attack before fleeing and the Confederate Colonel had declined to make a pursuit, as he felt his forces would be needed in case the Federals under General David Hunter, who had succeeded General John C. Fremont, would invade the Indian Territory. But Hunter was soon on a retreat from Springfield, Missouri, his army going into winter quarters. Colonel Cooper, under orders from General McCulloch, who had moved most of his army into Southwest Arkansas and Southwest Missouri, and with word that Colonel John Drew and Colonel Stand Watie would join his command, readied for another try at stubbornly resisting Opothleyoholo.

Clem Rogers, whose father had been killed by the Ross sector in the Cherokee Nation, and father of the great humorist Will Rogers, helped guide the Cooper column which left Spring Hill November 29 and on December 9 reached the Union Indians strongly situated at Chusto-Talasah, or Little High Shoals, on Bird Creek. This time Cooper's assault was well planned and Yo-ho-la was surrounded by several thousand attackers. The moment for revenge of Round Mounds was at hand.

But Colonel Cooper had not counted on Colonel Drew's duplicity. Drew had arrived with his Cherokee command a day before Cooper's main column. The Ross Cherokee leader had received word that the Old Chief desired peace and—with Cooper's permission—sent Major Pegg of the Cherokee regiment into Yo-ho-la's camp. Surprised Pegg was confronted with Union Indians in full warpaint!

News of the warpaint took its effect on Drew and his command. His five hundred Cherokees refused to attack the full-bloods and withdrew from the battle. Again, this time on the south bank of Bird Creek, Opothleyoholo, though having to give some ground, threw back Cooper's efforts to capture or rout the Union Indians.

Crippled Confederate forces fell back to Fort Gibson to await new supplies and ammunition from Fort Smith. Frustrated Cooper rode ahead of his men so that he could rush out request for aid.

General McCulloch was in Richmond trying to straighten out difficulties in command which conflicted with Sterling Price and his State Commissioned Missouri army. His second-in-command was James McIntosh, whose brother John was to lose a leg in the battle of Winchester and later he retired as a Brigadier General in the United States Army. Brother John fought on the side of the Yankees! When Ross hedged on forcing Drew and his men into action against the obstinate Old Creek Chief, McIntosh, an aggressive fighter, came to Cooper's aid from Van Buren, Arkansas, with over a thousand men who had participated in the triumph at Wilson's Creek.

Through the cold snow, Colonel Cooper's column advanced up the north side of the Arkansas River so as to get in the rear of the Union Indians. Colonel McIntosh led his column of 1,600 men, mostly Texas cavalry except for four companies of South Arkansas Mounted Riflemen and the South Kansas-Texan Regiment of Colonel Lane, up the Verdigris River.

On December 26 – four days after leaving Fort Gibson – McIntosh reached Shoal Creek and crossed the thin ice as fire came from four hundred yards down the prairie where the loyal Indians were hidden behind boulders and blackjack along the brow of a hill.

McIntosh, even though his supporting Indian column, failing to keep its paripassu, was not in sight, ordered his cavalry to dismount, then charge. The Confederates reached the shelter of rocks and trees and then methodically started their way up the hill under a shower of bullets. The real fight against Yo-ho-la had commenced.

Hurrying along their path beside the Arkansas River were three hundred Cherokee horsemen with Stand Watie riding at their head; at his side, Major Elias C. Boudinot. The Confederate Cherokees rode as hard as the weather permitted for they were alert to the possibility of striking a death blow at the feculent Union Indians. With the Texans advancing in another column the Rebel pinchers would close on Opothleyoholo!

At darkness Watie's men — behind them the Cooper column of Choctaws and Chickasaws — rode into Shoal Creek to find the Texans warming themselves before large campfires.

Jubilant McIntosh shouted a welcome to Watie, then said, "I'm going back to Fort Smith, Colonel Watie, the war's over!"

Watie's men, dismounting from their horses, could hardly believe what had happened. The Texans in a four hour battle and losing only nine killed and forty wounded, had routed Yo-ho-la. The victors pointed out their captives, several hundred men and women and a handful of Negroes as well as thirty-nine wagons, seventy yoke of oxen and over five hundred ponies.

McIntosh explained that some of the loyal squaws had escaped with the warriors who were able to flee on horseback. Among those who had slipped from the Texans' trap was the Chief himself.

Watie told his men to rest for the night, but the morning's light would find them in on the chase.

And so on the morning air, when McIntosh, winner of the battle of Chustenahlah, rode with his victorious Texans toward Fort Smith, Watie and Boudinot, followed by Douglas Cooper's Choctaws and Chickasaws, sped their vengeance.

In the wintery blasts — so cold that one of Cooper's men froze to death — retreating bands of Unionists were overtaken and, when they offered resistance, killed. The fleeing Indians, with supplies gone and hope of reaching Kansas fast disappearing, watched apprehensively across prairie and hill, wondering if approaching horsemen would be blue-coated cavalry sent to their rescue by Lane or the ill-uniformed, but hard-riding Cherokee Rifles under Watie.

And when the riders turned out to be the dreaded Confederate Indians, the dismayed mothers — even as some of them had bashed in prisoners' heads — threw babies into cold mudholes and tramped them to death rather than let them fall into mixed-blood hands. Yet Watie and Cooper were not making war on women and children and none who surrendered were slain. But as thoroughly as possible the Rebel leaders sought out the loyal bands; some hiding in brush shelters and some, having eaten their horses, hidden in the cover of their hides.

"Surrender or die!" was the ultimatum. The Seminole Alligator took his choice. He died

Terror rode the Indian lands as even the independent tribes were caught in the net spread by Watie and Cooper. Those Indians not with Yo-ho-la were released and many of the half-wild Indians, on their way to free Kansas, felt it prudent to speak up for the Confederacy.

The rout of the loyal Indians was complete. Not only were their warriors defeated at Shoal Creek, but some seven hundred of the fleeing Indians perished in the flight, either through the elements or under the guns of the Southern Indians. Opothleyoholo, though, reached safety at Leroy, Kansas.

Since Colonel Stand Watie was in the forefront of the chase he became the hero of the wild winter pursuit and Confederate newspapers erroneously had him "capturing and burning Fort Scott, Topeka and Lawrence."

Chief John Ross sulked in his mansion at Park Hill for Colonel Stand Watie was the hero of the Cherokee Nation and Albert Pike was now Brigadier General Albert Pike, commander of the entire Indian Territory.

One of Pike's first acts of importance was to obtain funds for the Indians and on January 28, 1862, he wrote from Little Rock to Major Elias Rector, Superintendent of Indian Affairs at Fort Smith:

"I have $265,927.50 in specie . . . Of course I must stay with it . . . about 150 gamblers are here, following up the Indian moneyes. I enclose an order requiring passports, that will keep them out of the nation . . . I have the $150,000 advance for the Cherokees, the $12,000 due the nation and the $10,300 due the Treaty party of Stand Watie's . . . also the $50,000 advance for the Choctaws."

Although the Indians received their money, Pike was unable to obtain uniforms even for Watie's top command. General Pike, knowing the psychological effect of putting the Indian troops into regular uniforms, pressed his demands.

In February 1862, Stand Watie's Cherokees were at McCulloch's camp at Cross Hollow, Arkansas. Price's "Patriots Army," which "Old Pap" had miraculously maintained for six months with no government to direct it, no weapons except those he provided himself and which had no regular provisions but lived on the country as it marched and fought, came into Cross Hollow with 50 pieces of artillery, 400 tents and a wagon train of stores. The stores had been captured from the Federals!

Price's captured equipment didn't include uniforms and his army was almost as ill-fitted as the Cherokees. Shortly after Price's arrival, new Confederate uniforms arrived. Although these were the ones ordered by Pike for the Indian allies, the uniforms were distributed to Price's men. Colonel Watie's unit remained in odd shirts and pants, moccasins and hats with feathers sticking in them. Pike, who wanted Watie's Indians to look as smart as they fought, was furious.

Throughout the war, the Confederates were unable to keep their army in proper uniforms whether it be on the Virginia front or the Indian Territory. Long before the end of the war the Confederates were wearing Yankee uniforms and overcoats in cold weather. Most of Jo Shelby's men were wearing Union blue and many were shot when captured in Missouri in these uniforms. Colonel John F. Phillips – one of Watie's chief opponents – said in a report on the battle of Marais de Cygnes that the Confederates captured wearing Union uniforms were "executed instanter on the battlefield."

Colonel Watie's troubles were much more extensive than having his uniforms appropriated by other Confederate commanders. Back at the Cherokee capital the hatred of John Ross for him was already penetrating the coverage placed over it by the Confederate alliance. From the Cherokee Executive Department at Park Hill, Ross wrote General Pike:

". . . I had intended going to see the Troops . . . in view of offering every aid in any manner within the reach of my power to repel the enemy. But I am sorry to say I have been disuaded from going at present in consequence of some unwarrantable conduct on the part of many base, reckless and unprincipled persons belonging to Watie's Regiment who are under no subordination or restraint of their leaders in domineering over and trampling upon the rights of peaceable and unoffending citizens."

Whereas it was true that the Indian officers did not demand the strict discipline adhered to by white officers, it was known that Watie's command was the best disciplined Indian troop. Later on in the war when his raiders would capture Yankee whiskey, Watie, if his men drank too heavily, dumped the remaining "likker" into the nearest stream.

Coming upon the horizon was the battle of Pea Ridge, the first time the Confederate Indians were to participate in the war "on a big scale" comparable to battles in the East and South.

5

JEFFERSON DAVIS IN order to circumvent the disagreement between Price and McCulloch over command, appointed Major General Earl VanDorn, a Mississippian and a nephew of Andrew Jackson, as the overall commander of Trans-Mississippi Department No. 2. Besides the contending Price and McCulloch, this Department included Pike's Indian regiments and M. Jeff Thompson's "swamp foxes." When Fremont, in an effort to stop the Southern enlistments for Price, had issued his own Missouri Emancipation in August 1861, and declared martial law in the state – men bearing arms without authority were to be shot – a few days later from the Missouri swamps came Thompson's proclamation that for every man executed because of Fremont's order he would "Hang, draw and quarter a minion of said Abraham Lincoln."

With 45,000 men under his command, VanDorn set to work to accomplish his directive from Jefferson Davis to defeat General Samuel R. Curtis, who, in turn, had determined to make up for General Fremont's failures in Missouri. Price, offering mostly a token of resistance, fell back until his army could join other Confederate commands.

The Confederates began to gather in the area near Pea Ridge. Here would start the Rebel campaign to sweep on to St. Louis where the society, openly favorable to the South, was planning gay receptions.

Brigadier General Albert Pike, instructed to bring his Indians to the aid of VanDorn, grumbled openly as he thought his army best operating in Indian Territory. He knew the shortcomings of his warriors and he did not think them adaptable to the conditions of major battles. But Pike felt it wise not to conflict with VanDorn's plans. And so the Indian column moved toward Pea Ridge. The most colorful description of this is, perhaps, in *Civil War on the Western Border* by Jay Monaghan, noted writer of Americana and former State Historian of Illinois:

"On another road, west of the Boston Mountains, Pike's Indian column was coming to join the Confederate army with from one to six thousand men – estimates vary as much as that . . . [a fair estimate is 3,500] . . .

"The Indians marched in a long straggling line, many mounted, some trudging on foot. At the head, in a carriage, rode poetical and bewhiskered Pike, decked out like a Sioux in feathers, leggins, and beaded moccasins. His Negro body servant, Brutus, accompanied him with the tribal papers and payrolls in carpetbags. With Pike rode conservative John Ross in frock coat and stovepipe hat like President Lincoln's. General Cooper brought his Choctaw and Chickasaw. One unit of the former called themselves the 'Blue Eyed Company,' but it would be a mistake to consider any of them not Indians. Both factions of the Cherokee Nation were represented. The mixedbloods, under Stand Watie and Elias C. Boudinet [author's spelling] rode with the Texas battalion – all veterans of the fights against Opothleyohola [author's spelling]. Twelve hundred full-blooded 'pins,' who distrusted Stand Watie's 'slick skins' more than they did the enemy, rode with John Drew. Pompous John Jumper, dignified as an archbishop, came with six hundred Seminole. The Creeks were led by long-haired Daniel McIntosh, with eight members of his family holding commissions in the regiment, among them the toothless Chilly with a battalion of two hundred. Surely as bizarre an army as ever rode into an American battle! A Van Buren, Arkansas, newspaper reporter described McIntosh's Creek regiment as being a mixture of all ages and colors, including many Negroes with no uniforms and few arms. They had practiced a unique drill unknown to the pages of Hardee's manual. For the newsman the tatterdemalion gang lined up and at a given command all emitted a savage yell, broke ranks, ran a hundred yards to timber, fired by squads, cleaned their rifles, and stood waiting further orders."

General VanDorn sat in an ambulance, his mare hitched to its side. "Old Pap" Price rode beside the ambulance as the Confederates advanced slowly through the scrub oak to the open country. VanDorn planned to push back Curtis' whole right wing held by Carr's divisions, its artillery firing from behind embankments of dirt and logs. Not long after the Confederate attack began shortly before 10:30 the morning of March 7, Carr, in a bad spot, was sending for reinforcements.

But VanDorn had planned an assault on the left, too. Peter J. Osterhaus with his Germans, under Sigel and who had ridden in with Jo Shelby's pursuing cavalry on his tail, sent scouts out beyond Leetown – a blacksmith shop, a grocery and a handful of homes – only to probe into serious trouble. Here on the left were a multitude of Confederate troops springing into action. As Osterhaus' scouts tumbled backward, the Southern horde caught the Germans without even time to retreat and soon the Union troops were breaking for their lives.

Bearing down on them, some units already into the Yankee ranks, were charging Texans, followed up by Stand Watie's Indians, advancing on foot, and behind them, the mounted Indians under Colonel Drew. The charging Confederates were fighting with guns, cutlasses and bows and arrows. Their German Infantry already having fled, Osterhaus' cavalry were soon streaking back through the ranks of the advancing Fifty-ninth Illinois shouting the warning, "Turn back!"

Colonel Watie's men, aided by some Texans, captured a Yankee battery and held it. Other Indians rushed up to see the "shooting wagon" as the Indians called the artillery.

One veteran of Watie's capture of the Yankee battery related this exploit to Mabel Washbourne Anderson, saying, "I don't know how we did it, but Watie gave the order, which he always led, and his men could follow him into the very jaws of death. The Indian Rebel Yell was given and we fought them like tigers three to one. It must have been that mysterious power of Stand Watie that led us on to make the capture against such odds."

Watie's exploit in capturing the Federal artillery lived long after the war's end and Judge James M. Keyes, of Pryor, Oklahoma, a Watie veteran, said:

"I regard General Stand Watie as one of the bravest and most capable men, and the foremost soldier ever produced by the North American Indians. He was wise in council and courageous in action. His charge alone at the battle of Pea Ridge, with his famous First Cherokee Regiment of Cavalry that resulted in the capture of a Federal battery should stamp him as one of the real heroes of that sanguinary affair . . ."

General Pike's Indians did more than charge a battery. Some fought in the woods and from treetops. And some indulged in such war whoops that one Northern newspaperman at the battle said the roar of the Indians "was hideous."

And, in the heart of battle, the old customs came to the fore and a few luckless Yankees were tomahawked and scalped. After the battle, Curtis protested bitterly to VanDorn about the Confederate Indian "atrocities" and Northern newspapers painted the battle as if it were a reacting of the French and Indian War. But even the most prejudiced writer laid nothing at the door of Colonel Watie. It was Colonel Drew's Indians — actually pro-Union though fighting on the Confederate side — who did the small amount of scalping in the battle.

Once the Texans and Indians had smashed the left, General McCulloch, dressed in a dove colored coat, blue pantaloons and Wellington boots, and with a Maynard rifle slung over his shoulders rode in front of the Sixteenth Arkansas Infantry and just in back of his line of advancing skirmishers.

Peter Pelican, of Company B, Thirty-sixth Illinois Infantry, had advanced across a field, taken a position with other Federal skirmishers behind a fence when the Confederate skirmish line approached. Infantryman Pelican took aim at a Confederate officer, fired and the Rebel tumbled from his horse. Soon the Secesh fell back and the Federals advanced, but the Southerners rallied. Peter Pelican saw the Sixteenth Arkansas break into a charge and he turned and fled along with other skirmishers.

The charging Arkansans came within fifty or sixty yards of the fence, some of the men halted under orders from Lieutenant Joseph M. Bailey of Company D. At their feet was a Confederate officer in a dove colored coat and blue pantaloons, but the dove colored coat was redding over the heart. His Maynard rifle and side arms were gone and so was his gold watch.

Peter Pelican had aimed well and his bullet had struck the officer directly in the heart, killing him immediately. The brave Texas Ranger, General Benjamin McCulloch, the colorful commander from the borders of the Indian Territory was dead.

With McCulloch dead, the command of the Confederate right fell to James McIntosh, the hero of the defeat of Opothleyoholo and the Creek rout. Fiery, bold McIntosh took his place at the head of his attacking troops. Soon he fell, mortally wounded, dying almost instantly. And, earlier, commanding on the extreme right of Price's army, General William Y. Slack, badly wounded at Oak Hill, led his brigade on an attack upon the enemy under Colonel William Vandever. General Slack fell fatally stricken by Union fire.

An officer of General Price's army wrote an article on the battle which appeared in the Richmond *Whig*. His description of the first day's action — its setting, sounds of life and sounds of death and feeling of movement in the Confederate charge — was a graphic personal reaction to the conflict and said, in part:

"After listening some moments to the terrible tumult in the distance [Price and the Federal right near Elk Horn Tavern], suddenly, and within 300 yards of me, two or three cannon opened their brazen throats hurling their missiles of death through the undergrowth in almost every direction. As the sound of the cannon came a third or fourth time, like the noise in springtime on the marshy margin of a lake, only more shrill, loud and apparently more numerous than even the frogs, came the war whoop and hideous yell of the Indians. Here I was unconsciously in the midst almost of McCulloch's charging squadron, and in range of a battery of three guns [Elbert's artillery] that were hurling death and defiance at them.

"The battery was speedily charged and captured, those supporting it being borne backward three quarters of a mile by the impetuous forward press of the Confederates. Their retreat, most of the way, was through a corn-field, down a road upon its borders, but continuing into woods adjacent, full of undergrowth, where the main force of the enemy's wing was posted. Here began the rattling musketry, which soon increased to a Niagara in sound. For hours there was hardly an intermission save that created by the stunning roar of the cannon, so close that the ears of both parties were deafened. Within this vortex of fire fell McCulloch and McIntosh. At one time, having concluded to make my way to General Price, after passing from the corn-field down to the edge of the woods, just as four of us entered the woods a shell was thrown at us, bursting in our midst . . . I then went leisurely over the corn-field and rode back to the deserted guns.

"About fortry-five men lay in the space of two or three hundred yards to the rear of the battery, all save one entirely dead, and all but three Dutchmen . . . Here was a sterner feature of war than any I had seen. The Texans, with their large, heavy knives, had cloven skulls in twain, mingling blood and brains and hair. The sight was a sad one, but not devoid of satisfaction to our exiles from home and wife. The character of the bloody victims, as denoted by their countenance, betoken victory for the South. I looked upon the faces of many dead enemies that day, and among them all, found no expression of that fixed, fierce determination which Yankees describe as belonging peculiarly to the heroic hirelings who enlist for pay to desolate our homes."

Despite the deaths of Slack, McCulloch and McIntosh and the capture of Louisiana commander Louis Herbert, the Confederates slept that night content of victory. True, Colonel Drew's Indian regiment had absconded and was already on its way back to Indian Territory. Later, when the final treachery of Drew's men occurred after the battle of Locust Grove, the Federals, to whom the Ross faction Indians had deserted, were told that "the killing of the white rebels by the Indians" in the Pea Ridge fight "was determined before they went into battle." In the excitement of the initial Indian charge and the capture of the Federal battery, the Drew Indians temporarily shunted their plans to turn against the Confederates.

Stand Watie and Chilly McIntosh preserved their commands

in good shape and they were ordered by VanDorn to take their post along the top of Pea Ridge. Tired, but comprehending a vital battle trend, Watie knew that all along the front the Federals had been pushed back. Not one Union commander could report an advance of his unit! Sigel was actually so despondent that he despairingly reported the only hope for Curtis was to order the baffled Federals to cut their way out to an escape!

On the following morning, Curtis, rather than test the possibility of retreat, threw a strong offensive against the weary Confederates. His cannons — under the command of Sigel — shelled Watie and McIntosh and, for a time, scattered the Indian forces. Fields and woods were set on fire by hot shot and wounded men burned to death unable to move beyond the inferno's grasp.

The Federal forces, regardless of their beating of the previous day, consolidated and moved forward with new confidence, now realizing that many of the Rebel arms were shotguns! Against the rifles of the Union troops, the Confederates short range shotguns were practically worthless. The Federal charge mounted in fury as the blue-coated soldiers sent a mighty column up the side of Pea Ridge. Over beyond Elk Horn Tavern, other Federal troops under Eugene Carr and Jefferson C. Davis, inspired by the advance on Pea Ridge, went forward and soon the out-gunned Confederates were breaking up.

Watie's men held their position on Pea Ridge as long as possible without being overwhelmed. Some of the half-breed Indians had been captured. In all, eleven of the Indians were taken prisoner and, after the battle, they were ordered to Rolla preceding a "tour" in which they would be exhibited before the taunting Northerners. But none went on the "tour" for none reached Rolla. Each Indian "made a break" for freedom — some writers say the Indians feared they would be tortured by the Yankees — and one by one each Indian was shot dead by his guards.

The Confederate Army was routed and in full retreat in three directions. Pike and his staff were cut off from the main body of Indian troops and were wandering in the hills, but Stand Watie, his command in good order, helped cover the Rebel withdrawal as did Jo Shelby. Sigel, who was following deceptive Shelby, became so confused about Confederate strength he warned victorious Curtis that VanDorn might yet rally and surround the Federals!

Watie's Cherokee Rifles reached Camp Stephens near which the baggage train had been left. To their dismay they learned that Drew's deserting Indians had looted the Confederate wagon train. Soon Watie and Pike were reunited at the little town of Cincinnati. Certainly the mixed-bloods at Pea Ridge had shown the highest valor possible.

Pike was delighted to be reunited with Brutus, his slave and body guard, who came into camp after the battle. Before the struggle had commenced, Pike entrusted into Brutus' safe keeping $63,000 in gold which his son, Walter Pike, brought from the Confederate treasury in Richmond to pay the Indian troops. Pike's orders to Brutus were that if the Confederates were defeated, Brutus was to go up the creek and hide until he could escape. To reward Brutus for his honesty, Pike freed him, but the Negro elected to stay on with his master.

The combined Confederate Indians had participated in their last — as well as their first — big scale battle. VanDorn ordered Pike to take his Indians back to their country "to cut off wagon trains, annoy the enemy in marches and prevent him as far as possible from supplying his troops in Missouri and Kansas." Later on Indian orders were "to maintain themselves independent . . . you will not give battle to a large force, but . . . fell trees, burn bridges, destroy supplies, attack enemy trains, stampede his animals, cut off his detachments . . ."

From his headquarters at Van Buren, Arkansas, on March 16, General VanDorn issued his report on the battle, saying:

"The major general commanding this district desires to express to the troops his admiration of their conduct during the recent expedition against the enemy. Since leaving camp in the Boston Mountains they have been incessantly exposed to the hardships of a winter campaign, and have endured such privations as troops have rarely encountered.

"In the engagements of the 6th, 7th and 8th instant, it was the fortune of the general commanding to be immediately with the Missouri division, and he can therefore bear personal testimony to their gallant bearing. From the noble veterans, who had led them so long, to the gallant S. Churchill Clark [grandson of the famous explorer], who fell while meeting the enemy's last charge, the Missourians proved themselves patriots and staunch soldiers. They met the enemy on his chosen positions and took them from him. They captured four of his cannon and many prisoners. They drove him from the field of battle and slept upon it.

"The victorious advance of McCulloch's division upon the strong position of the enemy's front was inevitably checked by the misfortunes which now sadden the hearts of our countrymen throughout the Confederacy. McCulloch and McIntosh fell in the very front of the battle, and in the full tide of success. With them went down the confidence and hopes of their troops. No success can repair the loss of such leaders. It is only left to us to mourn their untimely fall, emulate their heroic courage, and avenge their death . . ."

To carry out the avenging mentioned in his orders, VanDorn — tear-stained from his first defeat in eleven battles — was soon moving his army across the Mississippi for an impending conflict near Shiloh. Price — his arm bound from a severe wound — retreated with his Missourians eastward; the methodical engineer, Curtis, following him. Pike set up his headquarters some 250 miles from Pea Ridge at Fort McCulloch on the Little Blue River.

And a new Confederate commander to take over McCulloch's troops arrived in eastern Arkansas, five foot one Thomas C. Hindman, former novelist and Congressman, with rose gloves and a rattan cane, who vowed that Curtis' soldiers would never reach the Mississippi.

On the open prairies at Fort McCulloch, Pike erected fortifications and set up a sawmill. From his headquarters in the Choctaw Nation, Pike could direct the commands of Douglas Cooper, Stand Watie and Colonel Drew, the latter still maintaining his loyalty to the Confederate cause despite the serious deflections of his men. Pike in a report of May 4, 1862, states that "Stand Watie and his Cherokees scout along the whole northern border of the Cherokee country from Grand Saline to Marysville and send me information continually of every movement of the enemy in Kansas and Southwestern Missouri."

General Albert Pike's detractors said, in derision, that he "devoted himself to gastronomy and poetic meditation."

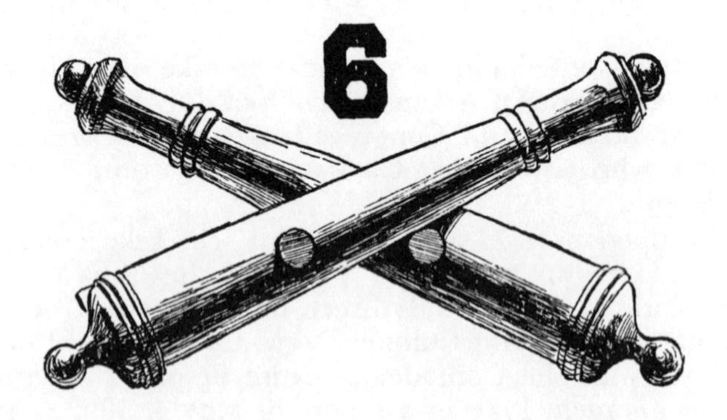
6

COLONEL STAND WATIE was scampering over the dirt roads of southwest Missouri. On April 26 Watie had fought the First Battalion of the First Missouri Cavalry at Neosho and on May 31, though Watie who had planned the attack was not present, his Cherokee Rifles had defeated a unit of the Missouri State Militia Cavalry through, reported one of the Federal officers, "screaming and whooping."

Watie raided through Missouri — Union officers feared this presaged a Confederate drive through northern Arkansas — and across into Indian Territory and fought again at Cowskin Prairie, June 8, near Grand River, when Colonel Charles Doubleday of the Second Ohio Cavalry with one thousand men and artillery sought to head him off. But Stand Watie eluded Doubleday under cover of darkness and soon was scouting in the Spavinaw Hills and O. E. Russell, of Pike's staff was reporting to General Hindman, "Colonel Stand Watie has recently had a skirmish . . . in which, as always, he and his men fought gallantly and were successful."

With Watie's Cherokee Rifles charging down dirt roads, across the countryside and ringing the air with their mixed-blood Rebel Yells, one can recall what Albert Pike wrote in *Ariel*:

"I shuddered for a time, and looked again,
 Watching the day of that eventful dawn;
Wild war had broken his adamantine chain,
 Bestride the steed of Anarchy, and drawn
His bloody scimitar; a fiery rain
 Of blood poured on the land, and scorned the corn
Wild shouts, mad cries, and frequent trumpets rang
 And iron hoofs thundered with constant clang."

Union commanders were growing weary of hearing tales of the iron hoofs and constant clang of Watie and his men. Too, the 6,000 refugee Indians, some of whom had fled with old Chief Opothleyholo, having endured a miserable winter, pled to be returned to their homeland.

On June 25, the Federal expedition against the Indian Territory moved out from Baxter Springs, Kansas; the Second Ohio Cavalry, the Sixth Kansas Cavalry, the Ninth and Twelfth Regiments Wisconsin Infantry, the Tenth Kansas Infantry, Rabb's Second Indiana Battery, the First Kansas Battery and units of refugee Indians. Colonel William Weer, who had been a lawyer with a liking for liquor and who had stolen Missouri horses when he had been a Captain with the Kansas Jayhawkers, was in command.

A few miles out of Baxter Springs additional Indians joined the column. Wiley Britton described these Indian troops in his *Civil War on the Border*:

"It was quite amusing to the white troops to see the Indians dressed in the Federal uniform and equipped for the service. Everything seemed out of just proportion. Nearly every warrior had a suit that, to critical tastes, lacked a good deal of fitting him. It was in a marked degree either too large or too small. In some cases the sleeves of a coat or a jacket were too short, coming down about two-thirds the distance from the elbows to the wrists. In other cases the sleeves were too long, coming down over the hands.

"At the time these Indian troops were organized the Government was furnishing the soldiers a high-crowned stiff wool hat for the service. When, therefore, fully equipped as a warrior, one might have seen an Indian soldier dressed as described, wearing a high-crowned stiff wool hat, with long black hair falling over his shoulders, and riding an Indian pony so small that his feet appeared almost to touch the ground, with a long squirrel rifle thrown across the pommel of his saddle. When starting out on the march every morning, anyone with this command might have seen this warrior in full war-paint, and he might have also heard the war whoop commence at the end of the column and then run back to the rear, and recommence at the head of the column several times and run back to the rear."

Colonel Watie's men were at Spavinaw Creek when his scouts brought news of approaching Federal Cavalry. With some three or four hundred men, including Major Brokearm and his Confederate Osages, Watie fell back, well knowing he could not withstand Colonel L. R. Jewell and the Sixth Kansas Cavalry. In the early afternoon Watie stopped for a meal with an Indian family, sending his men on. After supper Watie was standing in front of the house when one of his guards rode in with the alarm that the Federal Cavalry was on his heels. Watie leaped on his horse and raced down the road as the Yankees came into sight!

With the Yankees firing on him, Watie rode hard to escape, finally overtook his retreating command. One of his men slid from his horse, shot by the pursuing Yankees. Watie had no time to attempt forming a defensive line but, as the darkness was approaching, he ordered his men to escape as best they could. Colonel Jewel reined up, the Indian Colonel having eluded him. But the chase had driven Watie's men off the road to Locust Grove where Colonel Clarkson, newly appointed northern Indian Territory commander was encamped with Texas troops as well as Watie's commissary and camp supplies.

Colonel Weer, advancing against Clarkson, reached the drowsing Confederate camp shortly before daybreak. The chase of Watie had been so close that his Cherokees were not able to get through to warn Clarkson. Astonished Clarkson, surrounded, soon surrendered, though some of his men were able to pierce the

Federal lines. While Weer captured only a few over a hundred able-bodied soldiers, he took sixty four mule teams with the Confederate supply train. On July 4 the captured prisoners and supplies were exhibited as part of the Independence Day celebration.

State of the Cherokee country and efforts to combat the Rebel Indians were shown in the report of E. H. Carruth and H. W. Martin, Indian agents, written July 25 at Wolf Creek in the Cherokee Nation. This report, sent to Colonel R. W. Furnas, commanding the Indian Brigade said:

"The country bordering the Arkansas, Lee's Creek, and Sallison [Sallisaw] which is the best producing section of the nation, is ruined; and the families living there, whose fathers and husbands are in our army, are gathering at Park Hill, and are even now in a suffering condition.

". . . A regiment of Cherokees has already been raised, another is fast forming at Park Hill, and this will, we believe, give you force sufficient to hold the country until re-enforcements arrive; and we will call on you to protect the Cherokee people."

Mrs. Hannah Worcester Hicks, daughter of Reverend S. A. Worcester who had died in 1859 after living with the Cherokees over fifty years, in 1862 wrote in her diary:

"My house has been burned down, my horses taken . . . This is the ninth Sabbath that I have been a widow . . . left a widow at twenty-eight, with five children growing up around me, and oh! most dreadful of all, my dear husband murdered . . . [Abijah Hicks was murdered by a political enemy when returning from Van Buren with boots, shoes, tobacco and a barrel of sugar for his store at Park Hill. He was found hanging over the dashboard of his spring wagon and buried about forty miles from Park Hill and Mrs. Hicks was never able to locate his grave.] . . . This weary, weary time of War! Will the time of suspense never end? I know not what is to become of us: famine and pestilence seem to await us!"

Conditions at Park Hill became so unbearable that Mrs. Hicks left her home and took her children to Fort Gibson, some eighteen or twenty miles away. The Federals at the fort were operating grist mills, had built ferryboats and enclosed some sixteen acres with defensive works.

It must have seemed comforting to Hannah to be within the protecting stockades of the fort for here had been one of the liveliest centers of social activity. Many West Pointers were assigned to the fort upon graduation from the Academy on the banks of the Hudson and the pretty Cherokee girls were active in the social life of the post. In the main room of the commissary building the soldiers and the Cherokee girls would stage plays and entertainments. Many of the soldiers were excellent singers. The Army Chaplain often sent the post ambulance for the Indian girls and saw to it that they were well chaperoned.

Some of the soldiers remembered Hannah's late sister, Sarah, widely known as one of the most beautiful women in the Indian Territory, and it is said that when she was in Cincinnati, people stopped on the street to gaze at her queenly beauty.

Despite distraught Hannah's lamentations over the agonizing conditions brought to the Cherokees by the war, she was to find a new romance at Fort Gibson and married Sarah's widower, Dr. Daniel Dwight Hitchcock, surgeon of the Third Regiment of Indian Home Guards, who headed the general hospital at Fort Gibson.

But Hannah's sister Mary Eleanor, in her early twenties, wanted no part of Fort Gibson and turned to Stand Watie's territory for she opposed the "Feds" and gave her time and devotion to the Secesh cause.

After the defeat of Clarkson, Stand Watie's military hold on the Cherokee Nation was loosened. The Federals knew that Chief John Ross would tender them little trouble and in August 1862, Captain H. S. Greeno and a party of one hundred-fifty white cavalry and Indians were riding on the Cherokee capital of Tahlequah.

But when the Yankees rode up to Park Hill, four miles south of Tahlequah, a large troop of Confederate Indians was encamped around Chief Ross' expansive home. Colonel Greeno's cavalry slowed up, wondering if somehow Watie's men had lured them into a trap. But as the cautious Federals rode toward Rose Cottage no hostile fire greeted them. What was the situation?

Soon the Federals were aware that the Confederates wanted to surrender. And then it became clear as to exactly who were these Confederate troops. These were men from Colonel Drew's command — men who had failed the Confederacy at practically every chance except the early fighting at Pea Ridge — who awaited Greeno so that they could join up with him and help hunt down the malignant Colonel Stand Watie! Soon some two hundred of Drew's command were in Colonel Phillips' Third Indian Regiment. Colonel Phillips, a former anti-slavery reporter for the New York *Tribune,* had been offered $10,000 a year to be a war correspondent with the Army of Potomac.

Colonel Watie and the remainder of Clarkson's command were now south of the Arkansas River and the segment of the Indian Territory north of the river was practically free from Rebel command. Chief Ross, though seventy-two years old, a prisoner of war on parole, had walked the beautiful grounds of Rose Cottage convinced that finally he had eliminated his old enemy, the despised half-breed Watie.

Wisely, Chief Ross felt it not prudent to remain within riding distance — and possibly shooting distance — of the mixed-bloods, contemptuous of the surrendered Indians. Before long, Mrs. Ross and her sister, household treasures and archives of the Cherokee Nation were in Washington and Chief John was paying his respects to President Abraham Lincoln. Later Ross was to establish a Cherokee "government-in-exile" of sorts in Philadelphia in an old Colonial house, inherited by Mrs. Ross on the South side of Washington Square. The actual Cherokee government was far from the City of Brotherly Love. It was held by a gallant band of durable fighters who rode under the wind-tossed flag of the Confederacy. For as soon as Ross fled the Indian Territory, the Southern Cherokee put in a new Chief. There could be only one man — intrepid, valorous and gallant — to rule the Cherokee Nation — Colonel Stand Watie!

A letter dated September 15, appearing in the *Confederate Records,* stated, "In the meantime the serious feud existing between the Cherokees had terminated in the expulsion of Ross and the unsound faction and in the election of our tried friend, Stand Watie, as their chief."

Colonel Watie was to get unintended succor from an unanticipated source. Difficulties split Colonel Weer and his second in command, Colonel Frederick Salomon, who charged that Weer was either insane or plotting treason and placed him under arrest. Colonel Weer, like his soldiers, had suffered a morale breakdown because of the intense summer heat and the long periods of inactivity. Too often he had stayed drunk in his tent while his command slipped out of control. Colonel Salomon ordered the white troops back to Missouri leaving the three Indian regiments without any plan of campaign.

The three Northern Indian regiments were commanded by Colonel R. W. Furnas, Phillips — soon to become the Indians' commander at Fort Gibson — and Corwin. When Colonel Furnas marched the Indians, with the exception of some two hundred left at Fort Gibson — Jefferson Davis had served there under General Zachary Taylor — as an outpost, to the Verdigris River, several hundred Osages, members of the Second Indian Regiment, deserted and went buffalo hunting; and, if that were not bad enough, part of the First Indian Regiment became unmanageable. Some Indians complained they'd received no pay and were ill-armed. The reputation of Watie's fighting command may have had some part in disquieting the malcontent, loyal Indians.

Units of Watie's command had recrossed the Arkansas River as soon as news had been transmitted of the withdrawal of the white troops. They raided turncoat Cherokees and on July 27 at Bayou Bernard, near Park Hill, clashed with Phillips' column. The Confederates were repulsed, Colonel Taylor and Captain Hicks of Watie's command and two Choctaw captains being among the Confederate dead.

Colonel Phillips, the ex-reporter turned Indian fighter, Major Elias Boudinot with his Cherokees and Colonel McIntosh with his Creeks sparred and did a little in-fighting, but Colonel Douglas Cooper, commanding the Confederate forces at Fort Davis, ordered all Confederate Indian Territory forces again back south of the Arkansas River.

With the Confederates withdrawing, Colonel Phillips found he'd have to extricate himself from a dangerous position as his troops were out of rations and the Rebels had fallen back beyond his immediate reach. His horses were in poor shape as, indeed, were those of the white regiments which had withdrawn earlier. The hard marching and the lack of corn and oats had brought this about. Top cavalry horses could not stay in shape on wild prairie grass. Colonel Phillips ordered a retreat and distraught Indians flocked to the retiring Federal column for protection, even as loyal Indians had clung to Chief Yo-ho-la, as it reached Wolf Springs and then withdrew back to Baxter Springs, the main camp and the original jumping off point for the arduous campaign.

Colonel Douglas Cooper poured himself a couple of stiff drinks, then called out his Choctaws and Chickasaws and pointed the way northward over the Arkansas River. The Cherokee Nation must resume its place under the military forces of the Confederacy.

Confederate fortunes along the border were brighter. On August 11, Confederate raiders, mounted on the best horses in the country, and acting under Brigadier General John B. Hughes and Colonel Upton Hays, with support by Quantrill, rode into Independence, Missouri, Jackson county seat, occupied by the Federals since the fall of 1861. In fighting that raged from building to building, Hughes died, but Lieutenant Colonel James T. Buell and many of his defenders surrendered on the promise that the prisoners would not be murdered by Quantrill. Shortly after the battle, Quantrill – he of the broad smile but grim and deadly determination – had a Confederate Captain's commission.

Five days later at Lone Jack, twenty-five miles below Independence, Colonel Hays and Quantrill, with other Rebel officers, took on Major Emory S. Foster, Seventh Missouri State Militia Cavalry, who had won a bit of regional renown fighting the Secesh guerrillas in Central and Western Missouri. The Union soldiers were considerably roughed up as nearly every officer of Major Foster's command was killed or wounded. Major Foster, himself, led sixty of his men to recover abandoned Yankee artillery. Eleven of the sixty reached the guns and, as they were dragging them away, Major Foster was shot down and the new commander retreated to Lexington.

General Hindman, having harassed Curtis after Pea Ridge, on August 24 became official commander of the District of Arkansas. His energy was boundless. He had manufactured his own military and medical supplies when the eastern source was cut off and even aroused the Negroes at Van Buren to give a ball at fifty cents a head for the support of his Confederate program.

Since his new command encompassed Missouri and Indian Territory, Hindman, encouraged by the Rebel success at Independence and Lone Jack, soon, leaving Jo Shelby's men reorganized into the Iron Brigade, sent orders down to Fort McCulloch for General Albert Pike to pay him a visit with his Indians.

Still recalling how his troops hadn't received their uniforms prior to Pea Ridge and understandably smarting over the Indian losses there, Pike sent word back to Hindman that he planned to hold his troops for defense of the Indian Territory. There were threats of arrest for insubordination, but Pike, rather than order his command out of the Territory, resigned, saying, in part:

"I have resigned the command of the Indian Territory, and am relieved of that command, I have done this because I received . . . an order to go out of your country to Fort Smith and Northwestern Arkansas, there to remain and organize troops and defend the country; a duty which could have kept me out of the country [Indian Territory] for months . . .

"Remain true I earnestly advise you, to the Confederate states and yourselves. Do not listen to any men who tell you that the Southern states will abandon you. They will not do it."

So the brilliant diplomat to the Indians, the strong link between the Southern Indian leaders and the Confederacy—and who was arrested November 14, 1862 at Tishomingo, taken to Little Rock by a detachment of Shelby's men but quickly freed—retired from his command to take no more active part in the war although near the end General E. Kirby-Smith sought to employ him for service among the Plains red men.

After peace, Pike edited the Memphis *Appeal* for a short time. He then moved to Washington where he practiced law, edited *The Patriot* and, before his death in 1891, became the highest Masonic dignitary in the United States.

Unlike Pike, Douglas Cooper would fight the Yankees anywhere and he applied for Pike's post as Indian Commissioner and Brigadier General. Appointed acting commander, he moved his Chickasaws and Choctaws in support of Hindman. Working in unison with Cooper was Colonel Stand Watie who wasn't particular on what grounds he killed Yankees and Pins. Hadn't he whipped the foe in his stirring raids into their territory?

Stand Watie and Douglas Cooper moved north with Hindman's command in early September for the invasion of Southwest Missouri. Among those coming up to oppose them were Frederick Salomon, now a Brigadier General since his return from the Indian expedition and his old commander, Colonel Weer, back in official good graces after his unmilitary conduct following the capture of Tahlequah. Colonel Phillips' Third Indian Regiment was ready to cross swords with Watie and Cooper after Rebel cavalrymen had peppered Phillips' rear guard. Colonel Richie's Second Indian Regiment was encamped near Shirley's Ford so as to protect the right flank of Salomon and Weer. Some fifteen hundred members of families of the Indian soldiers made up a clumsy and ill-controlled camp following.

With Watie and Cooper prepared to strike, Jo Shelby sent Captain Ben Elliot on September 14 against a body of Pins and runaway Negroes encamped in the timber near Carthage. Elliot's men surrounded the camp and then charged in from all sides toward the center. The cowed Indians and Negroes made little resistance as they were ridden over and trampled down. Some even bared their breasts to the revolvers of the Confederate cavalrymen who silently and grimly exterminated the gathering. Few men escaped and only one prisoner was taken. In two hours of killing almost the entire craven band of two hundred-fifty Pins and Negroes was wiped out. The vengeance of the Confederates was not without merit. On the dead were found the scalps of a dozen or more white victims, at least one of whom was a woman, as the long, soft hair had still its silken gloss which shone despite the clotted drops of blood amidst the curls.

It was later in the war that the Confederates were able to repeat such a sanguinary victory over the Pins. Lieutenant Arthur McCoy rode out of the great blue hills of Cane Hill and surprised one hundred Pins rolled up asleep along a heavy rail fence. Only two Pins escaped. McCoy alone killed seven.

Some six days after Elliot's successful raid, units from Stand Watie's Cherokees, Colonel Hawpt's Texas Regiment and Major Tom Livingston's Rangers surprised Colonel Richie's pickets at Shirley's Ford and the Union Indian camp-followers romped, panic-stricken, into the main part of the camp. Although the Confederate retirement was preceded by an hour's fighting, Richie with no more stomach for the fray, permitted five civilian prisoners to be shot, ordered his regiment to fall back in the morning. Colonel Weer, wearied and out of patience with Richie, ordered his arrest and recommended dismissal from the service. Richie's Indians, often out of control, had plundered homes of Weer's command, burned country places indiscriminately and, to point up Richie's inadequacy, two of the civilians executed on the day of Shirley's Ford were Unionists!

There was fighting sporadically around Newtonia, Jo Shelby's Highlanders or Iron Brigade routed Union Missouri Cavalry, chasing them some ten miles northeast of Newtonia. But the Rebel horsemen suffered a serious loss in the death of bold fighter Colonel Upton Hays.

On September 28, the 7,000 Confederates moved up from Indian Creek to Newtonia, a little college town of four or five hundred population. The Federals were only fourteen miles away at Shoal Creek.

Union forces, unaware that the main Confederate force was at Newtonia, the next day marched openly over a ridge onto the town and landed in a Confederate trap. Soon the Southern cavalry and the Choctaw Indians were pursuing the fleeing Yankees. Behind the fast riding cavalry, among the several hundred Federal soldiers killed, wounded or captured, lay seven infantrymen of the Seventh Wisconsin, naked in death, stripped by the Choctaws.

This Confederate victory led off a series of small engagements which was climaxed October 4 when the heavily reinforced Union troops assaulted Newtonia — General John M. Schofield, commander of the Army of the Frontier, took charge of the offensive — and, on the heels of a heavy artillery bombardment, stormed against Cooper's men posted behind stone fences. Although these fences had been welcome protection in the earlier fighting, Cooper felt that his defenses were vulnerable. He looked over to where Lieutenant Colonel R. C. Parks was commanding the Cherokee Rifles in Stand Watie's absence, ordered a general scattering fire. Then he signalled for a retreat and the Confederate forces melted from Newtonia, marched down Indian Creek, reached Pineville and then crossed into Northwest Arkansas. That invasion of Missouri was at an end.

General Cooper rallied his troops once they were back in Indian Territory and shortly had orders from General James Rains, in or near Huntsville, to attempt another invasion; this time against Kansas and Fort Scott. Cooper was ready to act when word was received that General Blunt's expedition against the Confederates was in Indian Territory. The two forces clashed at Old Fort Wayne, four miles south of Maysville. Cooper and Watie had 3,000 men and four guns. The Yankees charged the Rebel line vigorously and, after hand-to-hand fighting, the Southerners fell back in confusion. Once again General Cooper was south of the Arkansas River and the Federals in control of the northern part of the Indian Territory.

Stroking his still black moustache and with victory in his deep-set eyes, General Blunt sent word to the refugee Indians to come home. But he wasn't satisfied that Watie and Cooper wouldn't strike back for Blunt's warning to the Union Indians was to report immediately any activity by the Confederate Indians.

In a matter of a couple of weeks or so, General Blunt had his report from the Union Indians. Colonel Stand Watie and his Cherokee Rifles had crossed over the Arkansas between Fort Gibson and Fort Smith. Blunt ordered Colonel Phillips to take the Federal Indian Brigade and harass him until he was forced across the river. Watie, leading Phillips a merry chase, was soon out of Indian Territory and back with Hindman, who was confident he could defeat Blunt in the Boston Mountains.

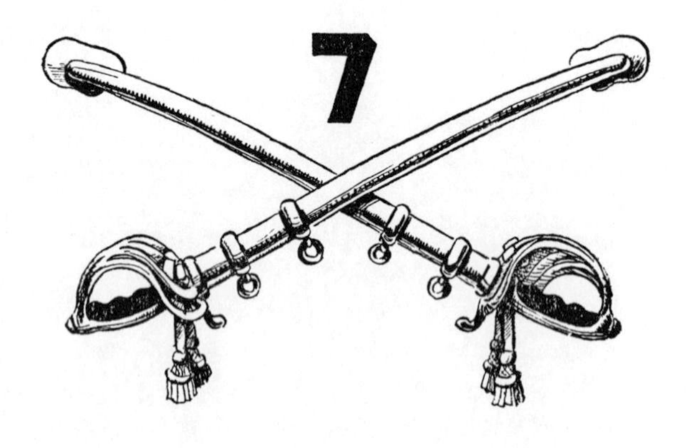
7

THE WARMISH FALL-LIKE weather of late November had changed and Watie's shivering men rode first in cold and ice and then in a pouring rain that drooped Jo Shelby's new black plume.

The Principal Chief of the Cherokee Nation must have pondered the fortunes of war as his men jogged along in the wet weather. Colonel Jewell's Sixth Kansas Cavalry had come close to capturing or killing him when they chased him down the road on the Indian Territory invasion, their fire tumbling one of his nearby horsemen. On November 23 Jewell had scouted almost to Van Buren and reported to Blunt at Lindsay's Prairie, thirty miles north of Cane Hill where Marmaduke with 7,000 cavalry awaited reinforcements, that Hindman and Watie were preparing to leave Van Buren and move northward. In a few days Blunt was forcing Marmaduke back from Cane Hill, but charging down a valley, Colonel Jewell fell wounded and on the 29th his body was shipped back to his family at Fort Scott.

As Hindman advanced against him at Cane Hill, Blunt wired General Samuel Curtis for reinforcements as Blunt had only about 8,000 men to oppose the 15,000 or so under Hindman's command.

General Curtis forwarded Blunt's request to Brigadier General Frank J. Herron at camp on Wilson's Creek, 116 miles from Cane Hill. To save Blunt, Herron would have to reach him before Hindman covered some sixty miles to Cane Hill.

Wednesday morning, December 3, Watie received instructions from Hindman which, in the light of coming events, actually took him out of the center of action. Colonel Watie, with part of his men — the remainder continued on with the main column — was sent to around Evansville where they were to open a communication with the pickets of the Confederate Army on the line road, and, if possible, occupy Dutch Mills. Hindman, apparently sensing the probability of a Confederate victory, desired Watie to be in a position to capture Federal supply trains if they should be driven by the Rebels into vicinity of Dutch Mills.

On Thursday, with about 400 men, Watie reached Dwight's Mission and the following morning his scouts killed several Pin Indians. That night Colonel Watie reached Peyton's Spring about four miles from Evansville. The next morning Watie's scouts entered Evansville just as a Federal scout was leaving. Citizens informed the Confederates that no Rebel pickets had been there for nearly a week and they could give no information about the location of the main Confederate Army.

Watie remained in the vicinity until that evening when, as he felt the enemy was in force at Cane Hill and had pickets near Dutch Mills, he considered it wise to retire down Lee's Creek. On Sunday, his troops heard cannonading in the distance. He returned to Peyton's Spring.

Dutch Mills fell into Watie's possession on Monday morning and Captain Wells was dispatched to take this news to General Hindman. The difficulty in maintaining Confederate communications was evidenced by the fact that Watie had received no reliable information on the battle of Prairie Grove the day previous. Actually, he did not know the location of General Hindman, but supposed him to be somewhere near Cane Hill.

On the night of December 6 — Herron had been marching on his relief effort for three days — Hindman had called a conference of his top officers. In a switch of strategy the Confederates were to send their main forces against approaching Herron with General Marmaduke — the same officer who had commanded at Boonville when Governor Jackson was retreating — using the men of Shelby and Quantrill and those of Watie not with the Colonel. A small force of Arkansas Cavalry under Colonel Monroe would engage Blunt at Cane Hill until the main force, having defeated Herron, could turn against Blunt.

General Hindman ordered leaflets he had printed distributed to his soldiers. These were instructions as to "Do's and Don'ts" in the coming battle and also contained a statement of principles for which the Confederates were fighting.

Secesh fighting men read, "Remember that the enemy you engage have no feelings of mercy or kindness towards you. His ranks are composed of Pin Indians, free negroes, Southern Tories, Kansas jayhawkers, and hired Dutch cut-throats."

Shelby and the cavalry rode out in the early morning about five with Quantrill's men — commanded in his absence by Dave Pool with Frank James and fifteen-year-old Jesse in the ranks — in front. In quick order, Quantrill's riders attacked Lieutenant Bunner's unit of the Sixth and Seventh Missouri Cavalry and routed it while Colonel Emmett McDonald's Confederate Cavalry defeated the rest of the Sixth and Seventh Missouri, killing the commander, Major Eliphalet Bredett, as well as Captain William McKee. Then McDonald and Quantrill's guerrillas routed the First Arkansas Cavalry and captured over a score of commissary wagons headed for Blunt's camp; Shelby, riding in to take care of the captured wagons was surprised by a rallied company of the Seventh Missouri and he, his staff and two artillery pieces were captured; but Confederates Major David Shanks and Pool with his men and Colonels Young and Crump, of McDonald's Cavalry, who had been chasing back on Herron and the advancing First Missouri Cavalry the routed First Arkansas mountain men — newly conscripted and gored with fear — returned up the road. Unexpectedly coming across the captured Shelby, the Confederate Cavalry, in turn, seized nearly four hundred of the Missouri cavalrymen and Shelby was free!

Such was the fast start the Confederates accomplished that morning. The Indian allies, meantime, were advancing with Hindman to the vicinity of Prairie Grove Church and there, much to their dismay, the unchallenged advance stopped. Eight thousand Confederates were placed in a two mile line along a high ridge covered with a heavy growth of young timber and underbrush to halt the forces of Herron on their way to General Blunt.

Had General Hindman continued his movement against the 6,000 almost exhausted soldiers in Herron's column, the odds for a Rebel victory would have been heavy as even the cutting up of the green Arkansas First Federals had almost thrown Herron's command off balance.

Herron's still weary men reached the Confederate line. General Herron in a display of courage even admired by the Confederates, with a sole staff member rode ahead to survey the land. Later his army, crossing Illinois Creek, doggedly charged the Confederate line time after time, but the gray troops – despite a two hour Yankee bombardment – held and shot down their foes advancing under the cover of fences and farmhouses. Shelby ambushed the Twenty-Fifth Illinois Regiment by abandoning four guns and when the Irish gathered around the "captured" artillery, Shelby opened up with concealed batteries and blew the Irishmen to pieces.

Cherokees, Marmaduke's cavalry and General D. M. Frost's – he was a West Pointer and former State Senator – and Monroe M. Parson's – he had started his career as a member of the Missouri militia in 1860 – Missourians impatiently waited to carry the battle forward. They sensed victory within reach.

General Hindman, sharing the feeling of confidence, started to give the anticipated command for a counter attack, even though he knew his whole strength was not available as he had detached General Parson's division of infantry to protect his rear guard and baggage from capture. Suddenly General Hindman halted in his command for something was wrong in the Confederate line. He discovered that Colonel Adams' Arkansas conscripted regiment, leaving only their officers on the field, had thrown down their arms and deserted! Hindman, instead of advancing, ordered the battle line held. Again and again the Union forces surged forward and were thrown back. Herron was becoming desperate, momentarily expecting an unblockable Confederate charge.

Meanwhile eight miles away at Cane Hill, Blunt, completely fooled, thought he was facing the entire Confederate command as Colonel Monroe's skeleton cavalry force was deployed as infantrymen in a wide battle line. But in the late morning the firing of the guns at Prairie Grove alerted him to the decoy planted by the Southerners.

Shortly thereafter Herron noted artillery fire falling among his skirmishers. To Herron this meant the failure of his effort as he had been outflanked. Quickly Herron revised his estimate after the fire was corrected. Blunt, arriving helter-skelter with 3,000 cavalrymen, twenty guns and double-quicking infantrymen, and not knowing the layout of the battle, had mistakenly fired upon the Federal skirmishers.

The arrival of Blunt's command to save Herron — an ironic reversal of the original situation — wrote the end to a Confederate victory although Hindman fought back all afternoon. Other conscripted Arkansas troops refused to charge and when Marmaduke's cavalry rode at their backs and forced them forward against Blunt's batteries, the spiritless sally failed and the unwilling Arkansas soldiers piled up like laid out cordwood as they died alongside one another. After the battle burial details found the pockets of the dead Arkansans stuffed with unshot bullets — these had been bitten from the cartridges so that the conscripts were firing only blanks at the Federals — and the propaganda leaflets issued by Hindman.

As night fell, fighting ceased, although General Blunt's powerful batteries continued to fire for some time, and the Confederate leaders held their lines against both Herron and Blunt; however, fresh Union troops under General Salomon were expected in the morning and additional artillery would throw grape and canister in deadly assault. Later Hindman said of the artillery fire, "There was no place of shelter upon any portion of the field . . . wounds were given and death inflicted by the Federal artillery in the ranks of the reserves as well as in the front rank."

Rebel Indians sternly watched as sweating Confederate gunners tore up blankets, wrapped them around artillery wheels. Then about midnight as silently as possible — but with the camp fires kindled to deceive the enemy — the fatigued Confederates slipped away.

Each side suffered battle casualties approaching thirteen hundred and the Federal dead and dying men were like wall-to-wall carpeting on the floors of the hospitals, churches and schools at Fayetteville. The Confederate wounded were taken to Cane Hill in ambulances furnished by the Union commanders. For their actions in the battle, Blunt and Herron were rewarded with major general's stars, Herron becoming the youngest such general in blue.

Blunt was to get his comeuppance at Baxter Springs in the fall of 1863 when Quantrill surprised his column, cut it to pieces, killing his fourteen musicians, as well as James O'Neal, special artist for *Frank Leslie's Illustrated Newspaper,* and making Blunt flee for his life. Chastised, Blunt was taken off his command of the Army of the Frontier and put in charge of recruiting Negro regiments.

And what of Colonel Watie? Since his camp in the vicinity of Dutch Mills was not, after all, on the route of the Federal Supply trains — in defeat or victory — the Cherokee Colonel found himself left out of the fighting engendered by the Prairie Grove action. But Watie's command near Dutch Mills was not to be devoid of contact with the enemy. On Wednesday, he learned that the Pins, concentrating at Manus', some ten miles from his camp were planning to attack him.

In Watie's report to Cooper, sent from Scullyville on December 19, he recorded his action to the news about the Pins:

"Early the next morning I moved upon them; soon dispersed them into the mountains, without any damage to our men, with the exception of three horses shot. We did not follow them far into the mountains. Three Pins were killed and 1 wounded. Quite a number of them were in uniform, thought to be soldiers. Sutler tickets were found in possession of some that were killed previous to this fight.

"Friday (the 12th) I moved back my command in the direction of Webber's Falls, in compliance with orders from you, Colonel [S.N.] Folsom's Detachment [which had come up from Fort Coffee] having been previously ordered to fall back with the train in the direction of Fort Coffee . . .

"On the expedition we killed 10 Pins and took 3 prisoners.

One being quite young and another badly wounded, were released . . ."

Dapper Hindman, for all his worthwhile work for the Confederate fortunes, paid for his failure to carry the attack to Fayetteville and he was soon on his way out as commander, replaced by General Theophilus Holmes, sixty-year-old friend of Jefferson Davis. In the reorganization of command, Douglas Cooper relinquished his temporary position replacing Pike — to General William Steele, formerly a Captain in the United States Army.

Colonel Phillips with twelve hundred Indian troops, two companies of white cavalry and an artillery unit, rode into Indian Territory to occupy Fort Gibson and then crossed the Arkansas River and attacked Fort Davis, which had been established by General Pike and named in honor of Jefferson Davis, and now defended by the forces of Cooper and Watie beneath the Confederate flag that flew on an Indian mound in the post's center. Phillips defeated the Texans and Indians and burned the million dollar Confederate camp, located on a slight hill north of what is now Muskogee. The Confederates fell back in the direction of Scullyville and Fort Smith, but Cooper, on orders from Hindman, retired deep into the Choctaw Nation at Johnson's Station, ninety miles northwest of Fort Smith on the Canadian River, and furloughed many of his Indian troops for two to three months. But before long Phillips was reversing his march under orders and the Northern headquarters in the southwest operated out of Fayetteville.

Camp Starvation became the Indian Territory winter headquarters for Colonel Watie. After the snows, heavy rains made the roads impassable and for six weeks Watie's men ate only parched corn and dried beef as no supplies could get through. The prized cavalry mounts which had carried Watie's Rifles on so many successful raids were fed on tree bark and branches.

Activity of the Civilized Nations was not confined to the battlefield. The mixed-breed Indians placed their representatives in Richmond to further any interests of their nations; S. B. Callahan represented the Seminoles and Creeks; Robert M. Jones, the Choctaws; Peter Pitchlin, the Chickasaws and Colonel Elias C. Boudinot, the Cherokees. There was ever the question of supplies and money for the Indians as well as obtaining the proper recognition for the support the Civilized Tribes were giving Jefferson Davis.

John Christopher Schwab wrote in his book, *The Confederate States of America*:

"The relation of the Confederate States to the tribes of Indians within their borders called for considerable legislation. Numerous treaties of peace had been framed beginning with some in 1861, which often created trust funds of which the Confederate government was custodian. These, in the shape of money or bonds, were held by the treasury and the interest was paid to the Indians in treasury notes and towards the end of the war in cotton at its market value. Apparently this small class of creditors were treated with special consideration."

The cordial relations between the Confederate States and its Indian allies, is brought out in a report by S. S. Scott, Confederate Indian Commissioner at Richmond, made January 12, 1863, to James A. Seddon, Secretary of War. Scott wrote:

". . . On the morning of the 13th of September, I left Richmond, but owing to the misconnection of trains upon certain railroads, and the difficulty at times of procuring suitable transportation, I did not enter the Indian country until the middle of October. I left it upon my return to this place about the 1st of December, having remained within its limits about a month and a half.

"During the time I had repeated interviews with Samuel Garland, the principal Chief of the Choctaws; Winchester Colbert, Governor of the Chickasaws; Stand Watie, principal Chief of the Cherokees; Motey Kinnaird and Icho Hacho, Chiefs of the Upper and Lower Creeks; John Jumper, Chief of the Seminoles, and other men of authority in the nations . . . it was evident that a spirit of dissatisfaction manifested itself prior to my arrival. This dissatisfaction did not amount to any real distrust of the good faith of the Confederate States . . .

"The task of removing it I found to be one of no great difficulty. Indeed, the mere fact of the Government having sent an officer from the Capital to their country charged with the special duty of conferring with them, and ascertaining by this means and through personal observation their wants and condition, was to them such a signal and conclusive mark of favor and good will, but little was left for me to do in the premises . . .

"The Choctaws alone, of all the Indian nations, have remained perfectly united in their loyalty to this Government.

"The Chickasaws have been less, but scarcely less, fortunate in this regard . . . About forty families in a body were induced to desert their country about the same time of the alliance of their nation with the Confederate States . . .

"Of the Seminoles, at least one-half have proved disloyal and have deserted their country. Their chief, John Jumper, however, has ever exhibited unshaken fidelity to the Confederate cause, and those of his people which remain with him are composed of the same staunch material with himself.

"The Creeks have lost about a thousand or fifteen hundred of their people. Hopoeithleyohola's deflection carried off almost all of these as well as the forty families of Chickasaws before alluded to, and the major part of the Seminoles.

"Of the Cherokees not less than one-half followed Ross when he deserted his country. Almost the whole of the worth and talent of the nation, however, was left behind him and now is clustered about Stand Watie, its present, gallant and patriotic principal Chief."

Several unusual facets of the Indian Territory, reported on by Scott, were:

"In reference to the condition and feelings of the small tribes located in the northeastern corner of the Indian country — the Osages, Quapaws, Senecas, and Senecas and Shawnees — but little is known. Their country, exposed as it is to invasion by Kansas desperadoes, has been completely under the control of the North almost from the very day of their having entered into treaties with this Government . . .

"Letters from the quartermaster of the Chickasaw battalion stationed at Arbuckle had just been received at Washita, giving an account of a serious attack on the reserve [homeland of the Comanches, Wichitas, Caddoes, A-na-dagh-cas, Ton-ca-wes, Ta-hua-ca-ros, Hue-cos, Ki-chais, and Ai-o-nais] by a band of marauding Indians . . . they made their appearance at the agency between 9 and 10 o'clock on the night of the 23rd of October . . .

"Four of the white employees of the agency were murdered . . . the agency building [was] burned to the ground . . .

"The following morning they attacked the Ton-ca-wes . . . killing their Chief, Placido, a good man, twenty-three of their warriors, and about one hundred of their women and children. The Ton-ca-wes, although armed with only bows and arrows, while their assailants had weapons of the latest design and best pattern furnished them by the North, inflicted upon the latter it was said, a loss of twenty-seven men killed and wounded . . .

"The remnant of the ill-fated Ton-ca-wes tribe, about forty men and less than one hundred women and children, made their way to Arbuckle a few days after the fight. They were in a most miserable and destitute condition.

"Before leaving the Chickasaw country I wrote to the Governor of that nation, asking permission to place them temporarily on Rocky Creek, about eighteen miles east of Arbuckle, where there was excellent grazing for the few horses owned by them, plenty of wood, and good water. His consent was readily obtained . . .

"Before dismissing the subject of the reserve agency, a few remarks in reference to the wild Indians will not be out of place . . . they have recently evinced no great disposition to wage war on the Confederate States. Indeed, with the exception of the Cai-a-was, they have never done so. This band, one of the most powerful and warlike of all the tribes leading a Nomadic life upon the prairies and Staked Plain, refused all propositions of peace made to them in July 1861, by the commissioner sent to them by this Government . . . and endeavored to prevail upon the Comanches to pursue a similar course. They were induced to act thus by Northern emissaries, who, at the same time provided them with rifles, six-shooters and knives to be used in murdering and scalping defenseless women and children. In their wicked and bloody designs, they failed to obtain the cooperation of the Comanches, several of the bands of which made a treaty with the commissioner. Latterly, however, even this tribe has manifested some desire to cultivate friendly relations with the Confederate States. . ."

The Northern Cherokees were plotting their political activity, too. On February 4, 1863, the Cherokee Council convened at Cowskin Prairie with Lewis Downing as its presiding officer and Thomas Pegg as acting Principal Chief. In a session which ran many days, the Council passed numerous resolutions including:

1) An Act revoking the alliance with the Confederate States and re-asserting allegiance to the United States.

2) An Act deposing all officers of any rank or character whatsoever, inclusive of legislative, executive, judicial, who were serving in capacities disloyal to the United States and to the Cherokee Nation.

3) An Act emancipating slaves throughout the Cherokee country.

For all the consideration given these acts by the Confederate Cherokees, the Council might as well have written them in the snow banks; that is, except the actions intensified the Rebel Indians abhorrence of the Pins!

As spring approached, Colonel Watie called in all of his men who had been on furlough for General Steele was proving to be an energetic commander — at least at the start — and he ordered the Southern Indian forces to be ready for renewal of the fight to control the Indian Territory. In March, Stand Watie's soldiers were back north of the Arkansas River. But Colonel Phillips' men were on their way back to Fort Gibson accompanied by a large flock of loyal Indians who wanted to be in their homeland. Phillips rode with anticipation of the greening grazing section of Cherokee lands. His cavalry horses had suffered from lack of forage so intensely that, in some cases, the horses had eaten each other's tails and manes.

Federal scouts, missing the Indian Confederate troops, reported no Southern Indians north of the Arkansas River, but in a few days a unit of Cooper's command was unsuccessfully skirmishing with the Federals. On April 9 the Union Indian refugee mile-long wagon train, which was guarded by three hundred Indian soldiers, reached Park Hill. And by the 13th, Phillips was back in Fort Gibson, but not until after a company of Stand Watie's was hemmed in and had to swim the Arkansas River to escape.

Highlight of the spring campaign was Watie's capture of a Yankee wagon train, bound from Fort Gibson to Fort Smith, at Webber's Falls. His men bested a Federal Cavalry unit which fell back to a battle line along a mountain top where infantry guarded the wagon train. Watie's beloved bugler, "Dutch Billy," sounded a charge and the men advanced up the mountain capturing the Federal supplies.

Colonel Stand Watie, as Principal Chief of the Cherokees, ordered a meeting of the Cherokee Legislature at Webber's Falls, twenty-five miles below Fort Gibson, and on the south side of the Arkansas River. Cherokee troops and leaders came in from around the countryside for the parley and, by night when Watie made the opening address, a sizable contingent was gathered. Nearby, at Northfolk, General Cooper stood by with his main command of Choctaws and Chickasaws.

And exactly what happened after that is disputed history. The Federal historians tell it this way:

Stand Watie was to contend with uninvited and most unwelcome guests who, at daybreak, broke up any hope of further convening the Cherokee Legislature and sent incensed soldiers and political leaders – often one and the same – reeling back into the canebrakes for protection. Colonel Phillips – a proclamation of the coming session having fallen into his hands – with no chivalric regard for political courtesy to the Rebel Cherokee Government, had led six hundred men – Indians and Sixth Kansas Cavalry – across the Arkansas on a night march. With Watie and the lawmakers scattered, gloating Phillips rode back to Fort Gibson.

General Watie's men, after the war, protested this story of the breaking up of the Cherokee Legislature. They did not accuse the historians of deliberately falsifying the story, but said apparently the Union writers had confused this supposed Rebel defeat at Webber's Falls with an actual one in the late fall of 1862 or the early winter of 1863 when Confederate Captain O.H.P. Brewster and a small party of Cherokees at Webber's Falls was attacked by Federal troops under Colonel Phillips. Colonel Watie, at that time, was at Camp Steel.

Be that as it may, if Colonel Phillips did disperse the Cherokee Legislature and ride in exaltation back to Fort Gibson, his countenance must have fallen when he heard the news there. The Yankees had abandoned their headquarters at Fayetteville and retreated to Cassville, Missouri. Because of that not only would Fort Gibson, which was established around 1830, and which held a commanding view of the surrounding territory, be a target for attack from Cooper and Watie, but also from General W. L. Cabell, new commander of the Confederate forces in Western Arkansas, who readily occupied Fayetteville with his cavalry.

Soon Cooper and Watie marched within five miles of Fort Gibson and watched the movements of the Union troops. Confederate Cavalry forded the Arkansas and Verdigris rivers and impertinently threatened to make life miserable for any Federal parties on their way to and from Fort Scott. General Cabell brought over his Arkansas troops and put them on the flank.

Inside Fort Gibson, Phillips was perturbed that Watie knew as much about the movements of Yankee supplies as the Federal supply officers themselves. The former newspaperman, through spies and scouts, learned that the next big wagon train bringing in supplies from the north would be in serious trouble.

Phillips' position wasn't made any more tenable by the knowledge that Major Tom Livingston's Partisan Rangers – the Major was to die soon, leading his "bushwhackers" on an attack on Stockton, Missouri – were making rapier thrusts against Colonel James M. Williams' First Kansas Colored Infantry at Baxter Springs, sixty miles south of Fort Scott on the military road to Fort Gibson.

Watie must have ruffled considerably any good humor Phillips had left by a raid on the Fort Gibson herds. The Confederate scouts, having observed that Union horses and mules were turned out to graze before daylight each morning, Colonel Watie's raiders swooped down in the early morning hours – death taking from the horsemen Major George W. West and Captain Buzzard – and cut off a vast number of horses and mules, capturing them under the Federal guns. The loss of the animals caused Phillips to revise his cavalry plans against the Confederates.

In mid-May, with their field glasses focused on Confederate activity in and around their camp, Union officers stood on the roofs of the stone buildings atop the bluff and speculated on where Cooper and Watie would strike and if Cabell could be held to his position.

For a week there were quick raids around Fort Gibson as news of the impending arrival of a large wagon train became known. The Federal commander of the train – which had two hundred wagons – marched at night with a reinforced escort of a thousand soldiers. About five miles from Fort Gibson, the Texans and Indians swooped down on the train, their mounted charge standing out against the lightening sky of the early morning.

When the wagon train pulled into Fort Gibson, later in the day, it had two wagons freshly loaded — Confederate Indian dead!

But in June another large train was expected. And the conniving Confederate Indians could wait for this one!

No one missed his family more than Captain James M. Bell, son of John A. Bell and brother of Sarah Watie, who was married to Caroline Lynch. His letters written to his wife brought out how much he wanted to be back with his loved ones, to live in the agrarian atmosphere of farm animals with their smells and noises amid the pastoral scenes of corn and wheat growing in a world which was only a memory as Captain Bell fought beside Stand Watie.

Even such memories were not to last long for a party of more than a score of Confederates, which set out in May 1863, on a diplomatic mission to the Plains Indians, and, who had ridden some 80 miles across Osage country, when they stopped to rest at noon in what is now Montgomery County, Kansas.

The Confederate mission was surprised by Osage warriors who wanted to take them to a Federal garrison. Between the hostile Osages and the prospect of being turned over to the Federals, the trapped Confederates had little choice. They fled under the fire of volleys of arrows.

But the unplanned flight was right into hundreds of Osage warriors coming from one of their villages. In dismay, the Rebel horsemen sought the comparative safety of the Verdigris River where they could rally on a sand bar.

Hopelessly outnumbered, the Rebels were unable to hold off the Indians and ran up a surrender flag. Better to be captured by the Osages and turned over to the Feds than to be pierced with Indian arrows and die on a sand bank.

Surrender was of no avail. The Rebels were soon stretched out in death, some beheaded, almost all scalped. One Osage hacked away at the beard of a dead Secesh as his victim was bald!

So ended the diplomatic mission, which, under orders from

General Steele, tried to resume the parleys with the Plains Indians commenced by Albert Pike in 1861.

News of the massacre reached the border from two sources. Osage leaders, fearful of what their warriors had done, reported the bloody affair to the Union authorities at Humboldt, Kansas, who sent investigators to the Osage village. There were found remains of the Southern diplomatic messages as well as some Confederate scalps.

The other news source was two survivors — they had dropped out of the race for safety on the sand bar — who walked into a Missouri settlement after days and nights of perilously crossing the prairie.

To keep the Federal Indians in a state of confusion and agitation, Colonel Watie commenced another lusty raid through the Cherokee Nation, killing loyal Indians who resisted and gathering supplies for the Confederate camp before Fort Gibson. Major Foreman and three hundred cavalrymen tried to trap Watie near Maysville, but Watie avoided a fight and headed back through Tahlequah and Park Hill with Foreman riding hard on him. Colonel Phillips, ever on the alert to catch Watie, sent out four hundred men to cut off Watie before he could reach the Arkansas River and then Phillips would have the elusive Cherokee Chief in his grasp.

But Cooper was equally bent on protecting his famed raider and he entertained no thought of letting Watie run any greater risks than need be. Cooper rushed out a force under Colonels Thomas G. Bass and Tandy Walker to cover Colonel Watie's racing withdrawal.

His horses worn out and not realizing that Phillips' aid was close at hand, Major Foreman slowed down his blue-coated cavalrymen and at Tahlequah gave up the chase and empty-handed turned toward Fort Gibson.

Safely back from his successful raid, Watie found a message from Texas in which Sarah was greatly disturbed over the report that Charles Webber, Saladin's nephew, and Saladin had killed a prisoner. Sarah asked that the boys be merciful to their prisoners, if they, in turn were to expect mercy themselves and she told how sad she became when such news reached her.

At the same time, although she knew the animosity toward the Waties and the Confederate cause by the Union Indians, and especially the Ross clan, she implored her husband to spare William Potter Ross, nephew of John Ross, if he should run across him, and make him a prisoner of war, as Mrs. Watie had a sympathetic feeling for his mother, Mrs. Jack Ross. Sarah Watie did not think it necessary for Stand Watie to kill his top enemies in order that they be removed from his path. But Sarah was being overly alarmed because of the reputed action by Saladin and Charles for Watie, although a raider, was not a wanton killer. Sarah urged her beloved husband always to do the right thing whenever it was possible.

"Do as near right as you can . . ." That was why Stand Watie risked his valuable properties, the welfare of the people who chose him their leader and the lives of those beloved to him. That he put his own life on the scales every time his raiders charged out against the Yankees was the price paid for leadership, yet a price paid equally by the stout horsemen who clashed with the blue-clad riders of bewhiskered Colonel Phillips.

These men who fought alongside Watie were not blank-faced strangers from a far state. These warriors were such men as, besides teen-aged Captain Saladin, Stand Watie's brother, Captain Charles Watie, and Major James M. Bell, his brother-in-law. And the acid-pen Yankee writers, blinded by the mechanisms of the abolitionists, had portrayed the Confederate Indian allies as border murderers and semi-savages. Charles Watie, Adjutant in the First Cherokee, at one time had been assistant editor of the Grass Valley, California, *Journal* when the famed John Rollin Ridge was its editor; and devoted Major Bell, ever at Stand's side, was one of the foremost leaders of Cherokee politics and culture.

No, these men of the Cherokee Rifles were not men with meaningless names who slept, sometimes very little; and ate, sometimes very little; and suffered from cold and sun, from absence from their loved ones and from love of their country; and who, far more frequently than it would seem just, died from a Yankee slash across their stomach, a Pin bullet in their chests or a neutral bug in their vital organs.

These were men who revered the brave flag of the Confederacy that marked defiance over their heads, pre-eminently proud of the high-born heritage of Cherokee and White South that ran in their veins, and possessors of an ironside determination that

ABOVE: Cherokee South Washington Delegation, 1866. From L to R: John Rollin Ridge, Saladin Watie, Richard Fields, E. C. Boudinot and W. P. Adair.

RIGHT: Stand Watie, "the foremost soldier ever produced by the North American Indians."

ABOVE: Col. E. C. Boudinot, Watie's nephew, Cherokee soldier and diplomat.

ABOVE LEFT: Gen. Jo O. Shelby, famed leader of the Iron Brigade.

LEFT: Gen. Albert Pike, scholar-soldier who raised the Stars and Bars over Indian Territory.

RIGHT: Chief John Ross (Cherokee), leader of the full-bloods, and long Watie's top adversary.

BELOW: Rose Cottage, Chief Ross's home at Park Hill, Indian Territory showplace.

ABOVE: Gen. William Steele, who could command white troops, but not Indians.

LEFT: Capt. George Washington, Commander, Reserve Squadron. (Caddo Chief)

ABOVE: Gen. James M. McIntosh, smasher of Opothleyoholo's Union Indian power.

ABOVE RIGHT: Gen. E. Kirby-Smith. Leading the Trans-Mississippi Army he followed a policy of losing a part to save the whole.

RIGHT: Chief Samuel Garland, (Chocktaws).

ABOVE LEFT: Gen. Douglas H. Cooper – with Watie, idol of the Indian troops.

ABOVE: Chief Samuel Checote (Creek).

LEFT: Gen. Earl VanDorn, at Pea Ridge suffered his first defeat in eleven battles.

ABOVE: Gen. W. Y. Slack, Commander of the Rebel Army at Pea Ridge – long enough to die.

RIGHT: Gen. Franz Sigel, (USA), defeated in first important battle in Missouri.

LEFT: Col. William A. Phillips, (USA). A former famed newspaperman, Indian Commander at Fort Gibson, he ever sought elusive Watie.

BELOW LEFT: Gen. Richard M. Gano. From Morgan to Watie he rode with them to victory over Federals.

BELOW: Gen. William L. Cabell, marched his Arkansas troops to aid the Southern Indians.

ABOVE: Chief Black Dog (Osage) and wife, on the side of Secession.

RIGHT: Chief Opothleyoholo, Creek foe of the Confederate Indians.

EXTREME LEFT: Col. W. P. Adair, Watie's daring Chief of Scouts.

LEFT: Gov. Winchester Colbert, (Chickasaw).

ABOVE: Chief George Washington Grayson, (Creek).

ABOVE RIGHT: Gen. John S. Marmaduke.

RIGHT: Col. Tandy Walker, Commander, Second Indian Brigade.

LEFT: Gen. Sterling Price, (CSA), "Old Pap," Commander of the Missouri Patriots Army.

BELOW: Capt. Saladin Watie, Cherokee Mounted Rifles, who rode in battle at his father's side.

ABOVE: Gen. Ben. McCulloch, up from Texas to command the Indian Territory at war's start.

RIGHT: Gen. James G. Blunt, (USA). Disliked by both the Rebel and Union Indians, he struck hard against the Cherokee Nation.

RIGHT: From L to R: Gen. Cadmus M. Wilcox, Gen. John B. Magruder, (CSA), Gen. Sterling Price, (CSA), Gen. Wm. P. Hardiman, and Gen. Thomas C. Hindman.

ABOVE: Gen. Francis J. Herron, (USA), the Yankees' youngest Major-General after Prairie Grove.

RIGHT: Capt. William Clarke (Charles) Quantrill. The border terror, his name was linked with Watie by fearful Unionists.

LEFT: Stand Watie's children.

ABOVE: Lt. Col. John Jumper (Seminole Chief).

RIGHT: John Ross – taken before the war.

LEFT: Minnehaha Josephine (Ninnie) Watie.

BELOW: Jacqueline (Jessie) Watie.

RIGHT: Stand Watie — during the war — who scored victories with torch, bullet and courage, and who lived a saga in Oklahoma history.

BELOW: Mrs. Watie (Sarah), whose thoughts were ever for her heroic husband.

ABOVE: Gen. M. Jeff Thompson, colorful border "swamp fox."

RIGHT: Gen. S. B. Maxey, capable Indian Territory Commander who called Watie "that gallant old hero."

their beloved land and their way of life would not fall to would-be conquerors who knew not either the Southern land or the Southern life. These were the men who answered the bugle-call of Dutch Billy when he signaled for an encounter with Death.

And new widows and orphans shed tears down along the Red River for their menfolk who perished in the Indian Territory for the same cause the men of Robert E. Lee and Stonewall Jackson died in the valleys of Virginia.

FORT GIBSON WAS practically under siege. Confederates raided the Union herds, Phillips' mounts were falling, both in number and quality, and soon the fear was that the Union retaliatory raids against the Confederates would cease. If conditions worsened, Phillips would have to retire from the Fort and Stand Watie's Cherokee Rebels would again be in full control. Indeed, there was some fear in Union quarters that the Texans and Indians might get impatient and attempt to storm Fort Gibson.

Phillips did the most practical thing. He called for help. General Blunt answered that the Negro regiment at Baxter Springs, the Second Colorado Infantry and some Kansas artillery would move to the relief of Fort Gibson with the next wagon train. Blunt knew that if the train fell, Fort Gibson would fall next. Colonel Phillips even sent six hundred of his cavalrymen from Fort Gibson to strengthen the train escort. Spies had reported an attack by Colonel Watie would take place before the commissary train approached the vicinity of Fort Gibson.

Cooper and Watie knew that Fort Gibson rations had been reduced to fresh beef, salt, rice and wheat, and sickness from the diet switch was spreading in the Union camp.

Stand Watie made adequate preparations for the proper reception of the wagon train. With 1,600 Indians and Texans he threw up embankment protection on the south side of Cabin Creek so that he could command the ford.

On July 1 the Federal train reached Cabin Creek, but after an exchange of picket fire, Lieutenant Colonel Theodore H. Dodd, Second Colorado Infantry, Union commander, ordered the train stopped as the high water made impassable a river crossing.

Watie perceived that the Federal train was determined to break through, but the Southern leader also was awaiting the arrival of some 1,500 men and artillery under Cabell who had come back from Arkansas for the explicit purpose of helping the Confederate Indians capture the wagon train. And General Cooper's column was marching toward Cabin Creek.

For forty minutes on the morning of July 2, Watie's men were shelled by the Second Kansas Artillery, but when Major Foreman led Union Indian and Sixth Kansas cavalrymen across the creek — which had now gone down — the Rebel fire drove them back and Major Foreman was wounded.

But the infantry, wading in water waist high, crossed the stream and the Ninth Kansas Cavalry was brought up to support the infantrymen. Watie's men were forced from their positions in the brush, but Watie reformed them on the edge of the prairie. If only Cabell and his column would come! But Cabell — only a few miles distant, wouldn't get his men over the swollen Grand — and Watie troops, without the planned reinforcements — for Cooper's force was also stopped by high water — did not withstand a strong Union cavalry charge. To the cheers of the semi-starved men on the morning of the 5th, the wagon train rolled into Fort Gibson; supplies, artillery, cavalrymen and Colorado and Negro infantrymen. Now Phillips could pay back Cooper and Watie for their seige of Fort Gibson!

Colonel Phillips' report on the engagement stated as to Watie's losses, "Part of the enemy's men and horses got drowned trying to escape by fording the Grand River. The dead men and horses floated past Fort Blunt."

The Confederates had some ideas of their own. Aging General Holmes, who had admonished General Price, "This is my fight. If I succeed, I want the glory; if I fail, I'm willing to bear the odium," had asked Jefferson Davis to relieve him after his failure to capture Helena. In Holmes' place his assistant, E. Kirby-Smith, commanded the Army of the Trans-Mississippi, cut off from the eastern Confederacy as the full length of the Mississippi was in Union hands with valiant northerner-in-gray, General John Clifford Pemberton, surrendering Vicksburg to General U. S. Grant.

When Vicksburg fell, some 10,000 stand of arms, ordered by Kirby-Smith, fell into Union hands. But General Josiah Gorgas, Confederate Chief of Ordnance, advised Kirby-Smith that he would have some 12,000 arms in Texas within three months. In Arkansas one-third of the organized troops were without arms and the Principal Chief of the Choctaws, Samuel Garland, was demanding promised arms.

Too, further east, General Lee was retreating from the "high tide" at Gettysburg.

General Kirby-Smith wanted Fort Gibson back in Rebel hands so as to ease the pressure on Little Rock. He ordered, through General Steele, a concentration of all Indian Territory Confederates supported by as many Arkansas troops as Cabell could muster. Eighteen miles below Fort Gibson, at Honey Springs near the present Muskogee, in the Creek Nation, the Confederates gathered.

At the same time, General Blunt, commander of the District of the Frontier arriving at Fort Gibson on July 11, determined he would defeat Watie and Cooper before the Arkansas troops arrived, and ferried some of his troops and ammunition over the Arkansas in flatboats.

When on July 17 the Federal force came in sight on the north side of Elk Creek, the Confederates were in position. The Twentieth Texas, dismounted cavalry, which supported the battery in front, Ninth Texas Cavalry and the Fifth Partisan Rangers formed the center. Stand Watie, unfortunately, was on detached service at Webber's Falls and Colonel Adair was absent through illness. Two able officers took over; Major Thompson commanded the First Cherokee and Lieutenant Colonel Bell, the Second Cherokee. These units made up the right wing. Colonel Daniel N. McIntosh led the left wing, composed of the First and Second Creek Regiments. The Choctaw and Chickasaw Regiments and two squadrons of Texas Cavalry made up the reserves.

Early in the fighting, the commander of a Texas regiment overheard the shouted order to fall back, given by Lieutenant Colonel Bowles, who had assumed command of the Negro troops when Colonel Williams was wounded. The Rebel officer, elated, ordered his own regiment forward. Twenty-five yards from the black troops, the Texans were met by a heavy volley of fire which killed their color-bearer and splintered their advance. In a few moments, the center of the Confederate line was broken by the continued fire. What had actually happened was that Colonel Bowles had instructed some Union Indians, who were riding between his unit and the Confederates, to fall back. And it was this order which the Texas commander had misinterpreted!

With the Texan center broken, through a strange quirk of fate, the Southern Indian troops were being pushed back and Colonel Watie's men loped over to the south bank of Elk Creek and, after making a futile stand, raced for their baggage trains near the Honey Springs depot, saving them from capture, though Watie's troops had to burn the commissary building in an effort to keep the supplies out of Yankee hands.

Two hours after the battle was over, General Cabell, marching along the old Pacific Mail route, arrived with artillery and a brigade of Arkansas Cavalry, 2,000 strong. But the Southern Indian forces were too shattered to reorganize quickly. Also, much of Cooper's ammunition — said to be Mexican powder — had been faulty, for in the damp weather it became paste-like and would not fire.

Such was the battle of Elk Creek or Honey Springs, lost in the Creek Nation through, perhaps, the odd combination of circumstances of a misunderstood enemy command, damp weather which, even if it did fill the canteens of the thirsty Yankees, made the ammunition unreliable and the tardy arrival of General Cabell with the reinforcements.

The loss was of serious consequences to the Confederate Indians for the courage of many pro-Rebel Creeks wavered after Honey Springs and now the initiative had been taken away from them. They had kept Phillips under close guard at Fort Gibson and he had ever been operating from a defensive base. Now the offensive could be launched by the Union.

With the defeat at Honey Springs and the subsequent withdrawal of the Confederate forces allowing the Yankee advance against the Indian Rebels, Watie became seriously alarmed at the turn of the tide. From his Executive Office, Cherokee Nation, on August 8, he sent an appeal for aid to S. S. Scott, Commissioner of Indian Affairs at Richmond, stating:

"In compliance with your request, I herewith submit a statement of matters relating to the Cherokee people. The history of military operations in this country and in the State of Arkansas, directly affecting the interests of our people, gives just cause for complaint. The Indian troops who have been true to the South from the very first have been treated in many instances as though it were immaterial whether or not they were paid as promptly and equipped as thoroughly as other soldiers. Money specially obtained for them has more than once been appropriated to the use of other commands. Clothing, procured at great trouble and expense, to cover the nakedness of Indian troops, has on several occasions been distributed among less necessitous soldiers. Notwithstanding this treatment has been such as to test to the utmost their fidelity, they have remained true as steel. I can point to my command, and show less desertions than in any of like size in the service. I am glad to be able to say that of late my command has been better provided for than formerly. In April last a small force of hostile Indians, negroes, and one battalion of Kansas troops, in all about 2,000 men, took possession of Fort Gibson, in the Cherokee country. They have held this place, and consequently the Cherokee Nation, ever since, almost unmolested. There have been no vigorous efforts made to dislodge them, and they have at leisure strengthened and fortified their position. This mongrel force has laid waste our country, driven the women and children from their homes, and kept the other Nations, which have yet escaped invasion, in a continual state of alarm.

"I cannot understand the soundness of the policy which allows a vastly inferior force of the enemy to ravage the land with impunity. The hardihood of our enemies in penetrating 200 miles from their base of supplies, and from all support from other troops, when it is well known we have a force at least three times as large, is only equaled by the lack of spirit, inactivity, and apparent cowardice with which they have been met. It was my opinion ten weeks ago that by a concentration of our available forces we could overwhelm and utterly destroy our foes. I wrote my convictions to Brigadier General Steele, who, unfortunately, was not cognizant of the true condition of affairs here, and to Lieutenant General Holmes. The former paid no attention to my suggestions; the latter assured me if General Steele did not think himself strong enough to move against the enemy he would make him do so in three weeks. Since then, although strengthened by infantry and artillery, the same lethargy and procrastination prevail, and our prospects look more gloomy than ever. These delays and novel movements around and about, but never against, a much inferior force have produced universal dissatisfaction and despondency. The most favorable time for repelling the invader has passed, but a little energy may yet retrieve our misfortunes.

"Nearly every able-bodied man among the Cherokees is doing service in the army. In a majority of instances their families have been robbed of everything, leaving them utterly destitute and only too glad to escape with their lives. They are scattered over the Creek and Choctaw Nations and in the State of Texas. A census will soon be made out of their numbers. I think it will not fall short of 6,000. It is proposed to colonize these families at some point convenient to the provision market of Texas. Some arrangement will have to be made to provide them with shelter and clothing. The Cherokees have, by an ordinance recently adopted by their convention, undertaken to provide for their own destitute people. Their agents, appointed for this purpose, can accomplish but little good without money. I suggest that the annuities due the Cherokees be turned over as soon as possible. There can be no question that such annuities are due from the States of the Confederacy. The difficulty of collecting them is another matter. The Confederate States have promised us full protection against our enemies. I have ever made due allowance for the many embarrassments and difficulties the Government has experienced in maintaining her own rights and fulfilling her engagements with the Indians, but I have always discouraged those who complain of neglect, and have done all in my power to maintain confidence in the ability and certainty in the intentions of the Government. Shall I continue to encourage them, or shall I at once unveil to them the dread truth that our country is to be hopelessly abandoned, and that they are to receive the reward of poverty and ruin for their unswerving fidelity to the Southern cause? . . ."

The following day Watie wrote to his allies in the Creek, Choctaw and Chickasaw nations. His message to the Governors of the Choctaw and Chickasaw nations was:

"I wish, through you, to present to the people of your country a few thoughts, which the present condition and future prospects of the Indians have brought to my mind. I have entertained the confident, but delusive, hope for the last year that ordinary energy and activity would take the place of sluggishness and delay in the military movements in this country, and that a proper use of the means in our power would enable us to regain that portion of our territory which has been overrun by our enemies. Relief and protection, so often cheeringly promised, has not been afforded us; but our strength has been frittered away without accomplishing any good. Every day drives the conviction to my mind that we, the Indians true to the South, must place small reliance upon the promises of assistance from abroad; indeed, I am of opinion that we should cast behind us all expectation of adequate aid from the Confederate Government, and test our whole strength to defend our homes alone. An insignificant force of the enemy has been allowed to hold the Cherokee Nation for five months, and every day's delay renders it more difficult to repel them. I do not think all is lost because officers in control here will make no effort to regain the country. We have suffered much, and I fear, are destined to suffer more, by reason of their culpable delay. If we are still to be the victims of incapable and slothful leaders, and our whole country devastated by a ruthless foe, we may have one consolation in knowing that, by a united and unyielding opposition of our Indian forces alone, we can make our fair country an unpleasant, if not an untenable, home for our enemies. The gallant Seminoles have shown what folly it is to try to subjugate and destroy a people determined to defend their rights. The bravery of the Choctaw and Chickasaw troops in this war has not been excelled by any troops in the service, and, by a proper understanding among ourselves, our country may yet be saved, despite the inertness and criminal delays of those who have promised to protect us. It is a mistake that the occupation by the enemy of the Cherokee country is of small personal consequence to the Choctaw people. If the Cherokee Nation is abandoned to the enemy, the Creek country falls the next victim, and, in speedy turn, your own country will share the same fate.

"I shall be glad to hear from you on this subject, and receive any suggestions as to the course most proper to pursue in the present discouraging state of affairs. . . ."

And to the Governor of the Creeks Watie wrote:

"The condition of affairs in the Indian country inclines me to address you upon the subject of paramount importance to Creeks as well as Cherokees, viz, the prospect of adequate assistance from the Confederate States against our enemies, and the ability of the Indians, unassisted, to maintain their rights and defend their homes. It is now more than a year since our foes invaded in force the Cherokee Nation. They have desolated the land and robbed the people, until scarcely a Southern family is left east and north of the Arkansas River. The friends of the South have almost as one man taken up arms in the Southern cause, and have, with their brothers of the other Nations, struck many blows upon their enemies. The promised protection of the Confederate Government, owing, I am compelled to say, to the glaring inefficiency of its subordinate agents, has accomplished nothing; it has been a useless and expensive pageant; an object for the success of our enemies and the shame of our friends. I fear we can reasonably look for no change for the better, but that the Indians will have at last to rely upon themselves alone in the defense of their country. I believe it is in the power of the Indians unassisted, but united and determined, to hold their country. We cannot expect to do this without serious losses and many trials and privations; but if we possess the spirit of our fathers, and are resolved never to be enslaved by an inferior race, and trodden under the feet of an ignorant and insolent foe, we, the Creeks, Choctaws, Chickasaws, Seminoles, and Cherokees, never can be conquered by the Kansas jayhawkers, renegade Indians, and runaway negroes. It requires at this time and will as long as the war shall last, all the Yankee forces of Missouri to hold that State against the friends of the South within her limits. The multitude of soldiers that the North has now, or may yet bring into the field, will have abundant occupation elsewhere, so that the only expectation of the North to conquer the Indian Nation is in the traitors that have deserted us, the negroes they have stolen from us, and a few Kansas jayhawkers they can spare from that detestable region. Shall we suffer ourselves to be subjugated and enslaved by such a class! Never!

"I have written to Lieut. Gen. E. Kirby Smith and the Commissioner of Indian Affairs upon these matters. I hope soon to know positively whether we are to receive effective assistance from the Confederate Government, or whether the Indians must defend themselves alone and unaided. . ."

A short time after Watie's message had been received at Camp Kanard in the Creek Nation, the fighting, eloquent leader of the Creeks, Moty Kanard, and his subordinate chiefs wrote their own appeal to the Confederacy. This was addressed to Jefferson Davis at Richmond and read:

"Dear Father: It was customary under the old Government for the Indians to address the President as their father, and if there were ties and relations which made it necessary in the old, it must be so in the new, where ties and relations are so much stronger. Then, in thus addressing you, we feel all we say; and presenting our wants to one we love, we have the utmost confidence that they will be respected and satisfied.

"In the late treaty concluded between the Confederate States and our Nation, it was stipulated that in the appointment of an agent for this tribe our wishes and preference in his appointment should be consulted, and a due deference paid to them in such selection. Believing it to be our right so to do, this preference as to a choice was expressed more than a year ago and forwarded to Your Excellency; but from some cause we have received no expression from yourself in regard to this choice, until the Commissioner of Indian Affairs came out here last winter, when the same choice was expressed to him. He assured us that the man of our choice, Israel G. Vore, should be appointed our agent in due time, as provided for by treaty, but from some cause unknown to us he received no appointment until the Commissioner came this time, when it was again promised us that I. G. Vore should be appointed our agent. Since we made this choice we have seen no cause for a change in choice; therefore urge it as a right, for since we made this selection, which was from a perfect knowledge of the man, we have seen no cause to change; hence urge and insist upon his appointment.

"And, again, in the same treaty it was promised that our country should be defended and protected and in order to do this most effectually, this people agreed to raise a regiment of men for the Confederate States, to be used only within the limits of the Indian country and for its defense. Since that time we have turned out another regiment of Creeks and several detached companies. Recently we have passed a conscript act, taking into the army all the men in the country between the ages of eighteen and fifty. The soldiers raised by us were to be furnished as white soldiers in the States. As to how they are furnished we know not; but our soldiers, until recently, were, with few exceptions, unarmed, most of the time without ammunition; bareheaded, barefooted, without bread, and body in rags. The most of the time we were hard pressed by the enemy, and no force near to aid and assist us, the forces under Brigadier General Pike having fallen back of our country some hundred miles. Under these great privations, which try the souls of men, a few of our people ran off from the country and joined the enemy, who were stationed in the Cherokee country just across our line.

"Since Brig. Gen. D. H. Cooper has had command in part, we have been assisted to some extent – as much, perhaps, as his unequal forces could give; and at this time (except the battalion under Lieutenant Colonel Wells) there is not a soldier within our limits except our own, while the enemy is stationed but a short distance from us, with a large and heavy force. Is there no remedy for our distressed condition? Will not our father, the President, aid and effectually assist his distressed and sinking children? We know he will. General Cooper has done all he can for the protection and defense of our country. We know he feels a deep interest in our welfare, and were the proper means placed in his hands, our country would be ably defended beyond a doubt; and as to a commander for this department, he is decidedly our choice and preference. This much we have thought proper to transmit to our father, the President, with entire con fidence that our wants in the premises thus sent will meet his approbation, and be completely met and satisfied. . ."

Despite the efforts of Watie and his compatriots, the Rebel Indian forces were not strong enough to hold off the assaults by the Federals and within six weeks or so after Honey Springs, the Confederate headquarters at Fort Smith was in Yankee hands.

The Confederate Indian allies were backed into the Southern portion of the Indian Territory as Federal occupation extended from the Arkansas to the Canadian River.

At Colonel Watie's headquarters at Boggy Depot in September 1863, the ragged condition of the Indian troops was apparent to the Confederate staff. Some twenty per cent of the Indian soldiers had no arms and countless were without a change of clothing or shoes and Captain James Bell felt his men looked more like Siberian exiles than military men, but he knew from experience that the Indian Secech would fight with a grit and determination which belied their tattered appearance.

With the success of General Blunt in recapturing the Cherokee Nation from Watie, the pro-Confederate civilians were forced to flee even as the Union Indians had fled when Watie's raiders took over the nation. Mrs. Watie, with the children and several of her male slaves, went to Rusk, Texas. Other Indian families, forced out of their homes by the return of the Yankee Indians, established refugee camps along the Red River and endured all the suffering of the Union Indians when they had been refugees in Kansas.

General Blunt returned to Fort Gibson in late September and, after dispersing troops in the northern part of the Indian Territory recently ruled by the men of Cooper and Watie, removed his headquarters to Fort Smith.

Steele's policy of inviting battle and then withdrawing — falling back after an advance skirmish or without a fight — was highly criticised. But General Kirby-Smith approved the policy as he was aware of the difficulties under which Steele operated and Kirby-Smith believed in "abandoning the part to save the whole."

Though Watie had been forced from his Nation, he concocted

plans to return as he felt Colonel Phillips' men no match for his Cherokee Rifles in raiding operations.

In the fall Colonel Watie's flying horsemen launched a drive into the Cherokee Nation and captured Tahlequah, killing all the armed Pin Indians who crossed their path. Then Watie burned the council house and next put the torch to beautiful Rose Cottage, Chief-in-exile John Ross' mansion. He remembered a letter from Sarah asking him not to kill William Ross if he captured him on a raid, for, although Sarah held no brief for William Ross, she didn't want his old mother to be hurt. On this raid, Stand Watie captured the brilliant editor William Ross, but remembering Sarah's pleas for mercy, he spared him (Ross added new laurels to his career after the war and in May 1876, edited the new intertribal *Indian Journal,* published in an effort to offset unfavorable, falsified stories on the Civilized Indians) as he did another Union Indian political leader, Dannie Hicks.

On this spectacular and successful raid, Watie was disturbed by the killing of Andy Nave, who had been friendly toward the Confederate leader prior to the war. But although Watie wanted to take Nave a prisoner, the Union Indian sought to escape and he was killed by Richard Fields. Andy Nave was Chief John Ross' son-in-law and his death is described in *Park Hill*:

"Nave attempted to escape [from his house] by running through a field at the back of his place, but while getting over a rail fence . . . Richard Fields shot him with a double-barrelled shotgun loaded with buckshot. The charge struck Nave in the back and he died hanging across the fence. Mrs. Nave would never allow the land upon which her husband met his death to be cultivated . . ."

Chief Ross received word of his son-in-law's death at the Willard Hotel in Washington at the same time he learned of the burning of Rose Cottage by what he termed "that notorious band of rebel robbers . . ."

While Colonel Watie was one who employed every military means to achieve victory, he was not a killer as were some of the border captains on both sides. Later on, Watie was falsely accused of being implicated in the murder of Lieutenant Colonel Robert C. Parks – he had commanded Watie's men at Newtonia – killed by another officer.

In protesting the charges to Sarah, Watie explained that, although he was supposed to be hardened by the fighting, that he was hurt over the false charges as he was most certainly not the murderer nor had he any part of it. If he was to be punished for the opinion of other people, he was certain that God would give him justice. Colonel Watie reiterated his devotion to his friends and his family even if some times he blundered in his intentions.

Around November, Colonel Watie was placed in command of all the Indian troops, except the Chickasaws and Choctaws.

In December 1863, Major General Samuel B. Maxey became commander of the Indian Territory replacing General Steele, who at the Headquarters District of the Indian Territory at Doaksville, immediately wrote Colonel S. S. Anderson, Assistant Adjutant-General:

"I received yesterday the order relieving me from command in the Indian country, complimentary in terms, but the effect of which is utterly destroyed by the accompanying letter, putting me in a subordinate position in the same command from which I have asked to be relieved. The slanders that have been industriously circulated through the Indian country and Northern Texas not only make it extremely disagreeable for me to serve here, but it impairs my usefulness. I think it only justice to me that I should not be required to serve in this region until I am cleared of the imputations referred to, particularly as serving in a subordinate capacity where I have been in command carries the idea that I have not given satisfaction, and have been superseded in consequence. The order relieving me will be seen by few, the fact that I am superseded will be patent to everyone. The belief expressed that General Cooper will be found to be the senior is an additional reason for wishing to quit the country. I cannot serve under him, as I may be required at any time to do. You have doubtless seen the article in the Houston *Telegraph* of the 5th instant, referring to matters here, and intimating that there has been complicity with the enemy. I have written to the editor for the name of the writer, with a view to a trial. This letter purports to come from the troops I am to be assigned to, and makes another reason why I should not take this command at present. I think I have lost enough already by accepting a command from a sense of duty, after it had been declined by several officers to whom it had been offered before me. Notwithstanding the fact that all the property I owned at the beginning of this war was at the North, and that I resigned from the army and cast my lot with the South, I am looked upon with suspicion as a Yankee, and am told that people will not believe that I am not a brother of the Federal general of the same name, that being one of the reports circulated. I had hoped to be able to quit this country and to have a short time to arrange the records of the district in such a manner that they would have formed my defense."

To precipitate action for the new commander, Colonel Watie took five hundred Cherokee Rifles into the upper part of the Indian Territory and Southwest Missouri and Yankee cavalrymen started polishing their swords as far north as Fort Scott, Kansas, for word was prevalent that with Watie rode Quantrill and the two were bent on a destructive raid that would leave Fort Scott in flames.

Though such was not the case, Watie's fleet horsemen – often with frustrated Yankee cavalrymen cursing in back of them – terrorized Union lands until December 18 when, at Barren Fork, in the Cherokee Nation, a brigade from Phillips' command at Fort Gibson edged Watie in a two-hour battle.

Captain Alexander C. Spilman, Third Indian Home Guards, wrote this report to Colonel Phillips on his clash with Stand Watie at Barren Fork:

"I have the honor to report that, in compliance with your instructions, I marched from Fort Gibson at 3:30 p.m., December 17, with a force of about 290 infantry, consisting of details from the First, Second, and Third Indian Regiments, and one howitzer. I took the Park Hill road, and, passing that place, went into camp at the crossing of the Illinois, at midnight. By inquiry at Park Hill, I learned that Col. S. Watie's force, variously estimated at from 500 to 800 men, after plundering Murrell's house and burning the negro cabins at Chief Ross' place, had moved during the afternoon toward the Illinois River, stating their intention to camp in the Illinois bottom that night. Morning came, and I was still ignorant of the exact whereabouts of the rebels, though satisfied that their camp was not far distant. I moved out of camp between 7 and 8 o'clock in the morning, taking the road leading up the Barren Fork. During the morning two small parties of rebels, one of 10 and another of 5 men, approached our column, mistaking us for their own men. They were fired upon, and 1 was killed, but not having mounted men to pursue them, the remainder escaped. I now became satisfied that we were in close proximity to the rebel force. The road lay first on one and then on the other side of Barren Fork, the valley of which was narrow, and covered with thick timber and underbrush, and walled in on either side by precipitous hills. About three-quarters of a mile beyond Sheldon's place the advance guard reported the enemy in force just ahead. I proceeded to the front, and discerned, through the thick undergrowth of brush, their line, formed in a heavily timbered ravine, of dismounted men, the right resting upon the road, and the left reaching up the ravine into the hill on the right of the road. I immediately brought forward the howitzer, supported by 95 men of the First Indian Regiment, under command of Captain Willets, placed it in position on the right of the road, and deployed the Cherokees, under command of Lieutenant (L. F.) Parsons. Third Indian Regiment, still farther to the right, between the gun and the foot of the hill.

"These preparations were not completed when the enemy opened on us a heavy fire from small-arms. This was replied to by our men with promptness and spirit. As soon as the howitzer opened upon the rebels, their line was completely broken, and they retreated in some confusion up the ravine, to the top of the hill. The Cherokees, under command of Lieutenant Parsons, followed them, and drove them about a quarter of a mile beyond the crest of the hill, where they again formed, and were a second time routed by our men. The road being now clear in front, I ordered the men back, and moved on about a quarter of a mile to take a better position, where there was higher ground and several log buildings, for the protection of our infantry. We had no sooner taken this position than the rebels, rallying, renewed the attack. A few discharges of canister and shell from the howitzer drove them out of the valley and they took possession of the adjoining hill, which was heavily timbered. Sheltering themselves here behind trees and rocks, the rebels opened a fire at long range upon our men, who replied from the cover of the log-houses. The fighting here lasted for more than two hours, without any decided advantage to either party. I saw that to drive the enemy from the crest of the hill by a charge would be difficult and hazardous. I also knew that if they came over the hill into the valley to fight, we had decidedly the advantage of them. Thinking to draw them out, I ordered the command forward on the road, as if to abandon the position. It had the desired effect. The enemy supposing, doubtless, that we were retreating, came over the hill, all dismounted, and in larger numbers than they had before shown themselves, and advanced toward the houses we were leaving. Our men were immediately rallied, and returned to their former position on the double-quick. The howitzer was quickly brought up, and opened fire upon the advancing enemy, who withstood the shock but one moment, and then turned and fled. Our men pursued them, driving them over the hill and beyond it nearly a mile. The rout of the rebels was now complete; they did not again make the least attempt to rally. Our casualties during the engagement were comparatively light. I regret that I must record the loss of Captain Willets, First Indian Regiment, who fell, mortally wounded, while gallantly leading his men in the early part of the engagement; Private Arch Benner, Company H, Third Indian Regiment, and———, Company F, First Indian Regiment, received severe, but, it is thought, not fatal, wounds. Two of the howitzer horses were wounded, one so badly that it had to be abandoned on the road; also 2 mules, belonging to the six-mule team, were wounded, one of which had to be abandoned."

Rallying his forces and whipping around the Yankees, Colonel Watie headed for Southwest Missouri and the tweaking of General Schofield's nose. Colonel Phillips again tried cutting off Watie and, as usual, Watie eluded him. Not only was Watie flaunting his cavalrymen in Schofield's face, but so were Jo Shelby and the daring "bushwhackers" under several commands, those of Captain Buck Brown often uniting with Watie for a raid. A former West Point Lieutenant and faculty member at Washington University at St. Louis, Schofield had long been at odds with Senator Jim Lane's policy of "Kill, confiscate and collect!" Lincoln no longer felt it wise to uphold Schofield and on January 22, 1864, William S. Rosecrans who had taken some buffeting himself in Tennessee, replaced the political Paw Paw, "moderate" Schofield.

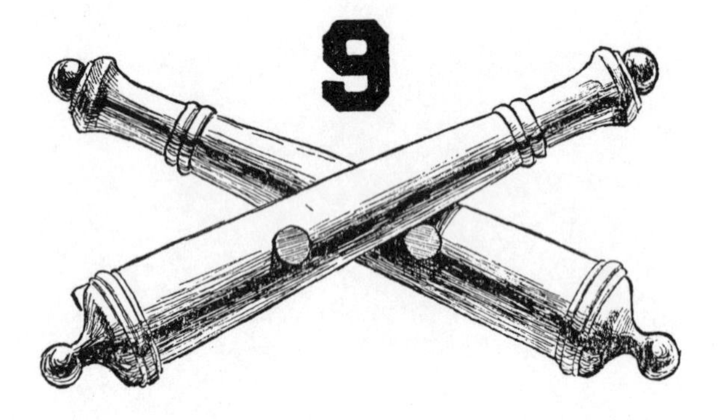
9

BACK IN TEXAS, General William Steele, who was put in command at Galveston, Texas, after he left the Indian Territory, began preparation of a report on his ill-fated command in the Civilized Nations. Steele had a well-desired military reputation which he did not want shattered by his failure to hold the Confederate Indian Territory against invasion. Colonel Stand Watie and the other Indian leaders had been highly critical of what they called Steele's policy of inaction and fall back.

Both Confederate General William Steele and Union General Frederick Steele, fighting in the same general area, were born in New York State—William was born in Albany and Frederick in Delhi, in 1819 and so came about the false story that they were brothers. A graduate of West Point, William Steele was in the Florida War, the military occupation of Tex ; and the War with Mexico.

Prior to the War between the States, he had served mainly on Indian service in Nebraska and Dakota. Despite his Northern birth, his sympathies were with the South and he resigned his commission in the United States Army in May 1861, and became a Colonel in the Seventh Texas Cavalry, C.S.A. After taking part in General Henry H. Sibley's expedition to New Mexico, he was made a Brigadier General and soon assigned to the Indian Territory command.

Himself a brave and competent leader of white troops, Steele, who after his command in Texas, headed a cavalry division in 1864 when he opposed General Nathaniel P. Banks' Red River invasion, was unable to cope with the unique military situation involving the Indian troops and their picturesque leaders. His report on his difficult command was:

"Having been relieved of the command of the Indian Territory, at my own request, I think it proper to report a brief summary of the military operations in that Territory during the past year . . .

"Early in the month of January, of the past year, in conformity with orders received from Lieutenant-General Holmes, commanding Trans-Mississippi Department, I reported to Major-General Hindman for duty in the Indian Territory, and, in accordance with instructions from the latter, proceeded without delay to Fort Smith, and, on or about January 8, 1863, assumed the command to which I had been assigned. I will premise by saying that I was fully and truthfully advised by Major-General Hindman of the exhausted condition of the country, as well as the undisciplined, ill-equipped, and demoralized state of the few troops over whom I was called to command. On my arrival at Fort Smith the appearance of everything was of the most gloomy description. The continuous occupation of the country by a large Confederate force from the beginning of the war had utterly exhausted its resources, and the retreat of General Hindman from that section immediately preceding my arrival had left the people desponding, hopeless, and, with a few honorable exceptions, thoroughly demoralized; insomuch that my anxiety and watchfulness was more taxed by the operations of traitors, deserters, and Union men known in common as "jayhawkers" (who were in the majority), than by the movements of the enemy in my front.

"The only force I found at Fort Smith was about 100 men, under Colonel (J. C.) Monroe, of the First Arkansas Cavalry, who had been sent temporarily to that point by General Hindman, and the remnant of Lane's (Texas) Partisan Rangers, under Lieutenant-Colonel (R. P.) Crump, numbering about 150 men, this being the entire number present for duty in a regiment originally consisting of fourteen full companies. This regiment had not a change of clothing nor an average of a blanket to the man. About 1,500 inmates, in a wretched condition, were officially reported in the numerous hospitals in the place. The quartermaster and commissary departments throughout the Territory were found in the utmost confusion. The officers serving in those departments, as a general rule, had derived their appointments from General Hindman or General Pike, were without legal commissions, and, in many cases, had executed no bonds. To have displaced these would have stopped all operations; therefore, having no others to replace them, I was compelled to continue them on duty. Many of these staff officers were incompetent and negligent. Orders were issued and re-issued demanding that their returns should be forwarded to headquarters without attaining the object sought. From Majors (Israel G.) Vore and (N. B.) Breedlove, quartermaster and commissary of subsistence, respectively, of Cooper's brigade, of some 6,000 men, on paper, returns were repeatedly called for, but never received. I may here also mention that I was unable to procure a single paper (nor did I ever receive one) in the way of a record, either in reference to previous military operations or the Indian superintendency.

"The few stores left by General Hindman on his retreat had been stolen and scattered to all parts of the country. In the quartermaster's department there was neither transportation nor forage. The best efforts of the officer in charge of the commissary department were only productive of a very limited supply of poor beef and corn meal. Of the latter, there was but a few days' supply on hand, and, to obtain the necessary supply for the subsistence of the troops mentioned, and the hospitals, it became imperatively necessary to reopen the navigation of the Arkansas River.

"I ascertained, on inquiry, that a considerable supply of flour, for the use of the Indian Department, had been purchased in Northern Texas by an agent sent by General Hindman for that purpose, but the deficiency in transportation and the condition of the roads forbade the hope of an adequate supply of breadstuffs from that quarter. The Arkansas River was, therefore, the only avenue for a supply left open to me, and this of corn. The territory on the northern side of the stream for a considerable distance was virtually in the possession of the enemy, whilst jayhawkers in considerable numbers were boldly depredating on both sides of the river between Little Rock and Fort Smith. Under these circumstances, I besought the lieutenant-general commanding to so dispose a sufficient force of cavalry along the north side of the river as to afford protection to such boats as might be employed in the transportation of corn. After no little delay and embarrassment, a sufficient supply of corn was thus obtained, not, however, until I was forced, through absolute want of subsistence, to send to Red River Speight's brigade, with a battery attached. The scarcity of forage and subsistence, together with the destitute condition of the command, involved the necessity, also, of ordering the remnant of Lane's regiment to a point at which there was a probability of subsistence, recruiting, re-equipping, &c. Bass' (Texas) regiment, of Speight's brigade, numbering some 200 men, was kept at Fort Smith for police duty, &c. This regiment, as was the case with most of the other regiments composing Speight's brigade, was found to be greatly demoralized, and in a very short time after being put on duty exhibited an effective strength of less than 100 men, this depletion arising, in the main, from desertion.

"The necessity of sending Speight's infantry brigade to the Red River, though deeply regretted at the time, was, nevertheless, imperative. Could I have retained that brigade at Fort Smith, I should have been enabled, in all probability, to have inaugurated the spring campaign from the line of the Arkansas River, and thus, perhaps, have materially changed the fortunes of war in that section of country. All of these many difficulties and embarrassments will be seen by reference to my official correspondence, to which I would most respectfully refer.

"Prior to my arrival at Fort Smith, General Hindman had directed Brigadier-General Cooper, in command of the Indian

Brigade, to adopt a universal system of furloughs. Very many of the Indian troops availed themselves of this privilege. There, however, remained quite a number who refused to accept furloughs, and whose subsistence, &c., added greatly to the then existing difficulties. Brigadier-General Cooper's official reports represented the troops under his command as being almost destitute of clothing; miserably equipped in all respects; poorly armed (many being without arms), and that it was impossible to subsist them on the line of the Arkansas River; hence I was under the necessity, also, of ordering this force to the southward. The alternative was thus presented to me either to proceed with the troops that had been ordered southward, and abandon the line of the Upper Arkansas, or remain in person at Fort Smith, and attempt, with the small force in garrison at that point, to hold possession of the place, and, to some extent, the line indicated, until such time as I should have it in my power to subsist such troops as were then in the country or as might be sent from other points. I determined, believing, as I did, that Fort Smith was the true strategic key to the Indian Territory, to adopt the latter course, trusting to the inclemency of the season and the waters of the Arkansas to shield me from an attack. During the winter the enemy made frequent raids, penetrating as far southward as the Arkansas, doing little other mischief than annoying and interrupting the river transportation. I became satisfied, however, that he had no design of attempting the permanent occupation of any point south of the Arkansas so long as our forces held possession of, and controlled, the navigation of the Lower Arkansas. Thus impressed, I ordered the main body of the troops in the Territory to encamp as near Red River as was convenient, in order, first, that they might be more readily subsisted, recruited, and equipped; and, second, that the available transportation might be used in accumulating supplies in the depots near the line of the Arkansas. I thus hoped to accumulate an ample supply of bread-stuffs for the commencement of the spring campaign at the earliest day, the artillery and cavalry horses being meanwhile recruited on Red River, where an abundance of forage had been placed, under my direction, by Maj. A. S. Cabell, chief quartermaster.

"In order to distract the attention of the enemy from an insight into these plans and operations, I resolved to have the enemy, then at Fayetteville, Ark., 55 miles northwest from Fort Smith, annoyed as much as possible, and to this end I gave every encouragement in my power to the formation of partisan companies. Colonel Monroe's First Arkansas Cavalry, about 400 strong, having been sent to my aid, I caused as frequent scouts to be made as it was possible for man and horse to endure. The greater portion of this cavalry was constantly employed watching over and defeating the operations of the numerous bands of jayhawkers who were committing daily deeds of violence and bloodshed.

"The full force of the enemy in Northwestern Arkansas and the Cherokee country during the winter and early spring did not exceed 3,000, inclusive of Pin Indians. Of the latter, some 1,200 or 1,500 were in the service of the Federal Government. To subsist this force and obtain forage, the enemy was under the necessity of scattering it over a large extent of country. In Northwestern Arkansas he was unable to mount a force exceeding 500 men. These facts were repeatedly urged upon the lieutenant-general commanding, and a movement in the rear of this force urgently pressed. I became satisfied that if the enemy was permitted to remain in quiet and uninterrupted possession of the north side of the Arkansas River during the winter and spring, he would, in the exercise of his customary energy, throw forward in the direction of Fort Gibson such quantity of supplies as would suffice to attempt a flank movement on Fort Smith in that direction. General Marmaduke's cavalry force was then occupying the country in the vicinity of Batesville. A brigade of cavalry, under Colonel (C. A.) Carroll, occupied the country in the vicinity of Roseville. From Batesville to Fayetteville was but a short distance, and from Roseville to the same point the distance was not exceeding four or five days' march. Had Marmaduke's cavalry been thrown rapidly in the rear of the enemy at Fayetteville while Carroll marched upon the front, it is quite sure that the result would have been either his capture in detail or his entire abandonment of Northwestern Arkansas and the Indian country. I mean no disrespect to the lieutenant-general then commanding, in making these statements, yet justice to myself and the subsequent verification of the correctness of the views then entertained and repeatedly urged, demand that I should record them. Had the movement indicated been made (its successful issue, in my judgment, being beyond the peradventure of a doubt), I should have been enabled to have had in store, in depots on or near the Arkansas River, an ample supply of breadstuffs, while the country south of that stream abounded in beef cattle of the best quality. In short, I could have assumed the offensive from the line of the Arkansas River with a force fully rested and recruited, both as regards men and horses, considerably earlier in the spring than the enemy could have begun his movements from either Missouri or Kansas. The moral effect of such a condition of affairs upon the people of Arkansas and the Indian Territory and Northern Texas, and its influence upon operations then contemplated and subsequently consummated in the direction of Little Rock, remains, of course, only a subject of conjecture.

"During the winter months I had caused workshops for the repair, &c., of arms and wagons (of which quite a number were fitted up from the debris found scattered about the garrison), as well as put in operation such other branches of industry necessary to the supply of the army as the resources of the country afforded.

"Repeated requisitions for the supply of arms and ammunition remaining unfilled, I assumed the responsibility of sending an officer of my staff to Texas, with a view of making an endeavor to obtain the necessary supply of ammunition and arms, if possible, from that quarter. A greater portion of the ammunition obtained by this officer had to be transported from San Antonio to Bonham, Tex., in ox wagons. The delay incident to this means of transportation was of very material prejudice, especially so, as it was found impossible to procure a supply from any other quarter. I also procured some 500 stand of arms from this source, these being the only arms brought into the Territory during the period of my command, other than a few repaired arms.

"I repeatedly urged upon General Cooper and the officer in command of Speight's brigade the necessity of straining every energy to the preparation of their commands for an advance movement at the earliest practicable period; and, in accordance with my orders, the march northward was begun by the entire force near Red River left under my command as soon as the condition of the roads, &c., would permit. Speight's brigade, together with West's battery (this being the only reliable battery then under my control), was ordered to Louisiana, after being some days on the march northward.

"Notwithstanding this sudden and important depletion of my effective strength, I determined to make every effort to hold the line of the Arkansas, and, if possible, by means of a superior numerical force of cavalry operating upon the enemy's rear, compel him to abandon his hold on the north bank of that stream at Fort Gibson, a point which he had strongly fortified and garrisoned with from 2,500 to 3,500 troops.

"General Cooper, in conformity with my orders, moved forward with his brigade, consisting of two regiments of Texas cavalry (De Morse's and Martin's), with the bulk of the Indian troops, and a battery of three mountain howitzers and one small prairie rifle gun, to the vicinity of Fort Gibson. Fully apprised of the difficulties experienced by the enemy in regard to his supplies (he being under the necessity of transporting them in wagons for a distance of several hundred miles), and being regularly and correctly advised of the departure of his trains from Fort Scott and other depots to the northward, I made such dispositions as I flattered myself would effectually cut off supplies and re-enforcements. Cabell's brigade, which had been placed under my command a short time before, was moved forward to Fayetteville, with the design of operating upon the rear and lines of communication from that quarter, whilst General Cooper was instructed to avoid a general action, and operate with his available cavalry from the west. Attempts to effect this object were accordingly made. With the conduct and results of these expeditions I was wholly unsatisfied. The failure of the first expedition, under Colonel McIntosh, sent by General Cooper, was attributable, in my judgment, to the command of the expedition devolving upon an Indian officer, deficient in energy and capacity, and who did not enjoy the confidence of the white troops under his command.

"A second expedition, under Col. Stand Watie, was sent to the west of Grand River and in rear of Fort Gibson, with the view of attacking a large train of the enemy and a number of re-enforcements, known to be en route for Gibson." [Steele then recounts the action at Cabin Creek.]

". . . In a few days (July 22) Cooper's and Cabell's brigades were concentrated about 25 miles in rear of the battleground

[Honey Springs] and by the 25th were placed in position at Prairie Springs, 15 miles from Fort Gibson, where I determined to await the arrival of a brigade from Texas, under command of Col. S. P. Bankhead, which I had been notified was ordered to report to me, and which was expected before the 10th of August. Upon the arrival of that brigade, it was my intention to take a position near enough to Fort Gibson to effectually prevent any further supplies or re-enforcements from going in. In a few days the desertions from Cabell's Arkansas brigade became alarming, without any apparent cause. They left by tens and hundreds (as many as 200 leaving in one night, several officers going with them). The weather at this time was good, and provisions (flour and beef) abundant; but another serious difficulty presented itself. The powder which had been received from Texas was found to be worthless when exposed to the slightest moisture, a night's heavy dew converting it into a paste. Under these circumstances, I determined to withdraw farther from the enemy, who might in a night's march attack us at any time, knowing, as he undoubtedly did, the condition of affairs with us, from several deserters who went to his lines. The whole force was accordingly withdrawn to the south side of the Canadian River, and Fort Smith being threatened by a force from Springfield, Mo., Cabell's brigade was posted within supporting distance of that place. My force being nearly all cavalry, and dependent entirely upon grass to subsist the animals, was necessarily much scattered; consequently, when a few days later the enemy was reported advancing in force, a move to the rear was made to a point where all could concentrate. The Creeks failed entirely to come to the point designated, and most of the Cherokees and several companies of Choctaws being absent, I found myself with not over 1,500 men, many of whom were unarmed (nearly all with indifferent arms), opposed to a force of 2,000 cavalry and about 3,000 infantry, the latter transported in 300 two-horse wagons. Instead, therefore, of risking an engagement, nothing was attemped but to keep the enemy in check until our supplies were moved to the rear. In this we were successful, nothing having been left to fall into the enemy's hands. He gratified his malice, however, by burning the little town of Perryville. From Perryville the enemy turned toward Fort Smith with a portion of his forces, where General Cabell contested his advance in an engagement of several hours' duration, most of his men behaving badly. A few hundred repulsed the attacking force, and then retired in the direction of Waldron.

"Whilst retiring before the enemy, near Perryville, I again received notice that Bankhead's brigade was ordered to report to me. It was hurried forward in the direction of Fort Smith, to the support of General Cabell, who had been instructed to retire, in case of necessity, on the road this brigade advanced upon. It was expected that if General Cabell had been obliged to evacuate, this re-enforcement would have enabled him to regain his lost ground. General Cooper's brigade, composed of a few whites and several different tribes of Indians, could not be moved. General Cabell's movements, by the way of Waldron, prevented his junction with the re-enforcements at a time when the enemy, feeling secure, had scattered his forces and offered an easy conquest. General Cabell reported that he had received orders from Major-General Price, which orders were never sent me, and thus his brigade was in some way disconnected with my command. Acting Brigadier-General Bankhead remained several weeks near Fort Smith, cutting off small parties of the enemy. General Cooper, with his brigade, was, as soon as possible, advanced upon the line we had retired upon.

"At this time I left General Cooper in command, for the purpose of having an interview with the commander of the Trans-Mississippi Department. On my return, I found that all the troops had been concentrated near North Fork Town, on the Canadian, and immediately after my arrival, and without consulting my wishes, General Cooper moved the whole slowly in the direction of Fort Smith, halting about 35 miles from that place, where I overtook him. The statements in regard to the enemy's force and position, sent to me during the few days previous to my arrival at his camp, had varied so much from day to day that I was in great uncertainty as to the best course to pursue. The troops had moved down with the expectation of a battle. I determined to attempt a surprise, upon learning that, owing to the annoyance given by the Choctaws, the enemy had no pickets on one road leading through the Arkansas Bottom, and gave orders accordingly, when General Cooper represented me that he could not bring up his brigade of Indians to take the part assigned to them. I then thought of making the attack from another direction, where a prairie, with several roads leading from it to the enemy's position, would obviate the objection urged. To this plan General Cooper demurred, on the ground that the ponies of his Indians, having been without forage for several days could not make the march in time. The distance was estimated at about 35 miles, to be traveled between 12 m. and daylight the next morning. Wishing to remove every objection, I moved my camp farther around to the south of Fort Smith, and to within 20 miles of that place, where I arrived on the 31st of October, having been delayed by a storm of rain and snow, and in cutting out a road through the Poteau Bottom. During this storm the various commanders of the regiments of Texas troops, composing the Second Brigade, came in a body to inform me of the suffering condition of their men from the want of proper clothing, and of their inability to keep the men together much longer under such circumstances. My force on the 31st of October, as I derived from inspectors' reports, was: Seminoles, 106; Chickasaws, 208; Creeks, 305; Choctaws, 1,024; Choctaw militia, 200, and whites, 999. Of the Indians, all but one regiment were armed with any kind of guns that could be obtained. Some were entirely without arms. The whole force was cavalry and artillery. General Gano arrived the next day with his escort and a portion of of Howell's battery, making my whole force nearly 3,000, about two-thirds of which was composed of at least three different nations, speaking different languages, and under no kind of discipline. The enemy's scouts had discovered us; consequently all hope of a surprise was at an end. General McNeil had arrived at Fort Smith with re-enforcements. I believe that to have made an attack would only have ended in disaster. Under these circumstances, I withdrew the white troops, and directed General Cooper to keep up, with his Indian brigade, a desultory warfare, to prevent the enemy from foraging or moving about at will. The Texas brigade, Brigadier-General Gano commanding, was withdrawn, and found its clothing at Boggy Depot, from which point it was moved at once eastward near the Arkansas State line. At the time of withdrawing the Texas brigade, the whole command was out of flour or other breadstuffs; 4 small wagon loads only arrived just as we were retiring.

"One of the most fruitful sources of embarrassment experienced in the command of the Indian country, and one which, instead of being repressed, constantly increased, was that of feeding the indigent Indians. The policy of feeding such Indians as had been driven from their homes, and whose country was in the occupation of the enemy, had been inaugurated prior to my arrival. The total failure of the crops throughout the entire Indian Territory had increased the number dependent upon the commissariat to many thousands. It became necessary to give these people bread or have them throw themselves upon the charity of the enemy, who lost no opportunity to gain ground by holding out liberal inducements of pardon, and of supplies of clothing and food. To resist the moral effect of these inducements held out by the enemy, I was compelled to yield with as much show of cheerfulness as possible to the very heavy demands that were made upon me, and, to meet these demands, large draughts were constantly being made upon stores accumulated for military purposes.

"An experience of twelve months in the command of the Indian country has convinced me that, with a few exceptions, the Indians are wholly unreliable as troops of the line. The officers, as a general rule, are ignorant, void of moral tone of character, and indisposed to enforce discipline among their men. Their allegiance to the Government seems to be regarded more in the light of a voluntary contribution on their part, susceptible of being withheld at their option, than the performance of an obligatory duty. In order to acquire the reputation derived from success, in the administration of the affairs of the Territory (according to the somewhat doubtful standard, success) it is necessary to pander to the opinions and sentiments of Indianized white men, and through such to coax and demagoguize with the Indians, rather than attempt the enforcement of discipline among the troops and system in the various departments. The ignorance of the main body of the Indians naturally subjects them to the influence for good or evil of a class of whites and educated half-breeds, who, living among them and having a knowledge of their language, feelings, prejudices, &c., find no difficulty in molding the masses to their generally interested views. I became satisfied that with those exercising the chief influence among the Indians, there was a settled design to subordinate white officers and white troops to Indian officers and Indian troops.

[Ill-feeling between General Steele and the Indians was in no way ameliorated by Steele's ordering for arrest and trial at Little Rock, Colonel W. P. Adair, Watie's courageous Chief of Scouts. The charge was "disrespect." Colonel Adair, in turn, threatened to have General Steele arrested. Adair was actually taken away from duty for a time because of his arrest.

It cannot be disputed that Colonel Adair may well have been guilty of disrespect technically, yet it was not practical for military leaders like General Steele to maintain the attitude that the Indian officers should have the same attitude toward army discipline as themselves. Indian officers and troops gave no deference to West Point training — either in Confederate or Federal officers — and they showed little regard for demands that they hew-to-the-line. The conflict between two different modes of military operations was mutually aggravating. Yet it is to be remembered that the Confederate Indians troops were not the sole Secesh soldiers with a carefree disregard for the rule books. Turner Ashby's cavalry, for an example, in Stonewall Jackson's Valley campaign, exasperated some of the old-line career officers by their lack of parade ground discipline. But, as with the Indian riders, Ashby's men, born to the saddle, were aggressive in operations and had the highest respect of the often baffled Yankees.]

"In suggesting these views, I would take occasion to state that there are serving in the Indian country a few striking exceptions. Among these I may mention Col. Stand Watie, whom I found to be a gallant and daring officer, but, as was the case in all other instances among the Indian troops, without the slightest discipline in his regiment. For some time prior to making the movement in the direction of Fort Smith, already referred to, I had discerned a growing disinclination on the part of the Indian troops to serve under my command. The ingenuity of my defamers had been taxed to the utmost in giving circulation to the most reckless falsehoods. I was charged with a determination to take the white troops out of their country and abandon them to their fate; that I only awaited a favorable opportunity to go over to the enemy in person; that I was Northern-born, and had no true feeling of sympathy with the South. With another class of troops such calumnies could have been successfully met, and my influence as a commander not, perhaps, have been thereby materially impaired: but among the Indian troops, with the influence mentioned operating against me, the consequence will be patent. An improper and unjust construction was given to almost every step I deemed it necessary to take for the good of the service; in short, nothing seemed to have been left undone by designing men and knaves to excite the most violent prejudice and distrust on the part of the Indians. The dark side of my picture, painted in their own colors, was kept constantly presented to their view. Explanations of my official conduct were never attempted to be made by those whose implied duty it was to give me their aid and comfort. The Indian command was also led to believe that I was illegally exercising the command of the Territory over Brigadier-General Cooper, who was represented as my superior in rank, and that he, being an Indian officer I was thereby trampling upon the rights, privileges, and wishes of the Indian troops.

"Concluding from these reasons, and many more of a similar character . . . I respectfully asked of the lieutenant-general commanding to be relieved of duty in the Indian country. . ."

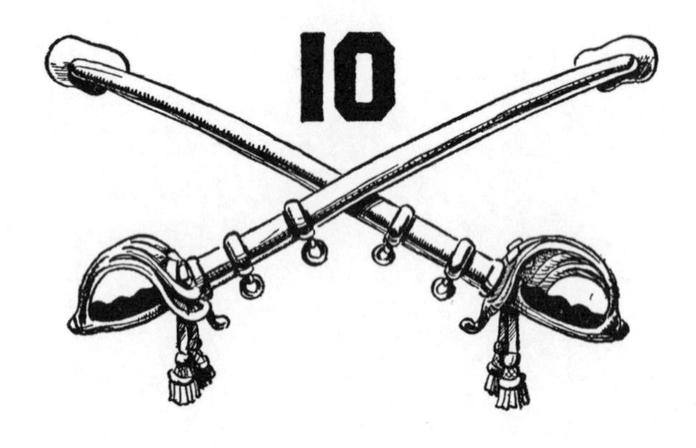
10

UP FROM TEXAS, General Samuel Bell Maxey, had high hopes for his new command. Born in 1825 at Tompkinsville, Kentucky, and a graduate of West Point, he fought in the Mexican War. A practicing lawyer in Texas when the South seceded, he declined election as a Texas legislator in order that he could enter the fight for Dixie. He organized the Ninth Texas Infantry and campaigned in Tennessee and Mississippi before becoming commander of the Indian Territory.

Following the war, he practiced law for ten years. After the White South threw off the hideous yoke of Reconstruction, Maxey was elected to the United States Senate and served there for some twelve years. He was well-known for his many speeches on Indian relations.

In the lands of the Civilized Nations, Maxey reorganized the

Indian forces and met with the Southern Indian officers February 1 at Armstrong Academy, Choctaw Nation. General Maxey advised the Choctaw people to remain in their homes and raise crops. Stand Watie's men had repelled the Federals from the borders of the Choctaw Nation and Maxey assured them that the Stars and Bars would stay over Choctaw territory. Maxey displayed a high respect for the Confederate Indian leaders. He felt that the Civilized Nations were aristocracies and that in them, as he thought it should be, the educated minority took the lead. Moty Kanard, political leader of the Creeks, praised Maxey's speech as "noble."

At about the same time, Colonel Phillips successfully campaigned against the Southern Indians pushing them back, even routing them at Middle Boggy, and continuing as far as Old Fort Armstrong himself.

On February 8, 1864, from his headquarters on the South Canadian, Colonel Phillips wrote Brigadier General Thayer, commanding the District of the Frontier:

"I have hopes now that I may be able, substantially, to crush and end the rebellion in the Indian Nation. I am adopting stern measures. The rebels have hitherto only trifled with propositions of peace. When next made, I have no doubt they will embrace them heartily."

A week later Phillips, from his Field Headquarters, Camp Kagi, Chickasaw Nation, sent out surrender appeals to most of the Confederate Indian leaders. The tenor of his approach may be judged from this letter to John Jumper, Chief of the Seminoles:

"I write you, not that I have any interest in appealing to you, neither because I admire your courage, which I recognize even among the disaster of your late defeat; nor do I refer to your humiliation in the late engagement to taunt you with what your personal bravery could not prevent. I write you because you are the recognized head of a part of the Seminole Nation, and in behalf of those who trust you I appeal to one whom I do not believe is dead to a just sentiment. I suppose you know the responsibility of power. I do not think you desire to see your people utterly ruined. I believe you do not wish the little remnant of their children to curse the day when you were their head. I think you and they know that neither you nor the rebels can overthrow the Government of the United States. I think you ought to know that so causeless a war to overthrow so good a Government is very wicked. I feel you have had no cause to rebel against the Government. Let me ask you, do you not see the end coming, and are you anxious to see your people destroyed in the ruins? Why let those demagogue rebels, who rose in arms against their Government deceive you? Do you wish to see the Seminoles perish to cover . . . and hide their crimes?

"The President of the United States has once more offered mercy, pardon, and peace. I strike hard, but not because the Government is cruel, but because everything must be destroyed that stands in the way of the glorious American Republic. For your people, then, I tell you to think of these things. The offer is honest; it is liberal, because the Republic is great enough to be generous. If you accept it soon, you may be preserved; if you do not, you and your people will be blotted out in blood. If you want peace, let me know. From your friend and the friend of the Seminoles."

The eloquent writing of Phillips did not deter Colonel Jumper from his determination to stay true to Dixie. But a section of the Choctaws in March held a convention at Skullyville, twenty miles from Fort Smith, and sought to win favor with the Union under President Lincoln's amnesty proclamation. They appointed a provisional governor, Thomas Edwards, and sent E. P. Perkins as a delegate to Washington where he endeavoured to shift all the blame for the Choctaw support of the Secessionists upon Douglas Cooper. The United States Government, nevertheless, realistic in its appraisal of the situation, realized that the rump delegation held no power and the Rebel Indians controlled the Choctaw Nation.

Richmond, well aware of the efforts of the Federals to disrupt the morale of the Rebel Indians was active. On February 22, Jefferson Davis sent a communication addressed to Israel Folsom of the Six Confederate Indian Nations and Samuel Garland, Creek Chief; George Washington, Caddo Chief; Winchester Colbert, Governor Chickasaw Nation; Stand Watie, Cherokee Chief:

"I have received and read with much interest your communication of the 24th of November, 1863 . . . your request, as well as your complaints, have received my earnest consideration

. . . the policy of constituting the territory of the Six Nations, a separate military department, outside of the control of the commanding general of the department west of the Mississippi, has been thoroughly considered and discussed by the Executive Department here with your delegates elect.

". . . I have caused the Indian territory to be designated as a separate military district, and the Indian troops to be placed under the immediate command of General Cooper — the officer of your choice. It was thought manifestly better for the interest of all concerned that your Territory should be constituted a separate military district rather than a department so that the commanding general of the Trans-Mississippi Department may be responsible for the defense and protection of your district . . . and will feel it his duty to aid and protect you with all the promptitude and efficiency that unity in the whole force will confer. This view has been presented to your delegates, and I hope, when fully explained, will meet with your approval.

". . . As there are not yet a sufficient number of Indian troops to constitute a division, a major-general cannot now be properly appointed; but as soon as there are three . . . brigades, I propose to appoint a major-general to command them . . . I earnestly urge upon you the policy of making the requisite number of Indian troops as rapidly as possible . . . Arrangements have been made with Major Le Flore to have a certain number of arms delivered to the west side of the Mississippi for the Indians and General Smith has been instructed to give every facility for their transportation.

"Your last resolution which instructs your delegates to assure the Confederate States of the unshaken loyalty of the Six Nations represented in the Grand Council . . . is highly creditable to them, is what I expected from them, and claims my grateful recognition. The soldiers and peoples of the Six Nations in treaty and amity with us are regarded by this Government with the same tender care and solitude as are the soldiers and people of all the Confederate States. . ."

R. W. Lee, Assistant Inspector General, reported to Maxey at Fort Towson, Choctaw Nation, in February:

"The Indians in this district are eminently faithful and zealous, and with good arms in their hands would be . . . able to protect themselves from all attack not more formidable than those which have hitherto assailed them . . . The necessity is immediate and imperative. Obtain arms for them, general, and their now gloomy faces will grow bright, and their cheerful voices will again soon ring around their now deserted homes."

Somewhat simultaneously, a most illuminating report on the condition of the Indians' arms was made by Captain J. J. Du Bose, Chief Ordnance Officer, at Doaksville:

"I have the honor to report the condition of guns in the First Brigade, Indian Forces, commanded by Col. Stand Watie, and also a portion of arms of the Second Brigade, Indian Forces, commanded by Colonel Walker and Lieutenant Colonel Wells' battalion, commanded by Lieutenant Colonel Wells. In each of these commands the appearance of the arms was very discouraging. The arms of the First Brigade were rather better than those of the latter commands. A few Enfield rifles were seen, with a few, very few Mississippi rifles in the line; the remainder were composed of double-barrel guns, Texas rifles, sporting rifles, etc. This is a very fine body of troops . . . What valuable guns they have, have been taken from the enemy, but a great many men are without arms entirely and are nothing more than camp followers. The First Choctaw Regiment of the Second Brigade are armed with an assortment of guns, more of the Texas rifles than any other class of arms . . . and I would call your attention especially to this arm. A regiment armed complete with these guns are armed but badly. These guns are nothing more than a cheat, badly put together and very unreliable, being liable, a great number, to burst. The remainder in the regiment were sporting rifles, which with a few exceptions, were badly wanting repair, double-barrel shotguns and a very few muskets. Lieutenant Colonel Wells' battalion were armed with Texas rifles, double-barrel guns, and a very few muskets with very few exceptions. I did not see a gun that was entirely serviceable."

South of the Indian Territory, Brigadier General W. R. Boggs, Chief of Staff for Kirby-Smith, was begging Major General Magruder at Houston, "General Smith desires you send him all the arms you can spare. He has 4,000 men."

Coloring their report to catch the ear of their captors, two deserters from the Rebel Indians, James Green Landon and Carter Warren Landon, told the Federals at Neosho in the summer:

"All supplies [for Watie] were drawn from Texas, from Bonham, about 140 miles, by ox and mule trains. Rations were short; about half in everything but beef, of which there were full rations. No supplies of importance are with the army . . . Stock is in poor condition. There has been no rain in Texas, except in the border counties, since winter, and there will be no corn or grain raised in Texas of any account south of the border counties. Corn and grain is very scarce throughout the State. His command [Watie's] is without discipline or order [a statement without foundation] and all the troops are clothed [false]. All are armed and seem to have plenty of ammunition [if that was true, and it wasn't, the main source would have been the Yankees]."

In the fall, Brigadier General Thayer, from Headquarters of the District of the Frontier at Fort Smith, made his own report on the Confederates in the Indian Territory, saying:

". . . The rebel troops in the Indian Territory are nearly all mounted. They appear to be in a very good state of discipline and are well armed [not by Union standards] with infantry muskets. They depend on subsistence upon fresh beef found in the country, with corn meal and flour. Their clothing is very poor and insufficient in quantity."

How completely true was that observation on the clothing! Only a few weeks before Thayer's report, General Maxey had written from Fort Towson to Kirby-Smith:

". . . Let me urge you, General, to stir up the clothing men on that question for this district . . . The command has been actively employed in the field ever since it started to Arkansas, 5th of April last, and is literally ragged and barefoot . . . I am uneasy about this thing . . . I think my arrangements for shoes will probably do . . . shirts, drawers, socks and pants are necessary for decency . . . Blankets are very scarce in this district. I hope provision will be made."

A unique supply situation existed with the Choctaws who found themselves without axes with which to get food for fire and building. Seminoles and Creeks with no arms and poor horses did their part in the Confederate effort by driving out beef for use of the Army. The whole supply movement in the Indian Nations was handicapped by lack of adequate wagons and the Confederate supply officers continually asked that captured Yankee wagons be sent to the Indian Territory.

The ambitious plans of Maxey were stalled as General Kirby-Smith ordered him to rush many of his men to the defense of Louisiana, threatened with a serious invasion. After the Yankee Red River move bogged down, most of Maxey's troops returned to their home territory.

In Louisiana Confederate Indian Territory troops had their first association with Major General Richard Taylor, veteran of Stonewall Jackson's Valley campaign, son of President Zachary Taylor and brother-in-law of Jefferson Davis.

An amusing observation on both General Taylor and E. Kirby-Smith was made by Lieutenant Colonel A. W. Hyatt in this excerpt from his diary which appeared in *Military Record of Louisiana*:

". . .We marched 300 miles last month, and none of us can see what this eternal movement is for. This is what is called strategy by some. We have evidently, a military genius in this Department. Old Kirby has a little too much on his hands, taking care of three states (even with the assistance of his immense staff) and at the same time watching over a bran new wife and going to pic-nics and blackberry and crawfish parties. General Taylor is a very quiet, unassuming little fellow, but noisy on retreats, with a tendency to cuss mules and wagons which stall in the road."

Taylor's army defeated General Nathaniel Banks' Red River expedition. Termed by Douglas Southall Freeman, "the Confederate General who possessed literary art that approached first rank," Taylor wrote on his smashing victory over army and ironclad:

"Long will the accursed race remember the great river of Texas and Louisiana. The characteristic hue of his turbid waters has a darker tinge from the liberal admixture of Yankee blood . . .

"Like generous hounds with the game in view, you have known neither hunger nor fatigue, and the hoarse cannon and the ringing rifle have replaced in this stern chase the sonorous horn and joyous hallo. Whether charging on foot, shoulder to shoulder with our noble infantry, or hurling your squadrons on the masses of the foe, or hanging on his flying columns with more than the tenacity of the Cossack, you have been admirable in all. Conquer your own vices and you can conquer the world . . .

"Soldiers! these are great and noble deeds, and they will live in chronicle and song as long as the Southern race exists to honor the earth . . ."

In April, Colonel Watie's men were back in the Cherokee Nation and a large unit under Colonel W. P. Adair, Watie's chief of scouts, moved up near Park Hill and Maysville, many of the men going to their old homes. At Huff's Mills, May 8, ten miles west of Maysville, Adair's riders were defeated and once again the Confederates turned southward.

In the meantime, Gano's Texas Brigade and Colonel Tandy Walker's Choctaw and Chickasaw Brigade were transferred to Arkansas under the command of General Maxey. With elements of Watie's command and Marmaduke's cavalry, they caught up with General Fred Steele's retreating column at Poison Spring, retiring from the ill-fated Union Red River expedition, washed out by flood waters in central Louisiana. On an April day the Confederates trounced the Yankee column with the Choctaws capturing both wagons and artillery. Steele's men continued their fall-back minus their wagon train and many of the 1,200 Negro soldiers who had guarded it.

General Maxey's concern for Watie and the Confederate Indians was evidenced in a letter of May 11, 1864, to Brigadier General W. R. Boggs at Camden, Arkansas:

". . . In my opinion, no effort should be spared to hold this country. Its loss would work a more permanent injury than the loss of any State in the Confederacy.

"States can be recovered — the Indian Territory, once gone, never. Whites, when exiled by a cruel foe, find friends amongst their race. Indians have nowhere to go. Let the enemy once occupy the country to Red River and the Indians give way to despair. I doubt whether many of the highest officials in our Government have ever closely studied this subject. It is a great barrier to the empire State of the South from her foe, now and in peace. Let Federalism reach the Red River, the effects will not stop there. The doctrine of *uti possidetis* may yet play an important part.

"I believe, from what I heard, that Mr. Davis has a fair knowledge of the subject, and I think from conversations with General Smith that he has, but his whole time, being occupied with his immense department—and empire—I trust he will pardon me when I say that no effort of commissaries, quartermasters, or anybody else should be spared to hold this country, and I regret it has not fallen into abler hands than mine."

That E. Kirby-Smith had a vastness of command that precluded, at times, his personal attention was to be the subject of an editorial in the Washington, Arkansas *Telegraph,* March 8, 1865, which gave this summation of the Trans-Mississippi commander's difficulties:

"He must quietly direct general operations from the centre, being himself almost unseen and unknown to the soldiers and citizens. Briareus-like he must from his position, reach forth a hundred arms in all directions, and strike with each. Hercules-like, he must fight a many-headed Hydra, one of those heads being lopped, two grow in its place . . . He must see at once the Rio Grande and the Missouri—the Indian Nation, and Bailze—the Mississippi and the Coast, and (sometimes weakening himself at one point) act in all, as may best subserve, the interest of the whole . . ."

For all his multitudinous responsibilities, Kirby-Smith did not neglect the spiritual life of his men. From his headquarters at Shreveport, Louisiana, on March 18, the General issued General Order No. 8:

"The Congress of the Confederate States having appointed April 8 as a day of fasting, humiliation, and prayer, military exercises will be suspended and a strict observance of the day is enjoined upon all troops serving in this department. On the eve of a campaign in which our resources will be taxed to the utmost, and upon which the destiny of our people will depend, we should humble ourselves before the Lord of Hosts, who giveth not the battle to the strong, but upholdeth the cause of the just. The lieutenant-general, commanding, therefore feels it his duty to invite the people of this department to join with the troops in invoking the blessings of peace and security upon our beloved country."

The Union refugees in Kansas were equally as homesick as the Confederate Indians who had occupied part of their homeland in April before being driven out in May. On May 16, 1864, the Indian refugee train moved out of the Sauk and Fox Reservation and headed for the Indian Territory. Graphically wrote Jay Monaghan:

"Three thousand men, women and children walked ahead and behind the wagons in a procession six miles long. Two thousand old people, mothers and babies rode in the wagons with bedding, coops of chickens and ducks, and at least five hundred puppies. Around the wagons and running along with the footmen trotted some three thousand grown dogs . . . Behind the procession came a private ox-drawn train of three hundred or more wagons with supplies for McDonald and Fuller, sutlers at Fort Gibson. From their perches on duffel in the wagons the travelers watched the sky line for guerrillas . . . The prospect of danger upset the travelers' nerves. Stand Watie and Quantrill were said to be waiting for them just below the horizon."

Thirty-one days later the Indian column straggled into Fort Gibson, its only molestation having been from a band of marauding Osage Indians who stole thirty oxen one night. Somehow the demons under Stand Watie had let them alone.

What they didn't know was that there was no longer a Colonel Stand Watie. On May 10, Jefferson Davis — to the ecstatic pride of Elias C. Boudinot — had signed a commission for a new Brigadier General. If ever a fighting man had earned his promotion astride a panting cavalry mount as he shouted defiantly to his men, "Charge back, boys! Charge back!" the gallant Cherokee warrior was that officer.

When news of Watie's rise to a General's rank reached the Indian Territory, his immediate command, the First and Second Cherokee — all his troops were soon to be known as Stand Watie's Indian Brigade — with whoop and yell and with screaming fife and beating drum — marched around Watie's tent in wild exaltation.

To hell with the devilish Pin Indians who would follow gasconading old John Ross, lolling in an easy chair up some side street in Philadelphia, or hovering about Lincoln as Union Cherokee agent in Washington!

How could the Rebel Cherokees lose when they fought on

Steammer "WILLAMS"

the side of Southern Right under a gallant soldier and gentleman whose whole military activity was motivated by love of his Cherokee Nation!

And another matter of which the refugee Indians had no inkling was that Watie planned to cripple them through a diverse route rather than direct attack. On June 15, a rise in the Arkansas River allowing a light-draught steamer to make the trip from Fort Smith to Fort Gibson, the steam ferryboat "J. R. Williams," loaded down with supplies, steamed fifty miles up the river.

At Pleasant Bluff, Cherokee scouts stealthily rode unseen by the approaching vessel. A nineteen-year-old Creek Lieutenant, George Washington Grayson, carefully inspected his three artillery pieces, masked one hundred yards apart by clusters of bushes.

When the "Williams" steamed opposite the center gun, the youthful officer — at eighteen he had returned to Indian Territory from school and enlisted as a private — shouted the command to fire and cannon balls crashed into the boat. Concealed Confederate soldiers opened up with a heavy volley of musketry.

In a few minutes the "Williams' " smokestack and pilot house were shot away and a cannon ball plunked into the boiler. From the shore, intent Colonel Watie (his General's commission hadn't reached him), watched the steam envelope the stricken boat. His well-planned ambush was a success! Run ashore on a sand bar a few yards from the north side of the river, the "Williams" — most of her men escaping — fell into Southern Indian hands as the clamoring Cherokees and Creeks waded out to take their plunder.

Barrels after barrels — some one hundred and fifty — of hominy, salt pork and flour were unloaded. Sixteen thousand pounds of bacon were taken off the "Williams." And Confederates could dress in captured new Yankee uniforms!

But Watie had no wagons and his men could carry away only what they could place on their horses. Watie fired the "Williams" and it floated off down the river, a delightful, fiery spectacle for the Confederates. How Watie would have enjoyed being in Fort Gibson when his capable and persistent adversary, Colonel Phillips, received the news of Watie's triumph!

After Watie's capture of the "Williams," Maxey, en route for Limestone Prairie, took time to write General Boggs:

"I have the honor herewith to enclose instructions from the chief quartermaster's office at Fort [Smith] to Lieutenant Huston, Fourteenth Kansas Cavalry, in regard to the freight of the Williams dated 14th instant; also the same to Col. W. A. Phillips, U. S. Army, commanding at Fort Gibson . . . the above papers, with some few prisoners, including Lieutenant Huston, were also captured by Colonel Watie. I am glad that the Colonel has so early given evidence of the correctness of my recommendation of him for promotion."

One of the men participating in the "Williams" capture told this story in Mabel Washbourne Anderson's little volume on General Watie:

"That night after we had all gone into camp, General Watie, who was small of stature, had wrapped himself in a long Union military coat, for the night was chilly. He was sitting near the edge of his tent in his customary attitude of deep meditation. The interior was in semi-darkness, and one of the soldiers passing by and peeking in saw the outline of the coat, but not the occupant. He hastily gripped the corner of the garment, thinking to make use of the same, when General Watie astonished him by saying, 'Hold on. There is a MAN in this coat!' "

Yes, Colonel Phillips and General Blunt well knew that there was a MAN in Watie's uniform whether it be his ragged Confederate gray or a bright new blue captured Union military coat!

The Federal river supply line was successfully broken and the Union Indians, hungry at Fort Gibson, learned that Colonel Stand Watie hadn't forgotten to give them a taste — not of their supplies — but of the bitter pill of his scheming and power. The gaunt Indians grew even sicker as they heard the news that the captured supplies — the portion that Watie couldn't remove — were floating down the Arkansas past Fort Smith. Stand Watie was making certain that if the Pins and the rest of the refugee Indians wanted to stay under the Union flag, they could stay — hungry!

With the Yankee river supply route disrupted, Watie and Cooper, having moved their outposts practically up to Fort Smith, went to work on destroying road-hauled supplies. All the military Cherokee units were summoned to Watie's camp at Limestone Prairie, June 27, 1864, and from this came a ringing resolution:

"Whereas the final issue of the present struggle between the North and the South involves the destiny of the Indian Territory alike with that of the Confederate States; therefore,

"*Resolved,* that we, the Cherokee Troops, C.S.A., do unanimously re-enlist as soldiers for the war, be it long or short."

General Maxey reacted enthusiastically, of course, to the re-enlistment and said:

"The earnest attention of the people of the Indian Territory is called to the action of the Cherokee troops in re-enlisting for the war.

"By the fortunes of war, the Cherokees are for the time being exiles. Their beautiful land is in the hands of a cruel and relentless foe. By a strange infatuation, and misguided by the treachery of their leaders, a portion of the people of this nation went over to the enemy. 'Watie and his men' have been from the very beginning as true as the needle to the North Star. Wherever opportunity offered, they have not failed to strike.

"In the midst of the unparalleled inclemency of the past winter they were battling with the foe.

"The enemy have felt ofttimes the blows of the Cherokees. They have made their names a household word. Now they come forward unanimously at the call of their country, and add fresh lustre to their renown by re-enlisting for the war. Men of the allied nations do likewise. By united and prompt action the whole Indian Territory will be redeemed and peace again smile within our borders."

On July 11, General Watie addressed the National Committee and Council of the Cherokee Nation as follows:

"Under favor of Divine Providence, to whom is due our humble and grateful submission, you, the representatives of the Cherokee people, are enabled to meet in general council, to promote, as far as may lay in your power, their best interests. In undertaking the work before us it is proper that we implore that wisdom and guidance without which human efforts are powerless and human calculations vain.

"Since the organization of the present government our people have been subjected to changes of condition consequent upon the war in which the nation has been engaged. Soon after the general mass convention, held by that intelligent portion of the Cherokee people who could not be infected with the deliberate treachery of their principal rulers, Confederate forces of this district made an advance northward, the enemy was expelled from our borders, and our prospect was fair for a continued possession of our country. The campaign upon the whole, however, proved disastrous to the common cause. All that portion of our country lying north of Arkansas River was wrested from us by overwhelming numbers, and our women and children forced to flee from the merciless traitors who had sworn with ourselves to protect them from the common enemy. The next spring saw the enemy strongly intrenched at Fort Gibson, and at the close of the following summer Fort Smith, the key of Western Arkansas and the Indian Territory, passed out of Southern possession. No efforts that could then be made by brave and zealous soldiers under truly able commanders could prevent or did prevent the whole navigable portion of Arkansas River with its contingent territory from falling into Federal hands. It was, we can suppose, the policy of our able commander-in-chief at Shreveport not to exhaust or expose the resources of the country by premature attempts to regain what had been lost, at all events the inhabitants of most of Arkansas on the Federal line of march were compelled to seek the rear of our retreating armies, and our own people, en masse with Creeks and the population of the Northern Choctaw counties, were driven to take temporary refuge on Red River and in Texas, where they at present abide.

"The destitute condition of the people had been represented to the authorities of the Confederate Government, and I am gratified to be able to state that measures had been taken to supply them with provisions, independent of the ordinance of convention to supply the destitute, passed May 30, 1863. The principal commissioner, Capt. J. L. Martin, who was appointed under that ordinance, was also appointed issuing agent under an order from General Steele, making provision for supplying the destitute with rations at the expense of the General Government. I have received no official report from the commissioner, and am only able to say in this connection that rations have been furnished him for distribution among needy Cherokee families, which have at short intervals of time been received and issued under his direction.

"During the last winter the Cherokee delegate to the Confederate Congress, Mr. E. C. Boudinot, succeeded in obtaining an appropriation or loan of $100,000 from the Confederate Government to supply the most pressing necessities of indigent Cherokees. Forty-five thousand dollars of this amount has been received by the commissioner on part of the nation who is now engaged in making purchases of such articles as their immediate wants require. It is expected that they will soon be at hand and ready for distribution. It lies within your province to take such action in this matter as your wisdom may judge best, for the uniform and best allotment of these articles among the actually and literally destitute, to which state many of the people have been reduced.

"The act of the general convention, entitled an ordinance to increase the military force in the Indian Territory, placed, with certain exceptions, all Cherokee male citizens between the ages of eighteen and forty in the service of the Confederate States for the term of two and three years. It is not necessary to inform you that it is of the most urgent consequence for effecting the re-establishment of our national rights that the war should be prosecuted with the greatest vigor, and that the whole of the population capable of bearing arms should take part in the common struggle. I therefore recommend, for the purpose of increasing our effective military force to the utmost, that an act be passed putting all Cherokee male citizens between the ages of eighteen and forty-five fit for duty, and not already enlisted for the war, in the Confederate service for that period, with such further provisions for fully carrying into effect such a law as in your judgment may seem best.

"The ordinance of the general mass convention establishing this government, held at Tahlequah, August 21, 1862, reaffirmed and adopted the constitution and laws previously in operation, and it lies within your province to make any amendments or additions to the same in the proper mode as you may deem expedient. I am, however, aware that the interruptions to which your present session is exposed, and the consequent necessity of dispatch, to which I respectfully urge upon your notice, will not allow you perhaps to exercise the requisite deliberation, except upon the most material subjects of legislative action affecting the immediate welfare of your constituents.

"A general council, to which all the Indian tribes are invited, has been called to meet on the 20th this month at Choteau's Trading House. Three delegates have been appointed to represent the Cherokee people, viz, Messrs. Tusy Guess, John Chambers and William Arnold. Copies of official letters will be furnished you for your information in regard to the object of this general council of all the tribes.

"Since the campaign opened last spring our prospects have been brightening. Confederate arms, so far as we have heard, have everywhere been victorious. In this department a vast and combined movement of the hostile armies toward Texas was signally checked and defeated early in the spring, a circumstance which should not be forgotten as explaining the seeming inertness for a time of our commander-in-chief, and as illustrating his consummate prudence and skill as well as the courage and discipline of the army. This success may well justify a hope that with the blessing of Providence upon the valor of our troops, our people may ere long return to their country and homes in peace.

"East of the Mississippi the war, at last accounts, was raging with the convulsive fury of a final struggle. The numerical strength of the enemy in the field is enormous, their means ample, and this power, raised for our destruction, is not contemptibly wielded. Against this threatening prospect are opposed an army which has not in all the terrible conflicts of this war failed to show a bold and progressive front; a general who has not his equal on earth, surrounded and aided by subordinate commanders scarcely inferior in capacity; and, above all, a cause which we know to be sacred. Whatever intelligence, therefore, we may receive of military operations in that quarter, we may securely expect a final triumph; and to this glorious result it is our privilege to conduce by a faithful and determined discharge of duty here in council and in the field."

Let General Blunt and Colonel Phillips — and President Lincoln — smoke that in their proffered peace pipes — and choke!

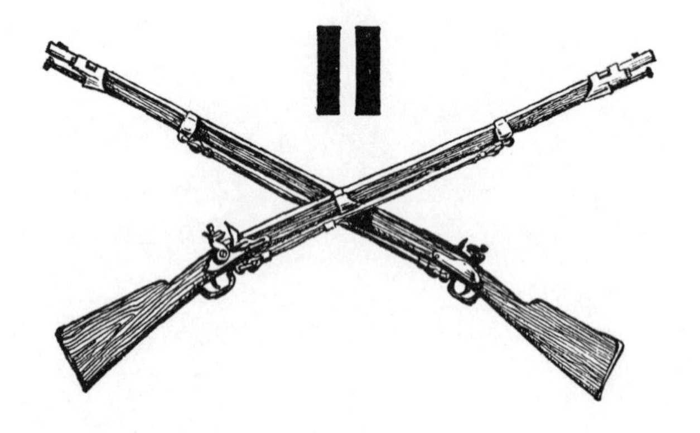
II

WATIE'S MEN — WHIRLING dust on the skyline — rode, continually raiding the Fort Scott-Fort Gibson road, killing Negro soldiers, burning mowing machines and Union hay stacks. General Watie's fame as the greatest of the Secesh Indian leaders became even more secure as his raiders scored with torch and bullet.

But Watie's most spectacular raid of all was still phantomlike on the coming fall winds — a strike against the Yankees which was to win Watie the official praise of the Confederate Congress; and Jefferson Davis was to speak with warmth to Elias Boudinot at Richmond concerning his uncle, the Cherokee cavalier.

Antedating this raid, though, was the Confederate victory at Massard Prairie, Arkansas. Early in July, General Cooper nimbly reconnoitered to within ten miles of Fort Smith and even audaciously attacked General Thayer's outposts near the fort. Under orders from Cooper, Gano and Watie expeditiously moved against Major David Mefford's Sixth Kansas Cavalry units, stationed about five miles outside Fort Smith. On the morning of the 27th, the spirited Indians and Texans charged in so rapidly that Mefford's horses were stampeded and his cavalry had to fight dismounted. After a fighting retreat of a mile, Mefford was unable to break the Confederate line which had cut across his rear and he and his men surrendered. Watie whirled his command back toward safety as already Thayer's reinforcements were on their way from Fort Smith. The captured Yankees—with no horses—marched double time for ten miles. The Confederates back across the Poteau River, deemed it safe to stop for the night.

General Cooper followed up the victory at Massard Prairie four days after, sending forward his whole army, Gano commanding his right wing and Watie his left, to within two miles of Fort Smith. But after an exchange of artillery fire and slight skirmishing, Cooper withdrew his army back into the Choctaw Nation.

In a summation of his operations around Fort Smith, General Cooper had this to say of Stand Watie:

"General Watie executed the order given him with his customary gallantry and promptness, sending Colonel Bell, with First Cherokee Regiment on the main and Colonel Adair on the road to the left known as the Line Road, both detachments charging with the impetuosity for which they and their men are noted. He not only routed the Federal pickets, but ran them up to the line of their entrenchments near Fort Smith, and returning, the men sat down to the plentiful dinner just prepared for the Federals at their camp.

". . .Having arrived at the camp lately occupied by the enemy, I found Brigadier-General Watie with his command in a position on the hill south of spring. General Gano soon arrived and Captain Humphreys, with his light battery, was advanced and opened fire on the enemy, then some 600 to 800 yards to the front.

"The enemy soon brought up a four-gun battery (Rabb's, I suppose) and commenced a furious cannonade upon our light howitzers . . . Captain Humphreys, being so unequally unmatched, was ordered to withdraw, and in the act of doing so a shell exploded directly amid the battery horses, killing 3, wounding one, cutting the leg off one of the men. Another shot swept off the head from the shoulders of one of Gano's men . . ."

Lack of the Confederacy to get adequate supplies, clothing, finances and ammunition to the Indian allies was beginning to create unrest among the ranks of the Indian troops, though in no way did it lessen their determination to support the Confederacy. The Indian soldiers did not realize that similar conditions were existing throughout much of Confederate-held territory. On August 8, General Watie wrote to General Kirby-Smith, complaining about what he considered subordination of the Indian interests and — a month later — Kirby-Smith replied:

"I know your people have a cause for complaint. Their sufferings and the apparent ill-faith of our Government naturally produces some dissatisfaction. That your patriotic band of followers deserves the thanks of our Government I know . . . Tell them to remain true . . . we must stand and struggle on together till that justice and good Providence, who always supports the Right, crowns our efforts with success . . . and I can only assure you that I feel the importance of your country to our cause."

Not long after he wrote Kirby-Smith, Watie's men rode on a routine raid, as reported in a letter written by Lieutenant Lynch of Adair's Company, Second Cherokee Regiment, "Gnl. Watie in command of about 300 of his braves crossed Arkansas river a few days ago and they attacked a small encampment of negro infantry as they thought, but they were more of them than he expected and consequently flaxed our General. Watie took twelve prisoners (white), killed several negroes and got only 3 wounded."

At the Federal hay camps at Flat Rock near Fort Gibson four companies of colored infantry — scattered over three miles of prairie — were cutting and putting up hay. Captain E. A. Baker with detachments of two Second Kansas Cavalry companies was in command. Scouts from these detachments rode in fast the afternoon of September 16, bellowing the alarm that a large Confederate force was sighted on the old military road — this road surveyed around 1824 ran from Fort Scott to Fort Gibson — advancing on the camp.

Indeed even then General Watie and General Richard M. Gano, the new commander of the district, stood on a high hill and with their field glasses, watched the big hay camp in operation. What a plum — especially the Corps d'Afrique as the Rebels called Negro troops — this was for the taking; something to whet their appetites for the main course these two Generals were planning to enjoy at the Yankee table!

With six pieces of artillery, the Confederates advanced on the camp — Lieutenant Colonel Welch and two Texas regiments on the right, General Watie and his Indians on the left, and General Gano commanding in the center.

Captain Baker, having fought vainly for half an hour, ordered all his men who had horses to break through the Confederate line at its weakest point; fifteen riders got through, but forty didn't!

The colored regiment, unmounted, was left to fight its way out on foot. Under Lieutenant Thomas B. Sutherland, First Kansas Colored Infantry, the Negro troops, fighting from behind natural obstacles, slowed down the Confederates for two hours. After that, the Rebels turned the engagement into a massacre. The veteran Confederate Indians, coming into close quarter fighting, shot down the blacks like rabbits. Some of the Negro soldiers ran out from tall weed patches and unburned hay stacks crying, "O! Good master, save and spare me!" But the Texans and Indians held no feeling of sympathy for Negroes in Union ranks and felt their cries for mercy sheer hypocrisy as only a few moments before the same Negroes had been trying to kill their "good masters."

After disposing of the Negro troops — about one in five was able to escape — the Confederates fired 3,000 tons of hay. Again Fort Gibson would smart under the sting of Stand Watie's whip.

The Confederate troops — with hardly a scratch from the warmup encounter — marched to Wolf Creek, approximately the location of Salina. With Watie in charge of the camp, General Gano and four hundred Texans moved north on the 18th, hid in the timber, and Gano sent word back to Watie to hurry forward and get in on the kill. For Gano had found the rich pickings for which he and Watie quested; a *million dollar* wagon train!

The search came about when General Watie, learning that this train was rolling down the Fort Scott road headed for Fort Gibson, asked General Gano to join him on an ambitious and bold venture to bypass Fort Gibson and destroy or capture this mobile Yankee treasure. General Gano readily agreed that here was the prize of all prizes. The Confederate column set out with Texans, Choctaws, Chickasaws, John Jumper's Creeks and Seminoles and, of course, the Cherokees.

Spies abounded throughout the Indian Territory and the Federals were not long in learning that venturesome Watie was really on the warpath for high stakes. Word was rushed to the train — "run for safety to any place with a stockade!"

Major Henry Hopkins, Second Kansas Cavalry, commanding the train, pulled it to a halt on the bluffs overlooking the military crossing at Cabin Creek. Quickly his soldiers and the wagon men piled hay bales into breastworks to reinforce the stockade. Major Hopkins worked with the assurance that Yankee men and guns were moving out from both Fort Gibson and Fort Smith to whip Watie and Gano for their arrogance in attempting to capture a million dollar train.

Without the expected reinforcements, Hopkins had about a thousand white and Indian troops to protect some four hundred wagons and about 1,800 mules and horses. Certainly, even if the support was tardy in arriving, Hopkins could hold off the attack. Hopkins was to get a quick testing. His scouts found Gano in a ravine three miles south of Cabin Creek.

The Confederate attack, like ghosts on the wind, flared out of the night at two o'clock in the morning. The advancing Confederates — Watie having arrived at midnight — could hear the noise of men drinking and shouting inside the stockade.

At three hundred yards, the Union defenders opened fire and the Confederates stopped as there was no need to lose precious men in the night firing. Captain Grayson — promoted since his participation in the "Williams" episode — walked boldly up and down his Creek line. He had no need for the "magic medicine" which some of the Indians had used earlier in the night for protection from Yankee bullets.

General Gano shifted his artillery so that it could cross fire the stockade and the Confederate shells crashed through wagon and timber, creating havoc within the stockade.

From the Confederate lines, individual Indians, anxious for plunder and a chance to plunge a knife into the hated Yankee Indians, would dash out toward the stockade, screaming their traditional turkey gobble challenge at the Pins inside.

In the inferno of disintegrating wagons, Confederate shells and screaming Indians, Major Hopkins realized that he could wait no longer for succor from Fort Smith or Fort Gibson. He must abandon his position and save what he could of the train by retreating to Fort Scott. This thought must have come to Hopkins and Watie at the same time. As Hopkins prepared to carry out this maneuver, two of Stand Watie's regiments took possession of the Fort Scott road, cutting off retreat.

With daylight, the condition of the Yankee encampment grew steadily worse as artillerymen for the six Confederate guns could more accurately direct their fire. Mules panicked, dashed through the camp, some falling over the one hundred-fifty-foot bluff. Federal soldiers threw themselves prone on the ground to escape the fire.

Yet Major Hopkins held out. Somewhere out of the haze might come those six companies of Indians and two howitzers from Fort Gibson. Watie and Gano, deciding to wait no longer, drove in the Union right – which originally faced south – until it faced almost west. Then Gano's Texans raced to flank the new position.

Billows of smoke reached into the murky clouds and, with this as a cloak, Hopkins, abandoning hope, shouted for his men to leave the wagons and fight their way onto the Fort Gibson road. This they did as the Confederates were more eager to capture the train than to stop escaping Yankees.

The ragged Confederates – the uniforms captured at the "Williams" were not plentiful – snatched new clothing out of the canvas topped wagons, sought new shoes for their scarred, bare feet, and poured Yankee brandy down their throats. And a few Indians, getting out of control in their detestation for their Yankee Indian opponents, killed and mutilated wounded men before the Confederate officers could stop them.

The looting and excitement subsiding, Watie and Gano felt it expedient to leave as soon as possible as they did not want to be attacked themselves by the tardy reinforcements. Half the wagon train stood fully loaded, but the mules — those which hadn't been killed or wounded — were hard to handle. Some would not take commands from new masters. Despite all the difficulties about one hundred and thirty wagons moved out of the camp toward Confederate Indian Territory. Gleefully, the raiders either put the torch to the remaining wagons or, pushing them over the bluffs, watched them shatter below. To put a spectacular end to the raid, 3,000 tons of hay went under the torch.

Nothing usable remained of the million dollar train except what was in Confederate hands. Watie and Gano with their Indians and Texans had given the damn yankees their worst disaster of the entire Indian Territory war. The Civilized Nations had scored their most impressive military triumph, one which resounded from Richmond to Texas and the Confederate Indian refugees down along the Red River and in Texas took new heart for the hopes of the Indian South.

As to the reinforcements for Hopkins, the six regiments and two guns from Fort Gibson headed for Cabin Creek passed the broken command of Hopkins coming in, but on another road, so that the two commands did not encounter each other.

The Confederates with clothing for 2,000 men and hundreds of thousands of dollars worth of supplies marched south and recrossed the Arkansas River about fifteen miles above Fort Gibson.

That night the victorious Confederates encountered Colonel J. M. Williams and his Negro troops with two Parrott guns on their way from Fort Smith to relieve the wagon train. Colonel Williams decided he'd recapture what the Confederates had won.

He didn't!

Watie's first effort to rush a report on the wagon train victory to Cooper failed when his messenger, sent from Bird Creek, September 21, failed to get through. But Cooper did receive word of the Confederate triumph elsewhere and on September 24 he wrote Captain T. M. Scott, Assistant Adjutant General, from his headquarters in the field:

"I have the honor to report that the expedition from this command under Generals Watie and Gano, north of Arkansas River is on its return, having destroyed several Federal camps and a large quantity of hay between Gibson and Cabin Creek on the Texas and Missouri road, and captured a train of between 100 and 200 wagons, with many prisoners. The above is from an old Uchee warrior, whom I know to be reliable who arrived yesterday at headquarters of First Creek Regiment, bringing arms, etc., he captured himself from a Federal officer. Generals Watie and Gano are returning slowly, the command being worn and tired. . ."

Later a message from Watie did come in and also one from Gano dated September 23 which said, "Our men behaved gallantly. The enemy had strong position at Cabin Creek and held it six hours. God has blessed us."

A later report from General Gano told of the efforts of the Yankees to retake the train:

"As we moved back with our train we met a reinforcement from Forts Smith and Gibson going up to protect the train, consisting of infantry, artillery and cavalry. We drove them back three miles and a half, held them in check all night, and created the impression that we had parked the train for the night by running an empty wagon train over a rocky place for two hours, while our train was being moved with all possible dispatch toward the Arkansas River. The day found us separating rapidly, we following our train while they were retreating to Fort Gibson. We expected to fight at Arkansas River, and hurried forward with all dispatch day and night. For three days and nights our boys were without sleep, except such as they could snatch in the saddle or at watering places. They dug down banks, cut out trees, rolled wagons and artillery up hills and banks by hand, kept cheerful and never wearied in the good cause, and came into camp rejoicing on the 28th instant.

"We were out fourteen days, marched over 400 miles, killed 97, wounded many, captured 111 prisoners, burned 6,000 tons of hay and all reapers and mowers — destroyed all together from the Federals $1,500,000 worth of property, bringing safely within our lines nearly one-third of this amount (estimated in greenbacks.) Our total loss was 6 killed, 48 wounded — 3 mortally . . . General Watie was by my side at Cabin Creek, cool and brave as ever. . ."

General Maxey at Fort Towson, in General Orders No. 61 referred to the victories on the expedition "by the troops under the leadership of the gallant and chivalrous Gano and the noble old hero Stand Watie" and also that "Throughout the expedition I am rejoiced to say perfect harmony and good will prevailed between the white and Indian troops, all striving for the common good of our beloved country." He called his men, "soldiers of the holy cause."

In a communication with General Boggs, Chief of Staff, at Shreveport, Maxey commented on the cooperation between Stand Watie and General Gano, who had been a star officer with the famous raider, General John Morgan:

"I also would call your attention to the noble course of General Watie. General Gano had been recognized a brigadier-general and acted as such before the date of General Watie's commission. General W., however, governed by patriotism, a feeling of delicacy, and, as he considered, justice, raised no issue, but acted in perfect harmony and concert for the common good."

General E. Kirby-Smith termed the capture of the wagon train "one of the most brilliant raids of the war," adding, "The celebrity of the movement, the dash of the attack and their entire success entitle the commands engaged to the thanks of the country."

Along with other reports of that time, which came through to Confederate headquarters at Fort Towson, was one proving the necessity of General Watie keeping an over-supply of liquor from his men. Captain J. N. Hildebrand, writing from Fishertown, to General Cooper, said:

". . . I have further learned that John or Johnson Thompson of General Watie's command, got drunk and went to sleep, and when he awoke, seeing a body of men and supposing they were Watie's men, went to them and finding they were Federals surrendered, was carried to Gibson and kept there until he was sober and then marched out and publicly shot."

The reaction of the Federal commanders to the Confederate triumph over the million dollar wagon train at Cabin Creek is reflected in these official communications. On September 20, Major General S. R. Curtis, at Fort Leavenworth, writing Major General Rosecrans, commanding the Department of Missouri, said, "The further advance of rebels toward our department is attested by the capture of train by 1,500 of Stand Watie's men . . ." On the same day Major General George Sykes, at Fort Scott, writing Major C. S. Charlot, stated "Colonel Blair reports that the train . . . was captured by the enemy at Cabin Creek, said to be 3,000 strong . . ."

Ever increasing was the size of the Indian Rebel attackers. Colonel C. W. Blair at Fort Scott communicating with Major Charlot, said, "Lieutenant Colonel Wheeler, who was with the train when captured at Cabin Creek yesterday morning, has arrived in one of my outposts . . . the rebel force was Stand Watie's and Colonel Wheeler thinks it 4,000 strong. . ."

In some quarters, the Confederate Indian victory created consternation and semi-panic. Colonel T. Moonlight, Eleventh Kansas Cavalry, at Paola, sent this urgent message to Major General Sykes:

"I have just received the following from Colonel Jennison from Mound City; 'Report of the capture of train troop. Two large bodies of troops, are moving north – one for Fort Scott, the other on Springfield. The force marching on Fort Scott numbers 3,000, and are reported to be from 75 to 100 miles below Fort Scott. It is reported that Fort Gibson has surrendered.'

"I believe there is some truth in the above, and would suggest the calling out of the militia of the three border tiers of counties immediately to replace the troops now on the border, who will be required to meet the enemy."

At Mound City, Colonel C. R. Jennison, Commanding First Sub-District, informed Captain George S. Hampton, Assistant Adjutant General, that with the victory over the train complete, Rebel forces were moving against Fort Scott and Springfield and "I will concentrate my forces at Fort Scott. I think I can hold that place. I will take the field in the morning in person . . . send as many troops to the southern portion of your district as can be spared. I will call out the citizens of this locality in the defense of their homes . . ."

Having taken the field, Jennison, two days later, from Fort Scott, wrote Hampton:

"From the loss of the supply train recently dispatched for the subsistence of the forces at Forts Smith and Gibson, the utmost difficulty is to be apprehended in procuring supplies, if indeed it can be accomplished. The presumption is that at this time the forces at the above points are reduced to scant rations, as they are reported to have had only sufficient to subsist them until the train should arrive. In this view of the case the evacuation of the post at Gibson and Smith becomes a matter of most reasonable supposition, and that the forces will fall back in this direction can hardly be imagined with large bodies of the enemy intervening. The probability is, therefore, that the troops mentioned will be sent to Little Rock or some other point in General Steele's command, thus leaving our whole southern and southeastern frontier entirely exposed . . . I have ordered the entire force of employees in the quartermaster and commissary departments at the post enrolled, armed and placed in charge of suitable and skilled officers. The citizen companies are being drilled, and every preparation is being made to resist . . ."

With his all-out efforts to repel attacks by the Rebels, Colonel Jennison even contemplated sending a column out against the supposedly advancing Watie. Higher headquarters quashed this move with the notation that Jennison had no suitable force for such a task. It must have been a somewhat chagrined Yankee Colonel who, in time, received the news that Stand Watie and his cavalry were safely back in their own territory.

But the exact location of Watie's activities was often a puzzle to his foes and, shortly, G. S. Smith, Adjutant Kansas State Militia, at Leavenworth City, advised Major General S. R. Curtis at the Headquarters Army of the Border at Wyandotte, "It is reported at Leavenworth City that a sergeant of U. S. Troops passed through Ottawa this a. m. with a dispatch for you, saying that Stand Watie, with 6,000 Indians, was within thirty miles of Humboldt and had burned the Osage Mission."

To which Curtis rather humorously replied, "This report about Stand Watie is undoubtedly a roorback. If true, it would have come to me by telegraph and not by a Sergeant."

The official Confederate report on the organization of the Army of the Trans-Mississippi Department, September 30, 1864, shows the makeup of the Indian Cavalry Division commanded by Brigadier General Douglas H. Cooper as broken into two brigades, the First Indian Brigade, commanded by General Watie and the Second Indian Brigade, commanded by Colonel Tandy Walker.

Comprising the First were: 1st Cherokee, Colonel Robert C. Parks; 2nd Cherokee, Colonel William P. Adair; Cherokee Battalion, Major Joseph A. Scales; 1st Creek, Colonel Daniel N. McIntosh; 2nd Creek, Colonel Chilly McIntosh; Creek Squadron, Captain R. Kenard; 1st Osage Battalion, Major Broke Arm; 1st Seminole Battalion, Lieutenant Colonel John Jumper.

Colonel Walker's Brigade was made up of the 1st Chickasaw Battalion, Lieutenant Colonel Lemuel M. Reynolds; 1st Choctaw Battalion, Lieutenant Colonel Jackson McCurtain; 1st Choctaw and Chickasaw Battalion, Lieutenant Colonel James Riley; 2nd Choctaw, Colonel Simpson N. Folsom; and the Reserve Squadron, Captain George Washington.

In addition, there were the unattached white troops, the 20th Texas, under Major John R. Johnson and the 1st Battalion, Texas Sharpshooters, commanded by Major James Burnet.

The Indians' artillery support was the Seventh Mounted Artillery Battalion in charge of Captain W. Butler Krumbhaar, and made up of Dashiell's (Texas) battery, Captain George R. Dashiell; Krumbhaar's (Texas) battery, Lieutenant W. M. Stafford; and Howell's (Texas) battery, Captain Sylvanus Howell.

Traditional Southern chivalry to the womenfolk had its place in the Indian Territory warfare, even as it did in the Confederate States. The honeyed words of a pretty girl could always bring a smile to a Rebel soldier no matter how hard the battle of the previous day.

But masked by the curving lips, the full figure and the protestations of devotion for the Johnny Rebs, was sometimes an entirely different woman than the one the gray-clad men held a friend, a confidante and – often – lover.

Commenting on the espionage agents in the War between the States, Harnett J. Kane, author of *Spies for the Blue and Gray,* wrote:

"The ladies were terrific. In this war they made their American debut in espionage, and never since have the nation's women taken such an active part as spies. No matter how raving a partisan a man might be, his wife or sister was probably still more impassioned . . . They connived endlessly, took great risks, and pushed through to success in ways impossible to simple males. They showed that the female is not only the deadlier of the sexes, but also the livelier.

"In the eighteen-sixties the double standard prevailed in spying as in other matters, and to the ladies' benefit. Neither side did a great deal about it, even when the identities of the women agents were well established. As the war grew slowly more bitter, men operatives were hanged one by one. The women received threats, or perhaps a prison term, and then freedom to try again . . . After all, a lady was a lady. . . .A gentleman could not bring himself to order her shot or swung from a gallows."

Colonel Phillips advised General Blunt, July 17, 1863:

"I have had for some time the utmost difficulty in getting information from the enemy over the river. My spies have been taken or killed . . . I have opened some new leads . . . I have just had a spy of Cooper's in camp. She brought up news of Scott and Sebastian counties and was recommended as a suitable spy for Cooper. He employed her and sent her over, giving her a good deal of information as to his modus operandi in getting news from our camp. She was passed over fifteen miles from here, and came in with my dispatches in her bonnet slits . . . ."

From Neosho, Missouri, September 16, 1864, Major Milton Burch, Eighth Cavalry, Missouri State Militia, wrote General Sanborn, Commanding District of Missouri:

"I have the honor, according to yours of the 4th instant requesting a lady suitable to act in the secret service as spy, to send you Miss Mary Martin, a lady of undoubted loyalty, ingenious and daring. I have information of Stand Watie being down near Spavinaw. I am going to start a lady, together with the boy Winfield Scott, in that direction today. I will use all the vigilance possible and inform you of every move in that direction. P. S. The news of Stand Watie being near is only from a rebel source, and I do not put any confidence in it, but I will soon know the acts and communicate with you."

Union reports on Mary Martin's ensuing activities indicated that she was held in high esteem as an agent. No name of the woman mentioned is given in an illuminating letter — which shows that it was not always brother against brother in the war — Brigadier General John B. Sanborn at Springfield, Missouri, wrote General Rosecrans, September 25, 1864:

". . . The [Union] woman scout has brothers in the rebel army and she always manages to get the confidence of their officers. She has spied a great deal for us from Neosho and always has been reliable and correct. She says she expressed great doubt to Colonel Speer about Price and his force coming to Missouri and to satisfy her that what he said was true he exhibited these letters to show the army was north of Batesville."

Apparently the female Union spy had forwarded to Sanborn the Confederate letters to Colonel Speer.

Sanborn continued, ". . . One of my secret agents has just returned from a trip down South. She reports having seen and taken prisoner by Major Piercy's [a leading Confederate bushwhacker] command . . . I have sent another agent down South, and if she can get through I think she will bring news of more importance . . . We hear nothing of Stand Watie at all; he may be down in the Choctaw Nation. If he is not there, I cannot tell where, but have all confidence in my agent that is gone down South bringing me news of his whereabouts."

One of the times a Union spy did locate Watie was told in a report made at Neosho by Major Burch to General Sanborn:

"I have the honor to inform you that I have the information there are some 800 to 1,200 rebels on Grand River, near Gilstrop's Ferry . . . This report came from a woman, who says she saw 60 of the rebels. She saw Stand Watie and talked with him, so she says. She says Stand Watie has 400 men . . . She also says they intend to attack the train that is now on its way from Fort Scott. She says that – they calculate to take my command in out of the wet, but they will have a hard time doing it. I can whip a thousand if attacked."

This account was made in May and actually tipped the Federals off about the plans of the Confederate Indians against the wagon train, the results of which were unsuccessful.

No less intent on spying were the Confederates and on January 15, 1864, General Maxey from Fort Towson wrote E. Kirby-Smith, "No man can be too cautious in the selection of men for secret service. I have a shrewd, intelligent Indian who spends his time in the cane brake between the Arkansas and Poteau, near Fort Smith and gets information through his women, who have the run of the town."

But the end for the spy, be he Union or Confederate? One such a finish was recounted by Colonel M. La Rue Harrison at Fayetteville to General Sanborn:

"One of Adair's [Watie's Chief of Scouts] spies came in yesterday; was followed by Lieutenant Rowe. He had a good horse, shotgun, 3 revolvers; left them all near town when he came in. He was killed near one of my pickets at 10 last night.

Wiley Britton, who after the war became the most widely known writer on the border conflict, was with Colonel Phillip's forces and in his book *Memoirs of the Rebellion on the Border, 1863,* related the following spy incident:

"A spy was caught today (23d) near camp, dressed in a woman's suit. He is a young fellow with light hair, fair complexion, of a rather prepossessing appearance, and I should think not over sixteen years of age. When I saw him in the Provost-marshal's tent he seemed to be badly frightened, in fact almost out of his wits. Two or three officers were putting questions to him in regard to his visiting our camp in disguise, but his excitement had not sufficiently subsided to enable him to give rational answers. He seemed ready to confess anything asked of him. He showed that he was unaccustomed to be goaded with questions of such a serious nature. From ancient times to the present day, it has been the practice of commanding generals of armies to hang spies immediately after being caught, so as to make it impossible for the enemy to gain any advantage from the information they have obtained. What disposition will be made of this young man, had not been determined. Colonel Phillips, as commanding officer of troops in the field, has authority to order him tried by a drum-head court martial, and, if found guilty, hung within the next twenty-four hours. It is possible that his youthful age may save him from the death penalty at present, and that he will be turned over to the Department commander, for such punishment as he may deem proper. He claims to have been sent here by General Cooper, who is now encamped near Webber's Falls, for the purpose of getting information in regard to our strength and intentions in the near future.

"It was by merest accident that he was detected. When several of our Indian soldiers first saw him near the limits of our camp, they thought he was a white woman, although there are now very few white women in this country. They also noticed his movements were peculiar and not like those of a woman, and when they came towards him, he started to run, but in the chase they soon convinced him that his only safety lay in absolute submission. His garments were probably an impediment in his flight, but as our Indians are generally fleet of foot, they would have soon overtaken him anyway.

"If I were going as a spy into the enemy's camp, to dress in a woman's suit would be about the last method I should think of adopting, even if I had as marked feminine features as some young men, which I have not. And as to the *time* of making such an adventure, I should prefer the night to broad daylight, particularly if there was anyone in the enemy camp likely to know me."

Although Britton's book leaves one uninformed as to whether the fair-faced Rebel spy was executed, hanging of spies was carried out by both sides and Private Sam R. Watkins, C.S.A., Maury Grays, First Tennessee Regiment, in his book *Co. Aytch,* described such an execution:

"I heard that two spies were going to be hung on a certain day and I went to the hanging. The scaffold was erected, two coffins were placed on the platform, the ropes dangling from the cross beam above . . . I wanted to see a Yankee spy hung. I wouldn't mind that. I would like to see him agonize. A spy; O, yes, they had hung one of our regiment at Pulaski – Sam Davis. Yes, I would see the hangings. After a while I saw a guard approach, and saw two little boys in their midst, but didn't see the Yankees that I had been looking for. The two little boys were rushed upon the platform. I saw they were handcuffed. 'Are they spies?' I was appalled; I was horrified; nay, more, I was sick at heart. One was about fourteen and the other about sixteen years old, I would judge. The ropes were promptly adjusted about their necks by the provost-marshal. The youngest one began to beg and cry and plead most piteously. It was horrid. The older one kicked him, and told him to stand up and show the Rebels how a Union man could die for his country. Be a man! The charges and specifications were then read. The props were knocked out and the two boys were dangling in the air. I turned off sick at heart."

So died the two youthful Yankee spies. But Sam Davis, one of the writer's regimental mates, had been hanged by the Yankees at Pulaski, it must be remembered. If they had been successful, doubtless teen-aged Confederate soldiers could have died because of the information they had gleaned.

And if the Rebel spy with the feminine features died at the

end of a taut rope in Indian Territory, doubtless there were Union men who turned away from the swaying body as "sick at heart" as was Sam Watkins.

From the Adjutant and Inspector General's Office, at Richmond, on July 21, 1864, had come Special Orders No. 171 signed by Samuel W. Melton, Assistant Adjutant General, which stated:

". . . XXXV. The Indian Territory west of the Arkansas is hereby constituted a separate district of the Trans-Mississippi Department, to the command of which Brig. Gen. D. H. Cooper, Provisional Army, C. S., is assigned."

This command change met with opposition from Kirby-Smith and he ignored it. Finally on October 1, 1864, from the Shreveport headquarters of the Trans-Mississippi Department, he wrote General S. Cooper, Adjutant and Inspector General at Richond:

"I have the honor respectfully to request that Special Orders, No. 171 . . . be revoked. I believe that serious injury would result to the service were this order enforced. I have delayed its publication. Awaiting further instructions. General Maxey, commanding the district of the Indian country, has with skill, judgment and success administered his duties. I have satisfactory evidence for believing that he gives satisfaction to both the Indians and the white troops. His removal, besides being an injustice to him, would be a misfortune to the department. General Cooper has been assigned to the division of Indian troops serving under General Maxey in the Indian Territory. I would respectfully refer this department to Colonel Scott, the Commissioner of Indian Affairs, for particulars regarding the administration of General Maxey's district."

The "Indorsement" to this letter by General S. Cooper merely stated, "Please inform General Smith, in answer to this letter, that Special Orders, No. 171, from this office, is deemed imperative and must be carried into effect."

It was a mighty long way from Richmond to the headquarters of the Trans-Mississippi and Kirby-Smith reckoned that it might be quite a spell before these orders "deemed imperative" were carried out by him.

And in the district of the Indian country General Maxey remained in command.

12

SUCCESSES OF THE Confederate Indians were to be offset in fighting adjacent to the Civilized Nations when "Old Pap" Price courageously sought to bring all of Missouri under Confederate control.

John H. Taylor, Supreme Commander of the State of Missouri, Order of the American Knights, from his St. Louis headquarters, in October 1864, called on support of Sterling Price, "that brave and true soldier, Missouri's favorite son," with "Remember our motto, 'Resistance to tyrants is obedience to God.' " This pro-Confederate "underground" organization claimed 30,000 members in Missouri.

General Price's hard marching and dogged fighters met their Waterloo October 23, at Westport, even though Marmaduke, Shelby and M. Jeff Thompson – of the ivory guns, canary vests and gay-colored coats — had fought until exhausted. Shelby battled hatless, with gun in hand, and his long hair blowing. So the South lost the biggest conflict fought west of the Missouri; 20,000 Federals and 9,000 Confederates in action.

And in rear guard battles after Westport, the Confederates put up strong resistance. At Mine Creek, the pursuing Federal Cavalry galloped only six hundred yards back of the Confederate rear cavalry. Suddenly, the Confederates, startled, reined to a halt, their progress blocked by one of their wagon trains, stalled by an accident, blocking the only creek ford. Hoofbeats of the approaching Yankees thundered louder and the trapped Rebel Cavalry, not having time to dismount and form a line, wheeled about to meet the charge armed mostly with long infantry rifles which, once discharged, were useless to the cavalrymen.

The Federal Cavalry drew its sabers and came in on the gallop. The Southerners fired, then weaponless as it was impossible to reload the rifles on horseback, turned their horses and, in an attempt to flee, unwittingly rode into their infantry coming up to help them.

In the ensuing confusion, the Yankees cut down Secesh cavalry and infantry with saber and revolver. Southern officers frantically and unsuccessfully tried to rally their men.

Private James Dunlavy levelled his gun at a big, disheveled Confederate in blue jeans, dripping with rain. One arm of the Confederate hung wounded and the private led in his captive, who, even in his battered condition, seemed to have a pride that rose above the indignity to which the fortune of war had brought him.

Private Dunlavy marched his captive to General Curtis, sitting in an ambulance. "Major General John Sappington Marmaduke?" spoke Curtis. The large wounded man nodded his head affirmatively.

So was brought in by his enemies the Confederate leader who had fought so aggressively in a number of battles alongside of Stand Watie and who, at the start of the war was described by Jay Monaghan as "A handsome six-footer with small hands and feet, he sat his horse with consuming grace. His eyes were kindly and intelligent, his mustache and beard soft. Fine hair was brushed smoothly down on his head and flared in a glorious ruffle around the back of his coat collar. Unmarried, he was the 'catch' of the river towns."

Wounded, drenched in rain and dressed in blue jeans — his unharmed arm grasping at his heavy pistol — so "the beau ideal his name denoted" — like many other Confederate Generals — even as the private soldier, fought and lost on the field of battle.

And the Yankees at Mine Creek caught another important leader, General W. L. Cabell, the Arkansas troops General who had cooperated within the Indian Territory with Stand Watie and Cooper.

"Old Pap," who had left his carriage, mounted his white horse and ridden back to Marmaduke's aid, ordered Shelby, the most successful of his commanders at beating Yankees, to make a covering stand at Little Osage; however, the pursuing Federals — their horses worn out — charged at a walk and by sheer numbers in a fierce conflict forced Shelby back. First pressed by the enemy under Alfred Pleasanton and then by a Curtis with newly-acquired vigor, Price's army, fighting most of the way, left a trail of broken men and equipment, finally seeking safety in the Indian Territory after blowing up its ammuniton train.

General Curtis, twenty-four hours behind Price, skirted into the Indian Territory as far as Pleasant Ford on the Arkansas River, fired a few artillery shots from McLain's Colorado battery and dissolved the organization of the Army of the Border, ordering his troops back to the Department of Kansas. No one seemed too eager to cross the Arkansas and tangle with General Stand Watie and his Indian Brigade!

Price's beaten and fatigued column marched for three days without food and even then all that some of the worn Confederates could find to eat was elm bark, acorns and a few fat Indian ponies. The proud army that had entered Missouri and marched with success on towards Kansas only a little over a month previously — until Westport — and which had thrown terror into even the populace of Kansas City, who despaired of Curtis, Pleasanton and Blunt saving them, wilted as hundreds of men perished on the prairies to the funeral dirge of the coyotes. Rain and snow pelted the column moving south through the Cherokee and Choctaw Nations.

General Price furloughed what was left of his Arkansas troops and they came out of the Indian Territory at Laynesport, Arkansas, but the Missouri soldiers, continuing to march through the Indian Territory, crossed the Red River on November 22 and reached E. Kirby-Smith's Texas domain. Wrote historian Jay Monaghan:

"Price could report optimistically that he had marched fourteen hundred and fifty-four miles, fought forty-three battles, and captured great quantities of Federal supplies. He did say not that he had lost five thousand stand of arms, all his cannon and the greater part of his army."

So it was that valiant "Old Pap's" major resistance to the Yankees was broken. But he still fought on with what troops he could rally, and M. Jeff Thompson's Swamp Foxes operated out of bayou hideouts, often in dugout canoes. With Hindman, Shelby and Quantrill still fighting, Stand Watie and his Indians could look to a continuance of their thrilling raids.

Though Watie's former tatterdemalions were now even better dressed than some of his Union opponents — for they were wearing the new uniforms captured at Cabin Creek — General Watie was deeply perturbed about the sufferings of the Southern refugee Indians. In an effort to aid his people, Watie sent his adjutant, Lieutenant Thomas F. Anderson, across the Mississippi to secure whatever medicine and cotton cards obtainable. The latter were necessary to make the cotton fibre ready for spinning.

An interesting comprehensive survey of problems in the Indian Territory, contained in the December 1 report of S. S. Scott, Confederate Commissioner of Indian Affairs, written at Richmond to James A. Seddon, Secretary of War, stated:

"I have just returned from the West, where I have been for several months, having left Richmond for the purpose of visiting the Indians in the latter part of May last under orders from the War Department. This visit was the third which I have made to the Indian country since the organization of the Confederate Government, the first being made in the year 1862, and the second in the year 1863. The funds appropriated by Congress at its last session, and its last session but one, for the Indian service I took with me and disbursed according to the intention of that body in making such appropriations. While in the West I made a close examination, as was my duty, into the condition of the Indian country, and I discovered that many changes had been wrought therein since my visit last year, which will be understood by what follows. General Maxey, at whose headquarters in the Choctaw county I passed much of my time, was assigned to the command of the District of Indian Territory by General E. Kirby Smith on the 11th of December, 1863, and commenced the discharge of his duties as such on the 24th of the same month. He has also been acting under orders from General Smith as superintendent of Indian affairs. He had in the district while I was there a brigade of Texas troops commanded by Colonel Gano, two or three unattached battalions and companies of Texans, and the Indian forces under General Cooper. Attempts were then being made — since, no doubt, carried into effect — to get all the able-bodied young Indians to enter the service. It was proposed to organize them with the other Indian troops into three brigades, to be called the Cherokee, Choctaw, and Creek brigades. The Cherokee brigade, composed of Cherokees, Chickasaws, and Osages, has been organized. The Creek brigade was about being so when I left, and the Choctaws anticipated no difficulty in being able to raise the number of men required to complete the organization of the Choctaw brigade.

"In the capacity of district commander, &c., General Maxey has attended to feeding the indigent refugee Indians of the various tribes within the limits of his command. The system of feeding these Indians out of the army commissariat was inaugurated, I believe, by General Hindman and it has been kept up to the present time. There was an urgent necessity for it at the time of its adoption, and, indeed, such has been the case ever since, as no provision has been made to feed them in any other way, and a failure in this respect would not only have entailed much suffering upon these people, but absolute starvation upon many, and produced an amount of disaffection within the several nations and tribes which would in the end no doubt have forever lost the Indian country to the South. In the beginning the task of feeding the indigent Indians was one of easy accomplishment, as the number requiring such Government aid were but few. Owing, however, to the occupation of the Cherokee country north of the Arkansas River, and the consequent insecurity of those portions of the Choctaw, Creek, and Seminole countries contiguous to the Arkansas River in the south, hundreds of families have been driven from their homes, and are now crowded in camps in the lower counties of the Choctaw and Chickasaw Nation, generally in a state of the greatest destitu tion. From papers furnished me by General Maxey I have ascertained that these indigent refugees at present amount to some 15,000 or 16,000. Of course the labor of feeding them, although they are located close to Red River, and within easy reach of the grain region of Texas, has become one of great difficulty. A plan to supply them with provisions was adopted by General Maxey soon after he assumed command of the district which has been found to work well in the main, but is open to one very serious objection. In order to secure regularity in obtaining the necessary supplies, their proper distribution, and to prevent frauds upon the Government, he has appointed a number of officers to supervise and attend to the matter, to wit, a superintendent of issues, an inspector of camps, and issuing agent, &c., but there is no law authorizing such appointments. It was necessary that some such system as the foregoing should have been adopted, however, and perhaps the difficulty just suggested could have been avoided had he made regular bonded agents of the commissary department, the superintendent of issues, inspector of camps, &c. The supplies, too, being drawn from the commissariat it is appropriate that they be managed by officers of the commissary department. I desire and respectfully ask advice upon this point.

"An act was passed by Congress at its last session and approved May 24, 1864, providing for an exchange with the loyal Indians by the Secretary of the Treasury of not more than $150,000 of the Treasury notes held by them on the 1st day of July, 1864, in notes of the new issue authorized by the act of February 17, 1864, without deduction. This law was enacted after my departure from Richmond for the Indian country. As it was known by Congress at the time of its introduction that I was about making that visit, the law empowered the Commissioner of Indian Affairs to supervise said exchange and see that no frauds were committed. I received, too, yesterday an official copy of this act referred to me by yourself on the 3rd of June, several days after my departure, with an indorsement made by the President May 31, 1864, calling attention to the liability of the execution of this act being attended by fraud, and advising care and caution. I did not reach the Indian country for several days subsequent to the said 1st of July, and I learned that the Indians had, on or about that day, turned over to certain depositories of the Treasury in the Trans-Mississippi Department the Treasury notes held by them and taken certificates therefore. They thus have been furnished with the strongest and most convincing evidence, to wit, certificates of depositories of the several amounts in their possession at the time specified in the law, and having no knowledge of the passage of the same at the time, they had no motive for, and consequently could not have perpetrated, frauds in making a deposit of the notes. The exchange referred to was not made with the Indians during my stay in the West, the agent of the Treasury for the Trans-Mississippi Department not having received the necessary instructions on the subject from the Secretary of the Treasury, owing, I presume, to the pressure of business on the Treasury Department, and the late changes therein. I wrote you a letter in regard to this fact on the 1st instant with the view of having it brought to the early attention of the Secretary of the Treasury, as prompt action on the subject is necessary in order to prevent dissatisfaction among the Indians. There is no Superintendent of Indian Affairs. The want of such an officer has given me much trouble and inconvenience, and been the cause of some complications in the administration of the affairs of this office.

"The President long ago, upon a suggestion similar to the above, instructed me to look for and recommend a suitable man for the position. The office is one of considerable importance and great care should be taken in the selection of the person to fill it. I have hitherto been unable to find one in every respect fitted for it, but hope to do so before the adjournment of the present Congress. The Superintendent of Indian Affairs has to be a bonded officer, as the greater portion of the funds intended for the Indian service has to pass through his hands. Finding it necessary to leave in the Trans-Mississippi Department funds to meet certain expenses with regard to the superintendency, &c., which I knew must accrue after my departure, and having no superintendent to take charge of them (and at the urgent solicitation, too, of General Maxey), I determined to call upon General Smith for assistance in making the necessary arrangements to meet the difficulty. On the 6th of October last I wrote to him as follows:

" 'It is necessary there should be some bonded officer at headquarters of the District of Indian Territory, to disburse certain moneys appertaining to the Indian service, in the absence of a regularly appointed superintendent of Indian affairs, to which officer such duty properly belongs. Could you appoint an agent of the quartermaster's department with instructions to attend to these disbursements and have him to give a bond which would cover them? Unless something of this kind is done I cannot conceive how it is possible for me to leave funds on this side of the Mississippi River to meet certain expenses of the superintendency which must inevitably arise during my absence.'

"In response to this letter General Smith appointed Mr. Robert C. Miller, who had been highly recommended for position in the Indian service, an agent in quartermaster's department for the disbursement of certain moneys appertaining to the Bureau of Indian Affairs, and ordered him to report to me. He gave the requisite bond, one fully covering the case, and immediately entered upon the discharge of his duties. This procedure was somewhat informal, but in my opinion strictly legal, and justified by the circumstances. All of the papers relating to this appointment which were forwarded by General Smith for ratification will be submitted by me in person. On the 23rd of August last, in my letter to you from Fort Towson, C. N., giving an account of the general condition of the Indians and the Indian country, I made the annexed statement in regard to arms for the Indian forces:

" 'The Indian troops are by no means well supplied with small arms, although by means of captures made by them at Poison Springs in Arkansas last April and recently in the vicinity of Fort Smith, they are in much better condition in this respect than they were when I was in this country twelve months ago. The 3,000 stand for which an order was obtained in Richmond about the beginning of last February by Campbell Le Flore, one of the delegates sent on by the Grand Council, &c., were not brought over by him as was expected both by the Government and the Indians. This was unfortunate, as the want of reliable arms has long been the most prolific subject of complaint with the nations.'

"On the 12th September General Maxey wrote to me as follows on this subject:

" 'I have in frequent conversations with you informed you of the lamentable deficiency of the Indian troops in arms. I have also shown you my letters to department headquarters on this subject. My wants have not been supplied. This is the source of anxiety with me, as the Indians feel that the treaty has not been complied with. They have recently turned out with great unanimity under the President's call. The wants have been thus increased. I would be glad if you would bring this to the notice of the proper authorities. At least 3,000 guns are needed.'

"The wants of the Indians in this respect, I would suggest, ought to be supplied if possible, and at an early day. By act of Congress approved February 15, 1862, the Indian country was divided into two judicial districts, called the districts of Cha-la-ki and Tash-co-homma, and courts for each of them established. These courts have never been organized. This is a misfortune just at this time, owing to the disturbed condition of the country, &c., and although it is a matter that belongs to the Department of Justice, I would respectfully suggest that measures ought to be immediately taken to correct it. I make the suggestions with the less hesitation because the want of these courts, as well as the want of reliable small-arms, the scarcity of good clothing, the irregularity with which the troops are paid, matters over which I have no sort of control and with which I have nothing to do as Commissioner of Indian Affairs, are the grounds and the only grounds of dissatisfaction on the part of many of the Indians with me, and have been made frequent subjects of complaint. The Indians in alliance with the Confederate States, especially those composing the five principal nations, were never more loyal than at the present time. This of course is generally known to be true of the Choctaws, Chickasaws, and that portion of the Cherokee Nation which has followed during this struggle the fortunes of the gallant Stand Watie; but the Creeks and Seminoles, about whose faithfulness some doubts may perhaps have been entertained, are in no respect behind the others in devotion to the Southern cause and Southern principles. On the 9th of August last I met all the principal men of these two nations and many of their warriors in council at Fort Washita, in the Chickasaw country. To show the sentiment of these people I give below extracts from the talks of the chiefs on that occasion.

Samuel Chekote [Checote], principal chief of the Creeks, among other things in his address to me, said:

" 'In reply to your encouraging remarks to-day I must say that it affords me more than ordinary pleasure to have an opportunity of seeing you, hearing you talk, and speaking to you face to face. I feel encouraged by your presence, esteeming your long and perilous journey to the Indian country to be prompted by no other motives than the welfare of the Indian people. And the assurances you have given us to-day, as on former occasions, of the good feelings and faith of the President and Government toward us, is an additional source of great encouragement. These manifest tokens of friendship I assure you, in behalf of the Creek people, are duly appreciated, and shall ever esteem it our high prerogative to cherish such feelings.'

"After alluding briefly to the sufferings of his people during the last year because of their having been driven from their homes by the enemy, he continues:

" 'These misfortunes and calamities I deem necessary incidents in the path of war. I am assured that many of my white brethren are suffering likewise. I, therefore, make no complaint, but assure you in behalf of my people that the cause of the South is our cause, her hopes our hopes, and whatever her misfortunes may be it shall be our pleasure to bear them patiently with her, even unto death. If she falls we fall, and if she prospers we only desire it to be our privilege to enjoy her prosperity. Being thus actuated we are enrolling every able-bodied man in the service for the war. Although many of those already enlisted are without arms, we shall persevere with the hope of getting them hereafter. I take this occasion to express my approbation of the officers over us in this department. I believe them to be men of patriotic and generous principles, willing to sacrifice personal ease and sectional feelings for the welfare of the Indians, and our common cause. Our numerous wants are, in a measure, being supplied. We believe that all is being done that can be done conveniently. We can see and appreciate the exigency of the times, and are willing to endure all that cannot be remedied.'

"Helma Micco or John Jumper, the principal chief of the Seminoles, a pure patriot, thus eloquently wrote me:

" 'In the fall of 1862 I first met you at Fort Arbuckle. You asked me if I had any requests to make the President of the Confederate States. I told you I had none. We were then by our firesides, living in comparative quiet; but war came to our country and drove us from these pleasant homes; we are now wanderers and strangers, yet the Confederate States have not deserted us; we have been provided for; our women and children are fed; our soldiers get all they should expect; the Government is engaged in a great war, she cannot do any more for us now than she is doing. Perhaps when the war is over we will be perfectly satisfied with her bounty; all claims will be adjusted. In view of all these things I again say to you that I have no request to make of the President. He will without asking do all for us that we should expect. I wish you, however, to assure the President that the Seminoles are yet true and loyal. Their treaty stipulations are sacred. The destiny of your Government shall be ours; if she falls we will go with her; if she triumphs no rejoicing will be more sincere than ours. Permit me to express to you the gratification we feel because of your visit. We thank you for the very friendly and satisfactory address of this morning. We feel strengthened and encouraged. We will remember your words when you are far away; we will profit by them. We wish you to visit us often; we think you are a good friend to us; we have confidence in you. May you have a pleasant and safe return to Richmond, and may you come again shortly to our wild western land. May the blessing of Almighty God rest upon our common cause.'

"The Indian troops, it may be well to remark in conclusion, have been doing recently good service, and have met with many successes. The achievements of the Choctaw Brigade in Arkansas and the Cherokee Brigade in the Indian country, have merited and obtained the high commendation in special orders of the general commanding the Trans-Mississippi Department. Before my departure from the Indian country, many of them, the Choctaws, Cherokees, and Seminoles, had re-enlisted with great uanminity [unanimity] for the war, and I doubt not that their example has been followed by all their brethren in the service."

13

WHEN THE WINTER weather began raging, destitute Indians in the area of Watie's headquarters sent in appeals for help and General Watie, saddling up a special command, himself escorted the Confederate Indian refugees across the Red River to Texas without the loss of a life.

Despite the Rebel money — inflated by this time until prices were fantastic — coming in from the Confederate Government, and the supplies being run past Yankee lines and river gunboats by Thomas F. Anderson and Reverend E. L. Compere, a chaplain in Stand Watie's Brigade, the problem of keeping the Indian refugees fed was mounting.

General Watie would anxiously await the return of Anderson from every foray for supplies into Yankee-held lands. Anderson, Watie's adjutant and close friend, of no Indian blood, was full of wit and humor, and always considered Mrs. Watie as his "Aunt Sallie."

The Cherokees, using every possible means to obtain money so as to buy supplies, were even transporting cotton to Mexico. This was carried on as a legitimate business and not as a wartime cotton speculation. Cotton bales were routed from Paris, Lamar County, Texas to Matamoros, Mexico.

At his winter headquarters at Boggy Depot, Choctaw Nation, General Watie was intensely lonesome for his "Dear Sallie" and in January he asked her to come up from Texas as he could obtain a house so that the Waties would not be dependent on friends for their domicile. Sarah, though, could not leave Texas and General Watie's desire to be with his wife remained unquenched.

Colonel William A. Phillips, Third Indian Home Guard (Kansas Infantry), harrassed but ever fighting back at Watie's raiders, briefly replaced as Commander of the Indian troops at Fort Gibson, had perplexing difficulties not originating with the Secessionists.

From Fort Gibson on January 16, 1865, he wrote Major General Francis J. Herron:

". . . I was summoned to General Thayer's headquarters and received orders to resume command of the Indian Brigade. They were reticent, and I sought to know no more than they felt proper to communicate. I could scarcely get an escort here, but I resumed command on the 29th ultimo. I would have preferred to meet and expose the powerful organization that I fear is not dead yet. I was willing to stake my reputation on the struggle, but God knows best. The orders to evacuate Fort Smith were issued and countermanded. I think the latter an error that time will prove. The orders to close the stores in Smith caused a remarkable sale. Goods were sold off in immense quantities to all persons from the 20th to the 31st of December, 1864. It has been stated to me by one of the parties that $2,000 on each merchant was levied by someone for that twelve days . . . I was directed to make needful rules to protect the rights of the Indians. This I shall do, but with the organizations above and below me it will be extremely difficult, and my limited authority and means will place me, to a large extent, at the mercy of those who are in league with the plunderers. Captain Vittum [David Vittum, Third Wisconsin Cavalry] was named by General Blunt provost-marshal of Southern Kansas. Only think of one of the most noted cattle thieves being police officer on the border. Blair [Colonel Charles W. Blair, Fourteenth Kansas Cavalry], is still at Fort Scott, and says he is not going from it. I have plenty in my hands, but think I ought to prefer charges and push the matter against both of them and others. Here I found matters in a frightful state. I had no idea that demoralization could have reached such a pitch in such a short time. I have the report and affidavit of an acting detective here implicating Colonel Wattles [Stephen H. Wattles, First Regiment Indian Guard], the provost-marshal, quartermaster and commissary. It seems they were regularly in the habit of throwing persons in a wretched prison and black-mailing them, the money being divided between Wattles, the provost-marshal and the detectives. Other articles were taken and divided. I placed the provost-marshal in arrest. He is a young man and refuses to admit, but does the same thing. He begs that I will not proceed against him and promises to refund his share of the money to the persons mulcted. Wattles I have not yet placed under arrest. I scarcely know what to do with him. I understand that my command will be defined as a separate command in orders, and I hope so, but I have no colonel, and he might raise the question of rank. I hardly feel like permitting him to resign. What should I do? My commissary carried on a frightful system. I find wholesale forging of vouchers. I have sent for Captain Peck to inspect and examine. Captain Gaylord left for Fort Smith before I began the inspection of his establishment. When he returns I will have to place him in arrest. The quartermaster's affairs I have not inspected sufficiently yet to speak fully, but he must be removed. Some of the officers have been leading a life of idleness, and go to work with a very bad grace, and the worthless soreheads caucus in McDonald's and McKee's Store for my removal. During the pendency of the contract nearly all the cattle killed, or a large portion of them, were contraband . . . I find that the corn bought at Fort Scott by Insley has been (part of it) shipped down here and put in the warehouse of McDonald here to be issued in another contract, part of it hauled in Government transportation. I got the affidavits of the wagonmaster and teamsters. I find that there has been a gigantic swindle by Coffin and McDonald in corn in the nation. I furnished seed corn to the Cherokees last spring, taken on South Canadian and Boggy. They raised nearly enough to do them. As the Creek refugees around Gibson were suffering, the President authorized the expenditure of $200,000. What do you think the rascals did? Coffin telegraphed that McDonald & Co. could furnish corn at $7 and beef at 6 cents, or 3 gross. He was allowed to take a temporary supply. He sends agents all through the Cherokee country buying at $2 and $2.50. If a man had 100 bushels they would buy it all and issue half of it to him, and give one of his neighbors an order for fifty of it to go and get it. It is paid for in McDonald's and McKee's checks, thirty days after date; 9,000 bushels were thus bought. Sometimes when there was no corn, they give checks for the corn and checks for what they pretend to buy. The contractor was killing contraband beef, forbidding them to kill their own cattle, and buying a few of these, about a tenth of what the contractors killed, at 2 cents. I have stopped all these irregular beef practices. It has been a perfect pandemonium broke loose. God knows when they would have stopped. I shall straighten it up as far as I have the power. My task is a thankless one, except the conviction of doing my duty. I am exposed to the interest of a powerful money corporation, and I doubt whether the Government will stand by me, but the thing of all others that I cannot afford is that anyone think I was unable to meet or afraid of any responsibilities . . ."

On February 16 from Fort Gibson Colonel Phillips was still irate over supply conditions and wrote Major General Canby at New Orleans:

". . . The Indian soldiers are more to be trusted for their own protection than are ours. They are amenable to each other as well as the Government. Most of the white regiments that have entered the Indian Nation commit more or less depredation. They treat it as if it were an enemy's country."

At the same time, Phillips continued to protest the questionable activites of Captain Vittum with contraband cattle.

Evidence to support the charges of corruption by Federal officers, contended by Colonel Phillips, was given in a letter written March 22 by John Ross, the "exiled" Cherokee Chief and Evans Jones and Daniel H. Ross, Union Cherokee delegates, at Washington. This correspondence to Lieutenant General U. S.

Grant, commanding armies of the United States, stated:

"The undersigned delegates of the Cherokee Nation, duly appointed by authority of the national Council to look after the interests of our people in the city of Washington, being informed that an effort is being made to get the Indian Territory attached to the Department of Missouri and Kansas, respectfully request the change asked for not be made. We are entirely satisfied to remain under the command of Major-General Reynolds, in the Department of Arkansas. When heretofore attached to Kansas our cattle and corn have been stolen and our country ravaged under the auspices the authorities sent to protect us, and we greatly fear that if we are again connected to that department our people will be still further impoverished by the same kind of misrule. We further request that Maj. Gen. James G. Blunt be not again placed in command of our country."

Efforts of Colonel Phillips to remedy the situation that distressed both himself and Chief Ross were, in the main, stymied by higher-ranking officers who reported that there were no Indian or Federal Courts in the Territory in which to bring charges against the accused.

General Maxcy worked arduously for the military welfare of the Indian Territory for he had contended the year previously, "If the Indian Territory gives way, the granary of the Trans-Mississippi, the breadstuffs, and beef of this and the Arkansas army, are gone, and the left of Holmes' army is turned, and with it not only the meat and bread, but the salt and iron of what is left of the Trans-Mississippi Department."

Under instruction of Kirby-Smith, P. B. Leeds, Acting Assistant Adjutant General, on February 14 issued Special Order No. 40, stating:

"XIII. Brig. Gen. Stand Watie will relieve Brig. Gen. D. H. Cooper in command of the Division of Indian Troops in the District of Indian Territory. In accordance with instructions from the War Department, Brig. Gen. D. H. Cooper, is assigned duty as superintendent of Indian Affairs in the District of Indian Territory."

That Stand Watie's surging horsemen were most feared by the Yankees is evidenced time and time again in the Northern reports. Even in early 1865 there was no diminution of alarm in Yankee-held territory when word spread that Watie was on the warpath. Major General Blunt at his headquarters in Paola, Kansas, on February 14, wrote Major General Dodge, commanding the Department of Missouri:

"In consequence of these facts [reports Watie was prepared for making a raid] the people of the settlements in the Neosho Valley are quite alarmed and not without some cause. The Neosho Valley is one of the best settlements in the State, and abounds largely in valuable stock of all kinds, which is a great inducement for raiding parties and the countries through which they will pass will be well supplied with grass and water as soon as the last of April or the first of May."

At the start of 1865, the situation with the Confederate Indians took a strange turn. The Plains Indians, who had made alliances with General Pike back in 1861 at the beginning of the war actually had done practically nothing to help the Confederacy. But with Watie's command fighting a desperate holding action — with their horses almost worn out and with the men sometimes riding night and day on raids — the Plains Indians suddenly wanted to don Confederate gray.

One plausible reason for the change in attitude of some of the Plains Indians resulted from Colonel J. M. Chivington's raid on the Cheyenne and Arapaho. These Indians, though known Confederate sympathizers were in their camp, had denied any participation in the mail and stage raids of the past summer. Nevertheless, on November 29, 1864, Chivington, with nine hundred volunteers out of Denver, who had crossed winter plains, struck without warning the Indian encampment at Sand Creek, forty miles below Fort Lyon. Hundreds of Indian men, women and children were either killed outright or driven onto the wintery plains to die of exposure.

If this were an example of the pious North "marching to make men free," then the half-wild and wild survivors of the massacre wanted none of it!

First hint of this new support came in January when news arrived at Boggy Point from the headquarters of the Osage Battalion at Camp Dorn that the Comanches and Kiowas of the Plains wanted to take the warpath against the Federals in the spring and summer, and the Osages, in poor uniforms, but good spirits, were hoping in the words of their adjutant, "to give Kansas hell in the summer."

Alert Northern spies had Union officers in the Indian lands trying to forestall any movement to the Confederacy. O-hop-ey-a-ne, Second Chief of the Comanches, reported to Tuckabatche Micco, Principal Chief of the Creeks, an Indian meeting held at Cherokee Town, around the first of 1865, in which the Creeks were visited by the Prairie Indians, the Comanches, Kiowas and Arapahoes. These Indians wished to meet the chiefs of the Confederate Indians, exclaiming they were anxious to see "you all."

The Plains Indian leaders at the Cherokee Town meeting told of several councils at which efforts were made to make the Prairie Indians take the warpath against the South. The Second Chief of the Comanches also stated the Prairie Indians had been assembled at a council by white Northern officers. The Yankees had large amounts of goods and presents for the Indians as well as a number of guns with ammunition. The Union officers told the Indians they could have all the goods and guns if they would make war on the South. Instructions were given by the officers to kill all the men and boys and take the women and children prisoners. Next, they were to drive off the cattle and horses. When they returned from their expedition, though, they must give up the white women and girls. But the Indian women could remain theirs. Mules and horses and cattle the Yankees would buy from them.

When the Union spokesman concluded speaking, the Comanche Chief answered that he had friends and brothers in the South and he would not make war on them. The Yankee Captain replied that if the Comanche Chief refused to fight the South, he would not be given the guns. That he would do without the guns and with his bow and arrows still kill buffalo and live on the Prairie, was the final answer of the Comanche leader.

Jesse Chisholm, the Cherokee Indian trader — who could speak fourteen different languages and who was helpful in winning Indians over to Pike — was interpreter at this Council and advised the Indians not to listen to the "Northern men's bad talk."

The Comanche's Second Chief ended up his message with the assurance there was a perfect estrangement between the Prairie Indians at the Council and the North. These Indians could be counted as true friends to the Secesh.

Shortly after receiving this information, which was forwarded to him by the Creek leader who was at Council on Washita River, Stand Watie, on March 19, wrote Creek Chief Tuckabatchee Micco. General Watie explained that he had received a letter from the Confederate States Agent for the Reserve Indians saying the Prairie Indians wanted to meet delegates from the Confederate Indian Nations. General Watie told how he had notified General Maxey, who sent Major Vore to the designated place, but the Prairie Indians had departed. Watie went on to state that on May 15 there was to be held a General Council of all the Indian Tribes friendly with the Confederate States to adopt plans for united and more vigorous prosecution of the conflict. With concentrated action the Rebel Indians would conquer and win peace with honor.

Before the conference, which was held at Camp Napoleon, there was another change in command. General Maxey was succeeded on March 1 by the heavy-drinking and heavy-fighting beloved by his Indians, Douglas H. Cooper. There was no denying that Maxey had done as well as could be expected, but the Indian soldiers had two idols, their own Stand Watie and their former agent Douglas Cooper. General Cooper, who before succeeding Maxey, had seen Jefferson Davis in Richmond, ever since General Pike's resignation and his temporary elevation to the top command, desired to have full control of the Indian Territory troops and, for all practical purposes, be ex-officio Superintendent of Indian Affairs for the Civilized Nations.

General Maxey well could have recalled a letter he had received from S. A. Roberts shortly after he had assumed command of the Indian Territory, which read:

"Northern Texas and the Indian Department have been neglected so long that they have become the most responsible commands in the Trans-Mississippi Department. I tremble for you. A great name is in store for you or you fall into the ranks of failures; the latter may be your fate, and might be the fate of any man, even after an entire, and perfect devotion of all one's time and talent, for want of the proper means. In military matters these things are never considered. Success is the only criterion – a good rule upon the whole, though in many instances it works great injustice. Good and deserving men fall, and accidental heroes, rise in the scale, kicking their less fortunate brothers from the platform."

From his headquarters of the Department of Missouri at St. Louis on April 12, General Dodge instructed Blunt at Paola:

"We have pretty reliable information that Stand Watie, under orders of the rebel authorities, has made a combination of all the southern Indians, except what are known as 'Pin' Indians, for operation against Kansas.

"How large a force he could collect, you can judge better than I can . . . You had better retain the Fifteenth Kansas until we can ascertain the facts. I expect the balance of Third Wisconsin soon, and they will be pushed out to you. Put some good man after Stand Watie if you can."

At the same time Dodge advised Brevet Brigadier General James H. Ford at Fort Riley, "If Colonel Blair is not strong enough [to fight Watie], you will have to move in that direction."

The next few days the Federal forces were constantly on the search for Watie and his raiders, but they never located him.

Yes, in late April of 1865 Stand Watie and General Cooper were carrying on their efforts against the evil Kansas abolitionists. "Give Kansas Hell!" The whoop and war cry, the shout and Rebel Yell came from aristocratic mixed-bloods dressed in patched Confederate gray, captured Federal blue, or else, as often General Watie dressed, in baggy old trousers with whatever coat he could find, and over this, when need be, a military cloak of mongrel classification. Indeed, the whoops and shouts resounded along the Plains from the half-wild Indians, who looked for omens of luck and restrained with impatience their Kansas assaults upon the Pins of the Indian long house culture.

But in shell-shattered Virginia towns and burned countrysides there was a strange quiet in the guns and a strange dismay in the hearts of the people. Jefferson Davis on April 5 had set up his government at Danville after his flight from Richmond, saying:

"Let us but will it and we are free. Animated by that confidence in spirit and fortitude which never yet has failed me, I announce to you, my fellow countrymen, that it is my purpose to maintain your cause with my whole heart and soul; that I will never consent to abandon to the enemy one foot of soil of any one of the States of the Confederacy."

On April 9 General Robert E. Lee surrendered some 26,000 men to General U. S. Grant at Appomattox Court House. An American Indian wrote with his own hand the articles of Lee's surrender; this was Captain Ely Parker, a Seneca chief named Do-ne-ho-ga-wa, who was on Grant's personal staff.

Colonel John Mosby and his famous Rangers capitulated to Major General Winfield S. Hancock on April 17 and then on April 26 General Joseph E. Johnston surrendered his army in North Carolina, an army that was slightly larger than that given up by General Lee.

Stand Watie, in the field, with his scanty forces overwhelmingly outnumbered still raided as a defensive measure and hoped that if General E. Kirby-Smith and the Army of the Trans-Mississippi would stand firm, then Watie could launch a counterattack with his new Indian allies. Then, too, word had reached the Indian headquarters that their beloved White Father, Jefferson Davis, was on his way to Texas.

True, Davis was on his way to lands still in Confederate control but on May 10 – the day after General Richard Taylor surrendered in Mississippi to Major General E.R.S. Canby – at Irwinsville, Georgia, Federal parties attempting to capture Davis and claim the $100,000 reward for his apprehension, became so confused they fired into each other, killing two and wounding four. Jefferson Davis and his party were seized.

A day later General M. Jeff Thompson surrendered his command of some 7,500 to General Dodge at Chalk Bluff, Arkansas.

And on May 13 the "last battle of the war" was fought, the battle of Palmetto Ranch, Resca Chica, Texas, near the mouth of the Rio Grande, when General James E. Slaughter, commanding 600 Confederate Second Texas Cavalry and light artillery, clashed with Colonel Barrett of the Thirty-fourth Indiana Infantry, assisted by four companies of the Sixty-second U. S. Colored Infantry.

The Federals were routed and Slaughter captured as many prisoners as he had Rebel troops!

Despite the Secesh victory, the news seeping into Indian Territory headquarters looked foreboding.

On May 18, a few days before the Indians were to hold their

large Camp Napoleon conference, Cooper advised Stand Watie:

". . . We must preserve order in the country, and I rely upon your aid and cooperation in that as well as all other things. We must keep cool and quiet and wait to see what course things will take. If the people of this Tery get into difficulties among themselves, it will be very disastrous. Let there be respect for private rights and forbearance one with another and all I hope will be well. Do not let your men get any whiskey. If excited by drink they will get into difficulties among themselves and their people. . ."

Three days later General Cooper was advising Watie, "The best policy is to keep them [First Indian Brigade, Creeks and Seminoles] all employed in front scouting and driving out beef from the Arkansas River."

And on May 23 Watie instructed Colonel Tandy Walker, "I do not desire collision with the Federals, but they must keep out of the Choctaw country until the grand council otherwise determine."

The compact made and entered into between the Confederate Indian tribes and the Prairie tribes of Indians at Camp Napoleon, on Washita River, May 26, 1865, stated:

"Whereas the history of the past admonishes the red man that his once great and powerful race is rapidly passing away as snow beneath the summer sun, our people of the mighty nations of our forefathers many years ago having been as numerous as the leaves of the forest or the stars of the heavens; but now, by the vicissitudes of time and change and misfortune and evils of disunion, discord, and war among themselves are but a wreck of their former greatness; their vast and lovely country and beautiful hunting grounds, abounding in all the luxuries and necessities of life and happiness, given to them by the Great Spirit, having known no limits but the shores of the great waters and the horizon of the heavens, is now on account of our weakness being reduced and hemmed into a small and precarious country that we can scarcely call our own and in which we cannot remain in safety and pursue our peaceful avocations, nor can we visit the bones and the graves of our kindred, so dear to our hearts and sacred to our memories, to pay the tribute of respect, unless we run the risk of being murdered by our more powerful enemies; and

"Whereas there still remains in the timbered countries, on the plains, and in the mountains many nations and bands of our people, which, if united, would present a body that would afford sufficient strength to command respect and assert and maintain our rights: Therefore, we, the Cherokees, Choctaws, Muscogees, Seminoles, Chickasaws, Reserve Caddoes, Reserve Osages, and Reserve Comanches, comprising the Confederate Indian tribes and allies of the Confederate States of the first part, and our brothers of the plains, the Kiowas, Arapahoes, Chivans, Lipans, and of the several bands of the Comanches, the Nocomies, Co-cho-te-kas, Le-na-weets, Yampankas, and Mootchas, and Jim Pock Mark's band of Caddoes and Anadarkoes, of the second part, do, for our peace and happiness and the preservation of our race, make and enter into the following league and compact, to wit:

"ARTICLE I. Peace and friendship shall forever exist between the tribes and bands parties to this compact. The ancient council fires of our forefathers already kindled by our brothers of the timbered countries shall be kept kindled and blazing by brotherly love, until their smoke shall ascend to the spirit land to invoke the blessing of the Great Spirit on all of our good works. The tomahawk shall be forever buried. The scalping knife shall be forever broken. The warpath heretofore leading from one tribe or band to another shall grow up and become as the wild wilderness. The path of peace shall be opened from one tribe or band to another, and kept open and traveled in friendship, so that it may become white and brighten as time rolls on, and so that our children in all time to come may travel no other road, and never shall it be stained with the blood of our brothers.

"ART. II. The parties to this compact shall compose (as our undersigned brothers of the timbered country of the first part already have done) an Indian confederacy or band of brothers, having for its objective the peace, the happiness, and the protection of all alike, and the preservation of our race. In no case shall the warpath be opened to settle any difficulty or dispute that may hereafter arise between any of the tribes or bands parties to this compact or individuals thereof. All the difficulties shall be settled without the shedding of any blood, and by suggestion of the chiefs and headmen of the tribes, band, or persons interested. The motto or great principle of the confederated

Indian tribes shall be, 'An Indian shall not spill an Indian's blood.'

"In testimony of our sincerity and good faith in entering into this compact we have smoked the pipe of peace and extended to each other the hand of friendship, and exchanged the tokens and emblems of peace and friendship peculiar to our race, this 26th of May, 1865."

Disquieting rumors reached Texas concerning General Watie. Some were that he had been captured, others were that Stand Watie was being sought out by the Federals bent on sheer revenge. Quantrill, who had started out on a wild ride, his men disguised as Federal Cavalry, to assassinate Lincoln, had himself been shot in a skirmish after being trapped in a farmhouse fifty miles southwest of Louisville. Partially paralyzed he lay moaning in a Louisville hospital and was to die at the end of May.

In the welter of conflicting stories and news, Mrs. Watie had sent word to the General that she could not keep living without hearing from him. Stand Watie quickly replied that his silence was because of the confusion among the troops and his efforts to keep as much control as possible. He had furloughed many of them home to avoid any potential outbreak against the authorities.

Watie's communication set at rest some of the fears for her husband's safety which had so torn Sarah. Rumors were rife in Texas that General Watie was a fugitive with a price on his head and that he was being hunted down by General Blunt's "Feds" like an escaped criminal. Sarah had worried that, if this were true, turncoat Indians might seize the General, if the Yankee Pins had not beaten them to it!

Honest, prayerful Sarah Watie had abhorred the speculation in government properties by some pseudo-patriots. She held a bitter detestation for those who had flown the Confederate flag only as a means of participation in whatever financial looting possible. Rather than have General Watie a party to questionable schemes which would injure those who had followed and trusted him, Sarah unstintingly proclaimed she would live on nothing but bread and water.

There was, of course, no iota of reason for Sarah doubting the course Watie would take. Stand Watie's actions had ever put his people before himself and if there were men in Confederate gray or Union blue whose colors were cemented to the expediency of profit-at-any-cost, Watie had only contempt for such charlatans.

Yet Sarah's fears – phantom though they were – could not be criticized as life was disintegrating around her in Texas. Would General E. Kirby-Smith continue to hold out? Would Texas fight on against the Yankees? And who could suppress the marauders and bushwhackers who robbed and stole from the defenseless Texas Indian refugees as well as the Texans themselves? Had not Sarah lost her black horse and any day her mules might be the next prize for the blackguards?

Sarah Watie's devotion and admiration for her warrior-husband is evident in her letters which appear in *Cherokee Cavaliers* as is General Watie's concern for his wife and children in Texas. For them there was no autumn for love as Albert Pike wrote in his poem:

"Love blooms but once and dies – for all –
Life has no second Spring;
The frost must come, the snow must fall
Loud as the lark may sing.

Oh Love! O, Life! ye fade like flowers
That droop and die in June;
The present, ah! too short is ours,
And autumn comes too soon."

Autumn's shadow was deep over the Confederacy! One day before Stand Watie had written Sarah, May 27, that he had no conclusive news on Texas, the vast and mighty empire of Kirby-Smithdom saw the Stars and Bars come down. When Kirby-Smith had decided to surrender, angered Jo Shelby and some of his aides threatened to arrest Kirby-Smith and the commander relinquished his duties to General Simon Bolivar Buckner. But a mere change in command couldn't be the magic elixir through which defeat was transformed to victory. Thus it was that at New Orleans on May 26 General Buckner surrendered the Army of the Trans-Mississippi to Major General Peter J. Osterhaus, a long time war favorite with the midwest Germans, who had lost his first major battle at Wilson's Creek and whose infantry was overrun at Pea Ridge by Colonel Stand Watie.

News of the surrender of Kirby-Smith's army must have stunned the Indian leaders. Hadn't General Kirby-Smith felt so confident he could hold out that he had issued a commission to Albert Pike so he could help in organizing the new Confederates allies, the Plains Indians? And hadn't General John Bankhead Magruder at Houston declared "I would rather be a Comanche Indian than bow the knees to the Yankees!"

Stand Watie still held the Choctaw Nation inviolate! The Southern flag was still the flag in power over much of the Indian Territory!

Out went the call to the leaders of the Confederate Indian nations to send their representatives to a Grand Council to be held at Cleata Yamaha, Choctaw Nation. Wild Indians had started on an expedition to attack trains on the Santa Fe Road, but they were recalled by the Confederate Indians so they could send other chiefs to the Grand Council.

From this council, on June 15, came these resolutions:

"Whereas at the grand council held at Camp Napoleon on the 24th day of May, 1865, the Cherokees, Choctaws, Creeks, Chickasaws, Seminoles, Comanches, Caddoes, Osages, Cheyennes, Kiowas, Arapahoes, Lipans, the Northern Caddoes, and Anadarkoes, did enter into a solemn league of peace and friendship; and,

"Whereas the object of this confederation of these Indian nations is to maintain the integrity of the Indian Territory as the present and future home of our race, to preserve and perpetuate the national rights and franchises of the several nations, to cultivate peace, harmony, and fellowship; and

"Whereas it is the earnest desire of this grand council that all strife, feuds, and hostilities among Indians should cease, and that our great principle, 'An Indian shall not spill another Indian's bood,' be universally adopted by all nations and tribes of Indians: Therefore

*"Resolved by the grand council of the united nations of the Indian Territory,* That the principal chiefs and governors of the nations here represented constitute a committee who are requested and authorized to extend, in the name of this confederation, the hand of fellowship to all nations of Indians.

*"Resolved further,* That the said executives be requested and

authorized to communicate the wishes and intentions of this grand council to the proper authorities of the Cherokee, Seminole, Creek, Osage, and all other nations of Indians now in alliance with the Government of the United States and at hostilities with these nations, and to invite the said Cherokee, Seminole, Creek, Osage, and all other nations of Indians to become parties to this confederation and to co-operate with this council in its efforts to contract anew friendly relations with the United States Government.

"*Resolved further,* That the governors or principal chiefs of the Cherokee, Creek, Seminole, Chickasaw, and Choctaw Nations, be and with the consent of their respective councils, be, and they are hereby, authorized to appoint one or more commissioners, not to exceed five from each nation, to represent the interests of such nation at the city of Washington, and who shall be clothed with full powers to negotiate with the United States Government such treaties as the exigencies of affairs may seem to demand.

"*Resolved further,* That any one or more of such persons authorized to be appointed may act as proxies for the remainder should it be out of their power to proceed in person to Washington City. Said delegates will be authorized and directed to invite the United States Government to send commissioners within this Territory to treat with tribes of this confederation who may not be represented at Washington City.

"*Resolved further,* That no treaty made under the provisions of these resolutions shall be binding until ratified by the national councils of the respective tribes making the same.

"*Resolved further,* That said delegates be instructed to communicate with the proper military authorities of the United States for the purpose of effecting a cessation of hostilities in order that there be time and opportunity to negotiate with the United States Government; also to obtain from said military authorities a passport to the city of Washington, and further urge upon said military authorities, in order to avoid collision, the propriety of sending no forces into the Indian Territory until they, the said delegates, may confer with the United States Government for the establishment of permanent peace."

One by one the Indian Rebels surrendered their forces. General Stand Watie as Chief of the Cherokees held out, a noble vexillary with his Secesh flag still flying.

Stand Watie knew that his subordinate commanders in the Indian Territory had given up with dignity and with pride. Military leaders of the Indian Nations had halted operations as unconquered chieftains, relinquishing their warfare against the hated abolitionists only because there was none left to fight alongside them. That was as Watie had planned.

It was not as Henry Wadsworth Longfellow wrote in *Hiawatha*:

> "Then upon the ground the warriors
> Threw their cloaks and shirts of deerskin,
> Threw their weapons and their war gear,
> Buried all their warlike weapons.
> . . .
> Then a voice was heard, a whisper:
> Broken are the spells that bound you,
> All the charms of old magicians,
> All the magic powers of evil."

As the oppressive, hot June days drew toward their close, Stand Watie rode his horse into Doaksville to meet with Lieutenant Colonel A. C. Matthews, United States Volunteers, and W. H. Vance, adjutant, United States Volunteers, commissioners appointed by Major General Herron.

So it was that on June 23, Brigadier General Stand Watie endured the hardest ride of his life. No Yankee guns were aimed at him and no sabers slashed close to his body. Unlike his truculent raids that had lashed the defiant Federal forts and snaking supply lines, this slow ride held no element of danger.

And the ending was written long before!

Yes, the end of the trail was written, mayhaps, back on July 4, 1863, when the wearied Confederates turned back from Cemetary Hill at Gettysburg, when hungry Vicksburg fell and Helena didn't.

Try as Stand Watie did — with raid and torch, with charge and countercharge — there was a path from which even the vicissitudes and caprices of fate would not let him escape.

His had been a bold dream — a dream that shimmered with

courage and valor. So bold the dream – so brave the dreamer!

And on June 23 in the old Choctaw capital the dreamer awakened and his days of glory were phantoms brought by the stroke of the surrender pen as if it were some evil Merlin's wand.

The last Confederate General to surrender his forces, General Stand Watie, with the full respect of his courteous victors, turned his horse back toward his headquarters.

Gone was the dream.

Somehow the Confederate flag that rippled in the wind over the virescent summer lands assumed a spectral-like quality there under the heavy June sun.

Stand Watie could see in the distance the burned homes of his beloved land with their monuments to the efforts of the Southern Cherokees. Stark against the horizon the lonely chimneys stood like giant gravestones in some gargantuan burying ground.

He had led his people – to this only?

General Stand Watie knew that though he had lost his fight, a hard struggle was thundering and pressing upon him. No shouts of Pins against Rebel Cherokees! No death cry of plunging mounts with minie balls through their lungs! No Stars and Bars above a Rebel Yell as the Secesh charged!

His new army to command was one of the sick, the maimed and the broken-spirited along the Red River; the wives and the children of the fighters, grown gaunt with fear and worry; the men of his old command who must survive with the Pins even as they had lived for years to kill the Pins.

Stand Watie, the military leader of the Civilized Indian Nations, the political leader of his people and the trusted cohort of even the half-wild Plains Indians, could never leave his land to the monuments of death. Even as he had led his people in war, he knew that somehow he must lead them in peace.

As the words of the beloved Father Abram Joseph Ryan were written for Robert E. Lee, they could have fitted the great patriot of the Cherokees:

> "Forth from its scabbard, pure and bright
>     Flashed the sword of Lee!
> Far in the front of the deadly fight,
> High o'er the brave in the cause of Right

Its stainless sheen, like a beacon light,
    Led us to victory

. . .
"Forth from its scabbard all in vain
    Bright flashed the sword of Lee;
'Tis shrouded now in its sheath again,
It sleeps the sleep of our noble slain
Defeated, yet without a stain,
    Proudly and peacefully."

14

FIFTEEN THOUSAND CONFEDERATE Indians were cast adrift with the end of the War between the States. Disconsolately some of them may have remembered lines from *Cherokee Rose Buds,* published by the students of the Female Seminary at Park Hill:

> "Like Roses bright we hope to grow,
> And over our home such beauty throw
> In future years — that all may see
> Loveliest of lands, — the Cherokee."

There was one in Stand Watie's family who did not live to see his father's army fall; Cumiskey, who died in Texas in 1863 when he was around fifteen years of age. But though Watie had lost Cumiskey, his prayers were answered when Saladin survived riding with his father on daring raids. Too, along with the girls, there was his youngest son, Watica, who someday could help rebuild the shattered Watie fortunes.

Applicable equally to the former Confederate Indian Nations as to the old Confederate States was this summing up of conditions at the end of the struggle by General Richard Taylor in his book, *Destruction and Reconstruction*:

"Extinction of slavery was expected by all and regretted by none, although loss of slaves destroyed the value of land. Existing since the earliest colonization of the Southern States, the institution was interwoven with the thoughts, habits, and daily lives of both races, and both suffered by the sudden disruption of the accustomed tie. Bank stocks, bonds, all personal property, all accumulated wealth had disappeared. Thousands of homes, farm buildings, work-animals, flocks and herds, had been wantonly burned, killed or carried off. The land was filled with widows and orphans crying for aid, which the universal destitution prevented them from receiving. Humanitarians shuddered with horror and wept with grief for the imaginary woes of Africans; but their hearts were as adamant to the people of their own race and blood."

After his surrender, Watie left immediately to visit Sarah in Texas and to confer with Elias C. Boudinot as to plans to obtain as favorable a peace as possible with the United States. He appointed six delegates to go to Fort Gibson in an effort to establish tribal harmony with the Union Indians.

To make it clear that this was no show of weakness on his part, General Watie provided his delegates with an escort of fifty armed men. Colonel John A. Garrett, of the Fortieth Iowa, who commanded at Fort Gibson, was amazed to see armed Rebel Indians arrive for the conference about July 8. Military authorities reported that the Southern Indians were "armed in the street and defiant." Efforts at reconciliation were a failure.

In the meantime, Watie had established his Executive Office for the Cherokee Nation in the Choctaw Nation, and he had ordered Colonels W. P. Adair and James M. Bell to Shreveport where they were to make whatever arrangements were practical with the military commander for the benefit of the Cherokees. These former Confederate officers were received with respect at the Headquarters of the Northern Division of Louisiana. Brigadier General James C. Veatch, commanding, advised General Watie as "Principal Chief of the Cherokee Nation," that Colonel Bell had been sent on to the Major General commanding the Department of the Gulf and Colonel Adair was being sent back to him with answers to the questions which the commissioners had laid before the military authorities.

It must be kept in mind that there were two Cherokee governments operating. In fact, there were rival governments in the whole Indian Territory. The Union Indians had re-established their governments in the former Rebel nations, but the Southern Indians — the Six Nations and their allies — had formed a United Indian Nations government completely in control of Stand Watie and his former Secesh officers.

On July 14 at Tahlequah, the National Council, under Lewis Downing, Acting Principal Chief in John Ross' absence, issued a pardon and amnesty "to all citizens of the Cherokee Nation who participated in the Rebellion against the United States, and against the existing Government of the Cherokee Nation . . . and invite all such citizens to return to the Cherokee Nation . . ."

There were some exceptions. Among them were all who had been in the military offices in the Rebel service above the rank of captain since the first of March, 1865, and all persons who "held the pretended office of Principal Chief and Assistant Principal Chief, Treasurer, and members of the National Council, in opposition to the existing Government of the Cherokee Nation."

Even as Colonel Phillips' offers as Northern Indian commander in wartime, for peace and amnesty to the Rebel chiefs had fallen on unresponsive ears, so did the efforts of the re-established Ross faction Cherokee government. At Armstrong Academy, the United Indian Nations headquarters in the Choctaw Nation, one would have never known these were the Indians who had surrendered!

Both the Southern Cherokee government at Armstrong Academy and the Tahlequah government agreed to meet with the Indian Peace Commission at Fort Smith which was to be comprised of Dennis N. Cooley, Commissioner of Indian Affairs; Elijah Sells, in charge of the Southern Superintendency; General

William S. Harney, Colonel Ely S. Parker and Thomas Wistar.

Present at the Peace Council which convened at Fort Smith in September were the still proud and completely confident former Confederate Indian leaders.

These warriors and diplomats had carefully mapped their strategy at their own conference held September 6 at Armstrong Academy. So when they moved out from the Choctaw Nation to meet the United States delegation, they were determined to maintain an aggressive action for what they considered their rights.

Southern Indian leaders of the various nations and tribes were Israel Folsom, President of the Grand Council of the United Indian Nations; John Jumper, Chief of the Seminoles; Clermont, Osage Chief; Co-not-sa-sonne, Comanche Chief; George Washington, Chief of the Caddoes; Luck-a-o-tse, Chief Arapahoes; Winchester Colbert, Governor of the Chickasaw Nation; Stand Watie, Principal Chief of the Cherokee Nation; Samuel Checote, Principal Chief of the Creek Nation; P. P. Pitchlynn, Principal Chief of the Choctaw Nation; and J. A. Scales, Secretary of the Grand Council.

Perhaps to show that they were still their own masters, the Southern Indians were late in arriving at the conference. When they did arrive, they were treated as equals and not as the conquered. At Fort Smith the Rebel Indians protested demands that they open up their territory to Negroes. The Seminoles, although "willing to provide for the colored peoples of their own nation" found most repugnant the idea that the Indian Nations were to become, in part, colonization grounds for the blacks of other states and other territories.

Ever seeking to throw their opposition off base, the United Indians projected a most unexpected line of attack when the scholarly, experienced Cherokee diplomat, Elias C. Boudinot, rose to speak. The politically suave Boudinot, equally as at ease in defeat at Fort Smith as when he had been in the Confederate Congress or conferring with Jefferson Davis at Richmond, paid his compliments to the United States Commissioners and then commenced to flay Chief John Ross, saying:

"The fact is the Cherokee Nation has long been rent in twain by dissentions and I here charge him [Ross] with it today and I will tomorrow . . . I will show the deep duplicity and falsity that have followed him from his childhood to the present day . . . what can you expect of him now . . ."

Chief Ross, who had only a short time previously been re-elected as Principal Chief of the Cherokee Nation by the inhabitants of the Nation — most of the Southern Cherokees were still afraid to return to their homeland and many of their homes had been confiscated by the victors — was astonished by the audacity of the assault. He was more stunned when the United States Commissioners, although cautioning Boudinot against opening old wounds, actually accepted his viewpoint. The Rebels decried the notion that Ross was faithful to the Union and built up a case against him to discredit the old Chief, their longtime foe, with the Commission.

And the United States Commissioners, as incredible as it was, actually suggested that Chief Ross had no right to occupy the Principal Chief's spot and contended that he had, in fact, enjoyed strong ties with the Confederacy.

General Watie, Colonel Jumper, and all the rest of the former Confederate Indian leaders making up the Southern Indian delegation knew how Ross had actually betrayed his allegiance to the Confederacy.

And now Ross was being penalized by the United States on the grounds he was too loyal to the Confederacy!

The political education and experience of the Rebel leaders was fomenting the possibility of a most unusual payoff.

Loyal Cherokees defended Ross with a declaration of dissent which stated:

". . . John Ross has never, as far as our knowledge extends, been an emissary of the States in rebellion, nor has used his influence to seduce our allegiance to the United States. On the contrary, long after all the tribes and States in our immediate vicinity had abjured their allegiance, when there was not one faithful left among the Indians, and all the troops in the service of the United States had been driven off by the enemies of the government, and all protection was withdrawn, he adhered to his allegiance, and only yielded when further resistance promised the entire destruction of his people. For three years past he has been our authorized delegate at Washington City and the recognized head of the Cherokee Nation . . . We also beg leave to assure the honorable commission that Mr. John Ross is not the pretended chief of the Cherokee nation, but is the principal chief in law and fact, having been elected to that position without opposition, on the first Monday in August, for the term of four years, by the qualified voters . . ."

But the commissioners brushed aside the petition of the Loyal Cherokees and the wily Confederate Indians brought forth Chief Black Dog of the Osages to discredit further Chief Ross in the eyes of the United States representatives. Black Dog related how the Osages had signed the Confederate Treaty after Ross had written them:

"My Brothers, the Osages, there is a distinguished gentleman [Pike] sent by the Confederate States, who is here to make treaties with us. He will soon be ready to treat, and I want you to come here [Tahlequah] in order that we may all treat together with him. My Brothers, there is a great black cloud coming from the North, about to cover us all, and I want you to come here so that we can counsel each other and drive away the black cloud."

Black Dog finished his statement and the United States Commissioners nodded their heads well convinced that they had been right about Chief Ross. Then Wah-tah-in-gah, Chief counselor of the Black Dog and Clermont bands of the Osages, solemnly endorsed the statement of Chief Black Dog.

No one doubted the words of the Osage leaders. Ross, himself, knew that what they said was true, but he most assuredly had turned against the Confederacy at his first opportunity to make his switch a success.

But the smiles of the Commissioners were all for their former enemies and the Rebel Indians looked with a condescending "the-pity-of-it-all" attitude at the thoroughly shocked and rejected Chief John Ross. General Stand Watie, as Principal Chief of the Cherokees, was back in the saddle and riding in triumph!

General Watie signed the Articles of Agreement drawn up at Fort Smith for the Southern Cherokees, but these were only preliminary in nature, and in November from his Executive Department Watie issued instructions to Colonel W. P. Adair to proceed to Washington as one of the Commissioners of the Cherokee south in the "free and final" negotiations between the United States and the Cherokee Nation.

All possible efforts were being exerted by the Cherokee south leaders to help their unfortunate people. Colonel Adair had appealed to General Henry J. Hunt, who in 1865 had been sent to command the District of the Frontier, for means to relieve the sufferings of the Cherokees. Formerly, the destitute Cherokees in Texas and the Choctaw Nation had been supplied by Confederate authorities and Adair maintained that the United States would be wise to assume the problem of supplies until the Cherokees could resume agricultural operations.

Elias C. Boudinot reported to Stand Watie in December, "I have been doing all that I could and am still working for what I believe to be the best interests of the Southern Cherokees and all other Southern Indians. I have already expended $600 on my own account for which I ask and expect no return."

In the Spring of 1866 the Cherokee delegation went to Washington. Besides General Watie, the members were all former members of his Rebel army; Saladin Watie, Elias C. Boudinot, W. P. Adair, J. A. Scales and Richard Fields. The secretary to the group was J. W. Washbourne. Soon John Rollin Ridge, who had been in California since 1850, joined them and was elected head.

The Ross delegation also was in Washington to uphold its claims and with the battle lines again drawn, both groups eagerly sought the attentions of the political leaders.

Noted Indian authority, Annie Heloise Abel, in her book, *The American Indian Under Reconstruction,* said:

"What the South Cherokees wanted was political separation, segregation, the assignment to them, in perpetuity, of a proportionate share of their tribal domain. It was what the elder Ridge had contended for, as leader of the Treaty Party years previous and what President Polk, with the facts all before him, refused to grant. Strange that at this particular time when a war against secession had just concluded, the thought of such a thing should be entertained a single moment, by the United States Government, and yet it was entertained and entertained seriously."

In the political tug of war the Ross faction consented to no partition of the Cherokee Nation, but they did agree to repeal their confiscatory laws and to restore the secessionists to full rights. The latter concessions were a major victory, but the Southern Cherokees kept pressing for their own independence.

In the meantime General Watie, having returned to the

Cherokee and Choctaw Nations, was urged by his Washington delegation to declare a South Cherokee country independent of the Tahlequah rule. J. W. Washbourne, at the orders of the delegation, sought Watie's action to organize the new Cherokee government in the Canadian District and to proclaim an election for all officers, even if only one thousand Cherokees had time to vote.

Utilizing his journalistic talents, John Rollin Ridge was fighting Chief John Ross — much of the time in a sick bed — through the New York press and both he and Ross strove for aid from Horace Greeley of the *Tribune*, though Greeley, himself, was pro-Ross.

The Southern Cherokees were most hopeful of victory; nevertheless Ross had managed to get a reversal of the stand taken by the United States Commissioners at Fort Smith and was recognized as head of the loyal Cherokees.

As usual, tempers sometimes were a bit short when the two parties conflicted and John Rollin Ridge was outspoken in his mind to the President. In fact, so outspoken, that he felt it wise to write Commissioner Cooley:

"I am satisfied upon reflection that the President did not correctly receive the idea that I intended to convey when I spoke of the blood which would ensue in the Cherokee country if the Government delivered us into the hands of the Ross dynasty. I did not mean — and did not say that *we,* the Ridges, Boudinots and Waties, would raise the flag of war and begin difficulties, but that the Ross power would certainly renew upon us the oppressions of old and dig graves for us as they did for our immediate ancestors, or try to dig them, and that in that case, we were men enough to resist and that we would resist, if it drenched the land in blood. I thought this observation just, manly and true, but not as it was probably understood by the President."

The delegations pressed their claims with the Senate Indian Committee and Saladin Watie wrote his father that the Chairman of the Committee had told the Southern delegation that it should be all right for the Cherokees in their faction to remain in the Choctaw District or in the Canadian District. Saladin considered such a statement both absurd and ridiculous and a revelation of the lack of true knowledge of the Indian problem by the Senate.

The Negro situation plagued all the Southern delegations of the various nations. The Choctaws and the Chickasaws settled for "forty acres of ground to heads of families of former slaves," but the Cherokees, Seminoles and Creeks were punished harder and they had to make equal distribution with their ex-slaves. Because of this the treaty was termed "The Dark Treaty."

Despite the tireless efforts of the Watie contingent, the Ross delegation finally prevailed and the hope of an independent Southern Cherokee nation was gone. The President approved the treaty and Saladin termed the treaty "a sad disappointment to our people." General Watie could never have succeeded in forcing Washington recognition for the Southern Cherokee nation, even if he had had the time to call the special election pled for by his delegation.

Elias C. Boudinot and Saladin Watie urged the acceptance of the treaty as the Southern Cherokees had won some points even though they had lost their plea for independence. Though the treaty recognized John Ross as Principal Chief of the Cherokees, the former Secessionists were restored to their full rights in the Cherokee Nation.

John Rollin Ridge and Colonel Adair opposed signing the Treaty and there was an open split in the delegation and Ridge, withdrawing, returned to California. But, realizing that the contest in Washington was concluded, the Southern Cherokees agreed to the July compact. They arranged to keep representatives in Washington to look after the interests of their people.

The Treaty of 1866 was signed on July 17, but was not proclaimed until August 11. In the meantime, on August 1, John Ross died in the Medes Hotel on lower Pennsylvania Avenue. At only around forty, the lovely Mrs. Ross had died a year earlier.

With the Treaty of 1866 guaranteeing their rights, the Southern Cherokees slowly drifted back to their homes. Stand Watie's family had remained on the Red River in Choctaw country, but General Watie moved them back into his beloved Cherokee Nation.

Wars . . . surrenders . . . treaties. Nothing could stop Cherokee politics. With the Southern United Indian Nations removed from any pretense of power by the Treaty of 1866 and General Watie completely retired from his rump position as Principal

Chief of the Southern Cherokee, the victorious Northern Cherokees then fought among themselves!

William P. Ross, nephew of the late John Ross, headed the National Party and Louis Downing, who had been a Lieutenant Colonel in the Union Army, and Reverend John B. Jones, son of the anti-Watie missionary, Evans Jones, were the leaders of the People's Party.

Of all the loyal Cherokee leaders, perhaps none had asked for fairer terms for his opponents than Louis Downing, who had maintained the Rebels should have their full rights restored. As a military man, Downing had a high esteem for the way in which Stand Watie had outwitted his opponents for four years.

Although the outnumbered Southern Cherokees could not elect their own men to office, they did hold the balance of power and, remembering the considerate treatment offered them by Downing — and still hating any connection with a Ross — the Watie faction threw its support to the People's Party and Louis Downing was elected Principal Chief over William P. Ross in the elections of 1867.

General Watie had been busy trying to resume his planting operations and he had cultivated many acres of corn along the Red River in Choctaw country. Saladin and the Watie family were back in Cherokee territory at Webber's Falls. In the summer a flood smashed up General Watie's acreage and over a hundred acres of his finest corn was destroyed.

Because of this disaster, Stand Watie planned to move back to his homeland earlier than originally set and from the new Watie home Saladin wrote his father that Sarah moved with all the energy and zest of a teen-age girl.

From the Red River Watie sent his wagons and early in 1868 he had back in cultivation some of his large plantation lands on the Grand River. He had to work hard and long in an effort to provide for his family.

General Watie also backed Elias C. Boudinot in a tobacco factory that his nephew established in the Indian Territory. Brilliant Boudinot had the assurance of the Federal officials that he would not have to pay an internal revenue tax as the internal revenue laws did not apply to the Cherokee Nation.

Notwithstanding this, when Boudinot was able to undersell

his Missouri competitors, his factory was confiscated for non-payment of internal revenue taxes!

Boudinot felt that Stand Watie should run for a political office in the government and, once seated, get the Cherokee Nation to defend both Boudinot's and the Cherokees' tax rights; however, General Watie was unwilling to run and eventually the United States Government paid Boudinot for his confiscated tobacco plant.

Stand Watie had built a new house about twenty-five miles below his old fighting ground at Fort Gibson and on the south side of the Arkansas River. Actually, as he wrote his friend J. W. Washbourne, he was flat broke and too old to work. Like most other planters who had been prosperous before the war, Watie was financially distressed and on one occasion didn't have enough money to buy shoes for one of his daughters so that she could attend school!

Yet he was still the leader to the Cherokee South. This whole region of the nation looked to him for guidance and felt that once the burdens had become too difficult for Stand Watie, much of the responsibility would be allotted to popular Saladin.

Suddenly, in early 1868, Saladin was taken ill and soon died. Some said he died of a broken heart over the death of Charles Webber, his intimate friend since childhood.

There remained Watica — sometimes called Solon — at school in Cane Hill College. This Arkansas institution, chartered in 1852, had been reopened after the war and was a favorite with the aristocratic but financially imperiled Indian leaders.

It took almost all of Stand Watie's last dollars to send Watica to school, but the youth rewarded the General with his good work and pride for his home located on a level sweep with large shade trees and a beautiful view of the river. True, the lad did write home for money — to buy a new hat! And for a horse — to carry him home for Christmas!

Some of Watica's letters which appear in *Cherokee Cavaliers* show the warm devotion of the Watie family.

Sallie E. Starr, daughter of Nancy Starr, Mrs. Watie's sister who died while they were refugees in Texas, was a student at Bell Grove Seminary at Fort Smith. Sallie nurtured high hopes for Cousin Watica. She wrote him in February, 1869, to get a book on Stonewall Jackson. Watica could emulate the life of the beloved Confederate leader and Sallie reminded Watica how she was depending on him to follow his father's example in courageous leadership of the Cherokees and the Cherokee Nation.

But in late March, Watica was more filled with homesickness than anything else for he yearned to be with his Mother and Father and his little sister. Yet he was determined to stay out his school term and then to enjoy the vacation fun at home. He dreamed of berry hunting and riding around the countryside with General Watie to see their friends, who would ask all about his experiences at Cane Hill College.

There was to be no such fun and berry-picking. Shortly after Watica had written home his anticipation of being with his family and the fun he would have riding with his Father, Watica was stricken with pneumonia. The General and Sarah hastened to Cane Hill.

Quiet, well-behaved Watica, General Watie's last son, failed to recover and the Waties took his body home for burial.

As for the Watie girls, Minnehaha Josephine ("Ninnie") for whom the General, determined that his children should have an education, had somehow found the dollars necessary to send her to the Sandles School at Fort Smith – died February 27, 1875, at the age of 23; and Jacqueline, who had attended Captain Isaac A. Clark's Academy at Berryville, Arkansas, on March 17, died at the age of only 18. Sarah Watie lived until 1880.

Broken-hearted General Watie, shocked and buffeted by the death of his two sons, had not slackened in his efforts to rebuild his fortunes to some semblance of his pre-war prosperity. Sarah and the girls deserved the best he could make for them. In September, 1871, General Watie was taken to his old home at Honey Creek and on the 9th died.

From throughout the old Confederate Indian Nations came tributes to their late leader and from the former Rebel lands in Missouri and Arkansas men in gray penned eulogies to one who had fought so well for the Cherokee Nation, the Indian allies and the Confederate States of America.

George Washington Grayson, the Creek Second Regiment Captain, who had been with Stand Watie at the capture of the "Williams" and the destruction of the million dollar wagon train at Cabin Creek, and who later became Principal Chief of the Creek Nation, wrote:

"Let me say . . . whatever else the Indians of the old Indian Territory may lose in the shock and crash of time, be it property, land or name; let it be provided . . . In stone and story that the name of General Stand Watie may never fade away. Let his memory and fame stand forth proud monuments to the virtues of patriotism and devotion to duty as exemplified in his life, as long as grass grows and flowers bloom . . ."

As a memorial to Stand Watie, Indian statesman and Principal Chief of the Cherokees, one could recall these words from *Hiawatha*:

> "And the evening sun descending
> Set the clouds on fire with redness,
> Burned the broad sky, like a prairie,
> Left upon the level water
> One long track and trail of splendor,
> Down his stream, as down a river,
> Westward, westward Hiawatha
> Sailed into the fiery sunset,
> Sailed into the purple vapors,
> Sailed into the dusk of evening."

And what words could fit better General Stand Watie, C.S.A., than those written by Virginia Frazer Boyle, which appear on the monument to General Nathan Bedford Forrest in Memphis, Tennessee:

> "His hoof-beats die not on Fame's crimsoned sod,
> But shall ring through his song and story:
> He fought like a Titan and struck like a god,
> And his dust is our Ashes of Glory."

Yes, as is written on the monument to the Confederate dead at the University of Virginia, "Fate denied them Victory, but clothed them with glorious Immortality."

Forever to those who loved the Confederacy there will be the remembrance of General Stand Watie.

*His had been a bold dream — a dream that shimmered with courage and valor. So bold the dream — so brave the dreamer!*

# Bibliography

Abel, Annie Heloise, THE AMERICAN INDIAN AS PARTICIPANT IN THE CIVIL WAR, Arthur H. Clark Co., Cleveland, 1910.

Abel, Annie Heloise, THE AMERICAN INDIAN AS SLAVEHOLDER AND SECESSIONIST, Arthur H. Clark Co., Cleveland, 1915.

Abel, Annie Heloise, THE AMERICAN INDIAN UNDER RECONSTRUCTION, Arthur H. Clark Co., Cleveland, 1925.

Abel, Annie Heloise, "The American Indians in the Civil War," *American Historical Review,* XV, No. 2 (January 1910).

Allsop, Fred W., ALBERT PIKE, A BIOGRAPHY, Parke-Harper, Little Rock, Arkansas, 1928.

Anderson, Mabel W., "General Stand Watie," *Chronicles of Oklahoma,* X, Oklahoma Historical Society, Oklahoma City, 1932.

Anderson, Mabel Washbourne, LIFE OF GENERAL STAND WATIE, Mayes County Republican, Pryor, Oklahoma, 1915.

Anderson, Mabel Washbourne, "Excerpts From the Life of General Stand Watie," *Southern Magazine,* Wytheville, Virginia, August-September, 1936.

APPLETON'S CYCLOPEDIA OF AMERICAN BIOGRAPHY, D. Appleton and Co., New York City, 1888.

ARKANSAS, Hastings House, New York City, 1941.

Bass, Althea, CHEROKEE MESSENGER, University of Oklahoma Press, Norman, 1936.

Britt, Albert, GREAT INDIAN CHIEFS, Whittlesey House, New York City, 1938.

Britton, Wiley, MEMOIRS OF THE REBELLION ON THE BORDER, 1863, Cushing, Thomas and Co., Chicago, 1882.

Britton, Wiley, THE UNION INDIAN BRIGADE IN THE CIVIL WAR, Hudson, Kansas City, 1922.

Burch, John P. Trow, Harrison, CHARLES W. QUANTRELL, Vegas, Texas, 1923.

Cathey, Clyde, "Battle of Pea Ridge," *Southern Magazine,* Wytheville, Virginia, July, 1935.

Commager, Henry Steele (editor), THE BLUE AND THE GRAY, Bobbs-Merrill Co., Indianapolis-New York, 1950.

CONFEDERATE STATUTES AT LARGE, Richmond, Virginia, 1864.

Dale, Edward Everett, "Some Letters of General Stand Watie," *Chronicles of Oklahoma,* I, Oklahoma Historical Society, Oklahoma City, January, 1921.

Dale, Edward Everett and Gaston Little, CHEROKEE CAVALIERS, University of Oklahoma Press, Norman, 1940.

Debo, Angie, THE ROAD TO DISAPPEARANCE, University of Oklahoma Press, Norman, 1941.

DICTIONARY OF AMERICAN BIOGRAPHY, Charles Scribner's Sons, New York City, 1933.

Eaton, Clemen, A HISTORY OF THE SOUTHERN CONFEDERACY, Macmillan, New York City, 1954.

Eaton, Rachel Caroline, JOHN ROSS AND THE CHEROKEE INDIANS, Monasha, Wisconsin, 1914.

Edwards, John N., SHELBY AND HIS MEN, Miami Printing and Publishing Co., Cincinnati, 1867.

Eggleston, George Cary, HISTORY OF THE CONFEDERATE WAR, Sturgis and Walton Co., New York, 1910.

ENCYCLOPEDIA AMERICANA, Americana Corporation, New York City, 1954.

Evans, Clemont Anselm, CONFEDERATE MILITARY HISTORY, Confederate Publishing Co., Atlanta, 1899.

Foreman, Carolyn Thomas, PARK HILL, The Star Printery, Muskogee, Oklahoma, 1948.

Foreman, Grant (editor and annotator), A TRAVELLER IN INDIAN TERRITORY, THE JOURNAL OF ETHAN ALLEN HITCHCOCK, The Torch Press, Cedar Rapids, Iowa, 1930.

Foreman, Grant, ADVANCING THE FRONTIER, University of Oklahoma Press, Norman, 1933.

Foreman, Grant, INDIAN REMOVAL, University of Oklahoma Press, Norman, 1932.

Foreman, Grant, SEQUOYAH, University of Oklahoma Press, Norman, 1938.

Foreman, Grant, THE FIVE CIVILIZED TRIBES, University of Oklahoma Press, Norman, 1934.

Foreman, Grant, THE FIVE CIVILIZED TRIBES, Indian Centennial Board, Muskogee, Oklahoma, 1948.

Foreman, Grant, "The Trial of Stand Watie," *Chronicles of Okla-*

*homa,* XII, Oklahoma Historical Society, Oklahoma City, 1932.
Freeman, Charles R., "The Battle of Honey Springs," *Chronicles of Oklahoma,* XIII, Oklahoma Historical Society, Oklahoma City, June, 1935.
Gittinger, Roy, THE FORMATION OF THE STATE OF OKLAHOMA, University of California Press, Berkeley, 1917.
Head, J. D., "Albert Pike," *Southern Magazine,* Wytheville, Virginia, July, 1935.
Henry, Ralph Selph, STORY OF THE CONFEDERACY, Bobbs-Merrill Co., Indianapolis, 1931.
Johnson, Charles H. L., FAMOUS INDIAN CHIEFS, L. C. Page and Co., Boston, 1909.
Johnson, Robert Underwood and Clarence Clough Buel (editors), BATTLES AND LEADERS OF THE CIVIL WAR, Century Co., New York City, 1887.
Kane, Harnett T., SPIES FOR THE BLUE AND GRAY, Hanover House, New York City, 1954.
Kline, Sherman J., "General Stand Watie," *Americana,* XIII (October, 1929), New York City.
Lindquist, G.E.E., THE RED MAN IN THE UNITED STATES, George H. Doran Co., New York City, 1923.
Loomis, August W., SCENES IN THE INDIAN COUNTRY, Presbyterian Board of Publication, Philadelphia, 1859.
Lossing, Benson J., HISTORY OF THE CIVIL WAR, The War Memorial Association, New York City, 1912.
MISSOURI, Duell, Sloan and Pearce, New York City, 1941.
Monaghan, Jay, CIVIL WAR ON THE WESTERN BORDER, Little, Brown and Company, Boston, 1955.
Moore, Jessie E., "The Five Great Nations," *Southern Magazine,* Wytheville, Virginia, August-September, 1936.
O'Flaherty, Daniel, UNDEFEATED REBEL, University of North Carolina Press, Chapel Hill, 1954.
OKLAHOMA, University of Oklahoma Press, Norman, 1941.
Parks, Joseph Howard, GENERAL EDMUND KIRBY SMITH, Louisiana State University Press, Baton Rouge, 1954.
Pollard, Edward A., THE LOST CAUSE, E. B. Treat & Co., New York City, 1866.
REPORT, Commissioner of Indian Affairs, Washington, D. C., Various years, 1844-'72.
Richardson, James D., (editor), MESSAGES AND PAPERS OF THE CONFEDERACY, United States Publishing Company, Nashville, Tennessee, 1906.
Rose, Victor M., THE LIFE AND SERVICES OF GEN. BEN Mc-

CULLOCH, Pictorial Bureau of the Press, Philadelphia, 1881.
Royce, Charles C., THE CHEROKEE NATION OF INDIANS, Bureau of American Ethnology, Washington, D. C., 1887.
Rutherford, Mildred Lewis, THE SOUTH IN HISTORY AND LITERATURE, Franklin-Turner Co., Atlanta, Georgia, 1907.
Schoolcraft, Henry Rowe, INFORMATION RESPECTING THE HISTORY, CONDITION AND PROSPECTS OF THE INDIAN TRIBES OF THE UNITED STATES, Lippincott Grambo and Co., Philadelphia, 1851.
Schwab, John Christoper, THE CONFEDERATE STATES OF AMERICA, Charles Scribner's Sons, New York City, 1904.
Scotterill, R. S., THE SOUTHERN INDIANS, University of Oklahoma Press, Norman, 1954.
Seymour, Flora William, THE STORY OF THE RED MAN, Longman's, Green and Co., New York City, 1929.
Starkey, Marion L., THE CHEROKEE NATION, Alfred A. Knopf, New York City, 1946.
Starr, Emmett, HISTORY OF THE CHEROKEE INDIANS, The Warden Co., Oklahoma City, 1921.
Stickles, A. M., SIMON BOLIVAR BUCKNER, University of North Carolina Press, Chapel Hill, 1940.
Street, James, THE CIVIL WAR, Dial Press, New York City, 1953.
Taylor, Richard, DESTRUCTION AND RECONSTRUCTION, Longman's, Green and Co., New York City, 1955.
TEXAS, Hastings House, New York, 1940.
Thoburn, Joseph Bradfield, A STANDARD HISTORY OF OKLAHOMA, American Historical Society, Chicago-New York, 1916.
Thoburn, Joseph Bradfield and Holcomb, Isaac M., A HISTORY OF OKLAHOMA, Doub and Co., San Francisco, 1908.
United States Indian Office, REPORT OF THE COMMISSIONER OF INDIAN AFFAIRS, 1859 to 1865, Washington, D. C.
Van Deventer, Horace, ALBERT PIKE: A BIOGRAPHICAL SKETCH, McCowat-Mercer, Jackson, Tennessee, 1910.
WAR OF THE REBELLION (THE): A COMPILATION OF THE OFFICIAL RECORDS OF THE UNION AND CONFEDERATE ARMIES, Washington, D. C., 1880-1901.
Wardell, Morris L., A POLITICAL HISTORY OF THE CHEROKEE NATION, University of Oklahoma Press, Norman, 1934.
Watkins, Sam R., Co., AYTCH, McCowat-Mercer Press, Jackson, Tennessee, 1952.
Wise, Jennings S., THE REDMAN IN THE NEW WORLD DRAMA, W. F. Roberts Co., Washington, D. C., 1931.

# Index

C

J



K



L

Mc and M

N



O



P

Q



R

U



V



W

Y